£18.99

Endurance Athlete's Edge

Marc Evans

Human Kinetics

To Mom and Joseph, Dad and Joan, my sister Cynthia and my brothers Tony, Jr., Michael, Lamont, and Joseph—may God bless each of you and grant you peace.

LIBRARY OF CONGRESS CATALOGING-IN-PUBLICATION DATA

Evans, Marc, 1953–
   Endurance athlete's edge / Marc Evans.
     p.   cm.
   Includes bibliographical references (p.) and index.
   ISBN 0-87322-938-X
   1. Endurance sports--Training.   2. Endurance sports--Psychological aspects.   3. Athletes--Nutrition.   I. Title.
   GV749.5.E83   1997
   613.7'1--dc21   96-40338
                                                      CIP

ISBN: 0-87322-938-X

Developmental Editor: Julie Rhoda; **Assistant Editors**: Sandra Merz Bott and Coree Shutter; **Editorial Assistant:** Jennifer Jeanne Hemphill; **Copyeditor:** Barbara J. Field; **Proofreader:** Erin Cler; **Indexer:** Joan Griffitts; **Graphic Designer:** Judy Henderson; **Graphic Artist:** Tom Roberts; **Photo Editor:** Boyd LaFoon; **Cover Designer:** Jack Davis; **Photographer:** Photophile; **Illustrators:** Roberto Sabas, Sara Wolfsmith, and Katherine Galasyn-Wright; **Printer:** United Graphics

Human Kinetics books are available at special discounts for bulk purchase. Special editions or book excerpts can also be created to specification. For details, contact the Special Sales Manager at Human Kinetics.

Printed in the United States of America   10 9 8 7 6 5 4 3 2 1

Human Kinetics
Web site: http://www.humankinetics.com/

United States: Human Kinetics, P.O. Box 5076, Champaign, IL 61825-5076
1-800-747-4457
e-mail: humank@hkusa.com

Canada: Human Kinetics, Box 24040, Windsor, ON N8Y 4Y9
1-800-465-7301 (in Canada only)
e-mail: humank@hkcanada.com

Europe: Human Kinetics, P.O. Box IW14, Leeds LS16 6TR, United Kingdom
(44) 1132 781708
e-mail: humank@hkeurope.com

Australia: Human Kinetics, 57A Price Avenue, Lower Mitcham, South Australia 5062
(08) 277-1555
e-mail: humank@hkaustralia.com

New Zealand: Human Kinetics, P.O. Box 105-231, Aukland 1
(09) 523-3462
e-mail: humank@hknewz.com

CONTENTS

FOREWORD

One of the odder reactions that has plagued my 20-year career as a professional athlete is the look of disbelief many people express when I tell them what my job entails. They seem to want to comprehend my workload but can't quite fathom how someone could consistently train so much, let alone why he would ever want to. More often than not, they wrinkle their nose, cock their head to the side, and naively ask, "Just what is it like to have to swim, cycle, run, lift weights, and stretch 50 hours each week?" I usually cop out with the retort, "It's good work; if you can get it."

Endurance athletics, for lack of a better term, is a relatively new category in the broad spectrum of human-movement study. After all, the aerobic training phenomenon is barely over 25 years old. Triathlon as a recognizable sport has not yet been around for even 20 years. Endurance athletics is a continually evolving activity in which new ideas, theories, and protocols are continually being introduced. Since I fell into high school distance running in 1972, I have watched endurance training evolve from vague concepts and a form of punishment for errant players into a multibillion-dollar arena touching many aspects of the fitness industry.

Unraveling the mystery of it all—the hows, the whys, and the what fors—has until recent years been equal parts experience, intuition, hearsay, and luck. Fortunately for the enthusiast, though, solid, proved, and empirical information in an understandable (even to the layman) and approachable form has arrived.

I've had the opportunity over the years to share information with a variety of talented individuals, to learn and hopefully to improve. Marc Evans was one of the first people I knew who tried to make sense of endurance training and the sport of triathlon in particular. You see, in the early 1980s there were no books, no how-to videos, no clinics—and no coaches except Marc. He worked for a few years with a small group of professional triathletes in northern California who did very well. Since then Marc has continued to improve his unique knowledge of endurance sports and special grasp of the sometimes vague concept of cross-training. Endurance sport has changed much in the past 15 years, and Marc has grown with it.

After a series of subpar performances in early 1994, I asked Marc to review my program and suggest ways to get back on track. This was difficult for me; for many years I had been entirely self-coached and had great success. Marc recognized this. He was able to use my work ethic and extended base and add to them a healthy dose of new training concepts that he had developed over the years. His knowledge of the technical aspects of training, along with his relaxed commonsense attitude, helped me get my career back on track.

Endurance Athlete's Edge is Marc's finest work to date. It is a compilation of nearly 20 years of research, trial and error, and hands-on, practical experience. There is a great deal of information in this book, but ultimately it is all useable. Time- and athlete-tested, it should prove easily adaptable to all ability levels.

Even with all my experience, I learned quite a lot reading this book. I can still recommend it, however, to beginning triathletes, swimmers, cyclists, runners, and endurance athletes of any ability.

Marc does a great job of putting together a wealth of material into a concise, reader-friendly format. I'm sure you will enjoy reading *Endurance Athlete's Edge* as much as I have.

Scott Tinley

ACKNOWLEDGMENTS

I would like to thank a few individuals who "made a difference." Human Kinetics developmental editor Julie Rhoda was tirelessly energetic, thoughtful, and intelligent at each step while acquisitions editor Kenneth Mange helped pilot the lengthy process.

INTRODUCTION

Endurance sport training methods are now highly sophisticated. That's because endurance athletes now have extensive research on sport science to guide them. Sometimes it's hard to know how to apply that knowledge coming out of the lab. This is one reason many leading endurance athletes are now turning to professional coaches.

A good coach can make sense out of the research, developing an organized training program based on scientific principles as well as on the individual athlete's current levels of fitness and ability, intended goals, and preferences. A good coach will be competent and knowledgeable in such divergent areas as biomechanics and technique, periodization, sport nutrition, sport psychology, and supplemental training. My own training program has developed over 15 years of successfully working with premier endurance athletes. My program has raised the performance level of multisport athletes coming from varied fitness levels and sport specializations to new heights of endurance for their professional and age divisions.

Achievement in endurance sports takes hard work, but it takes smart work, too. And it takes a lot of planning. To train successfully for endurance sport events like triathlons and duathlons athletes must be organized and have a strategy.

Endurance Athlete's Edge guides you in your overall training plan and offers specific drills and workouts to hone your sport-specific training. Part I highlights four levels of training intensity, forming the foundation for understanding the specific workouts, drills, and form techniques that follow in parts II and III. You'll learn how to recognize training in each intensity level and how to plan your training to get the right amount of each intensity. Part I prepares you for the details of the training program that has produced great results for world-class athletes. Part II addresses the mechanics of swimming, cycling, and running. Each chapter in this section provides tips for technique and drills to help you develop the most efficient form. The model workouts I've designed show you how to incorporate the drills as well as the four intensity levels into your sport-specific workouts. I also provide you with detailed supplemental training information. You'll find out how isokinetic, isotonic, calisthenics, and flexibility training can make a difference in your fitness, strength, and injury-prevention efforts and result in improved performances. I then help you put this information to use: You'll have an innovative system of organizing training intensity and managing workouts through using the table of periodization. You'll have tables and charts that can be adjusted to your own level of performance and that spell out exactly how much, how hard, and how often to train—and when to rest. This information helps you organize your season so you come to the starting line of the most important events in peak fitness: fine-tuned and ready to race.

While my background as a coach is basically in triathlon, this book is for endurance athletes from nearly any sport. The program philosophy presented here will help you achieve better results. You'll find that the training program managers and the table of periodization can be adapted for distance runners, swimmers, cyclists, ultra-distance athletes, cross-country skiers, in-line skaters, mountain bikers, and nearly any person of whatever ability level who wants a proven, successful approach to endurance training.

My goal in writing this book was to make each and every sentence be of value to readers. From the first to the last chapter, you'll find an organized and instructive program for achieving *your* endurance edge.

PART I

PLANNING YOUR PROGRAM

1

ENERGY FOR MULTIENDURANCE SPORTS

Many endurance athletes train randomly, not really knowing how hard or easy their training should be for each workout. Just showing up and going with the flow, or following someone else's training plan and going like heck, is the misguided recipe for many. But optimal endurance fitness and performance comes from planning. This is brought about by managing training through periods of emphasis on volume, technique, and perhaps most importantly, on training intensity. *Endurance Athlete's Edge* will help you avoid mistakes in training by showing you how to organize your training into a long-term, successful, and individualized program.

THE STRATEGIES FOR TRAINING

Everyone realizes improvement in a sport requires training for that particular sport, but there are many different training methods, and they are not all equally effective. Three notable rules for physical training and design of the endurance athlete's training plan provide the principal foundation:

Right Practice—Progress (improvement) in any sport must involve the training of that sport.
Specificity of Practice—Training effects are limited to the specific muscles and movement patterns trained.

Intensity of Practice—Peak performance is achieved through training at the right intensities.

These rules should form the basis of any complete training program. The first and second rules may seem obvious. Swimmers, for example, spend most of their training time in the water, and they focus on working the swimming-specific muscles such as the triceps and lats when they train in the weight room. The third rule, intensity of practice, is often overlooked by athletes but may be the most important of the three. This book provides the multisport endurance athlete with a clear plan for effectively implementing the right training intensities to improve performance.

THE INTENSITY OF PRACTICE AND PEAK PERFORMANCE

Several years ago, on an early-morning jog, professional triathlete Scott Molina and I talked about the infamous Wednesday group bicycle ride in San Diego. Fifty or more aspiring triathletes would gather regularly with Molina, Scott Tinley, Mark Allen, and others for what often turned into an exhausting ordeal. It wasn't that the professional riders would ride at an intensity too high for the rest of the riders, but one of the wanna-bes would invariably try to make an impression by pushing the pace.

Other newcomers tried to hang on longer than their training had prepared them for. Scott stated, "I've seen them all come and go, showing up and doing our pace without having any real training basis. After a couple of weeks, or even a day, you never see them again. They've injured themselves because of their ego perhaps. You simply can't train effectively within another person's program."

Not only must your program suit your fitness level and goals, but you cannot expect to do what the big-name athletes do without first going through basic training. A simple example of this is weight training. An earnest weight lifter would agree that you can't walk into the gym and lift massive weights on the first day without risking injury. What would be the point anyway? What can this training possibly prove, and what physiological benefits are achieved?

Rather, the wise weight trainer starts with lighter loads and more repetitions, progressing gradually to heavier weights as strength, power, and endurance increase. A stair-step progression is an excellent example of training periodization or, for the endurance athlete, preparing for competitions in specific sequences of varying intensity and training volume. Periodization refers directly to this variation of work (intensity) and rest (recovery) and how those training loads (volume) are adjusted during a season. The purpose of periodization is to attain maximum performance when it matters most—at important competitions.

TRAINING CYCLES: THE ESSENCE OF PERIODIZATION

There is much research confirming the importance of training cycles of varying intensity. And along with hard work, rest is also important for the athlete trying to achieve peak performance. The body needs a periodic breather to adapt fully to the workload of training. Without adequate rest, athletes become fatigued and can't maintain high-intensity workouts. Yet with too much rest and too little high-intensity training, they lose conditioning and fail to achieve their best results.

Any well-designed training program adjusts the volume of training. An athlete will build volume progressively to adapt physiologically. Adaptations to training are most effective when an overload stimulus is applied that challenges but does not under- or overtrain the athlete. Additionally, this training volume and intensity should be adjusted upward and downward each week, permitting greater adaptation. Most athletes are familiar with the concept of "tapering," reducing training volume prior to an important race or series of races, but the intensity of training needs to be changed too.

True athletic periodization involves adjustments in the volume, frequency, and intensity of training to achieve peak performance at just the right time. In this program, the training intensity zones are adjusted and managed similar to your weekly training volume; that is, they change each week and during each training period. The program managers and table of periodization, explained fully in chapter 2, prescribe how much of each kind of training to do in any particular week—no more guessing about the intensity, volume, and frequency of training at any time of the season. These tools provide exactly what all athletes and coaches want to know: how much training, how hard, how often, and with how much rest.

THE BODY'S BASIC ENERGY SYSTEMS

To understand the importance of proper training intensity, some understanding of the body's energy systems is necessary. Two energy systems within the body supply energy for muscular contraction and movement lasting more than a few seconds. One is the lactic acid system, also called the *anaerobic system*, because it works without oxygen. The other is the *aerobic system*, which requires oxygen. Both operate at the same time but at differing levels, depending on exercise intensity.

The basic fuel for muscular contraction and movement (aerobic and anaerobic) is a molecule called adenosine triphosphate, or ATP. Foods provide the potential energy, but first need to be broken down into these chemical

molecules. When one of the phosphate bonds is broken in a chemical reaction, it releases energy that fuels the working muscles. The remaining adenosine diphosphate (ADP) molecule can be recycled into a new ATP molecule by either the aerobic or the anaerobic system. When the aerobic system does the job, it does so by metabolizing fats. This is very efficient, because you get a lot of energy from just a little bit of fat. The problem is that this process is limited by how fast your body can get oxygen to the working muscles. The anaerobic system produces ATP much more quickly by metabolizing glycogen (a form of glucose) stored in the muscles and liver. This metabolism doesn't require oxygen, but it produces a by-product called lactic acid, and the stored glycogen gets used up within two to three hours of high-intensity exercise. In contrast, fats are virtually an unlimited source of fuel with enough reserves to last several days. However, fats need carbohydrate to metabolize efficiently. When

endurance athletes talk about "bonking" or "hitting the wall," they are describing what happens when the glycogen is used up and the anaerobic system can't contribute anymore.

So we have two energy systems. The anaerobic system is good for high energy demands (speed), and the aerobic is better suited for long-duration events (endurance). Endurance athletes need both. Their training programs must include work at several intensity levels for optimum training of these energy delivery systems and the balance between them.

FOUR TRAINING ZONES TO PEAK FITNESS

With the right kind of training, you can improve the efficiency and capacity of both systems and effectively raise your threshold pace. I have adopted four distinct intensity zones for training using work by David E. Martin and Peter N. Coe (1997). My program has further described each of these zones by separate acronyms, intensity, and durations in order to quantify predictable training for each zone.

1. Aerobic conditioning zone (O_2)
2. Anaerobic conditioning zone (LVT)
3. Aerobic capacity zone (VO_2)
4. Anaerobic capacity zone (LAC)

Each of these training intensities produces certain adaptations in the body that may not be duplicated at a higher or lower intensity. Low-intensity aerobic training, for instance, improves the circulatory system with the formation of more capillaries to carry oxygen-rich blood to the working muscles. Higher-intensity training doesn't do this, but each zone has its own benefits. In determining the physiological benefits of these training zones, my work with Jaci L. VanHeest, PhD, Director of Exercise Physiology for U.S. Swimming, has been particularly beneficial in helping provide references for nearly all of the physiological and biological training benefits described for each intensity zone.

In the descriptions that follow, you'll see workout intensity defined by percent of maximal heart rate and rating of perceived exertion (RPE). We'll discuss these and other indicators later in this chapter. As you read through the descriptions of the intensity zones (table 1.1), keep in mind that the boundaries among them often overlap and depend on an individual's fitness level.

Aerobic Conditioning Zone (O_2)

Heart rate: 70 to 80 percent of maximum
RPE: Fairly light to somewhat hard

The highest volume of an individual's training will be done within the aerobic conditioning (O_2) zone. The O_2 zone is the lowest intensity, but athletes can't afford to discount its vital importance to overall training. Each of the multisport disciplines needs extraordinary amounts of this training. Training in this zone provides the physiological foundations that enable the body to handle the higher intensity levels. Training effects are achieved by long-duration, easy-distance training of very light intensity.

Training in the Aerobic Conditioning Zone

Longer-duration and moderately intense uninterrupted swimming, cycling, running, rowing, mountain biking, climbing, hiking, in-line skating, or cross-country skiing are the ruling guide for this intensity zone. Durations are from 20 minutes to several hours of training. A major advantage beyond the indicated physiological benefits is the training of technique. Although this intensity is not similar to race conditions, it is an excellent time for working on optimizing technique. With the lower oxygen requirements associated with the aerobic conditioning zone, an athlete can perform the proper technical habits more easily. Always work on at least one element of technique when doing this type of training. In each week of training, depending on the discipline and periodization stage, anywhere from 59.5 to 100 percent of training will be in the aerobic conditioning zone. This is a significant portion of the overall training volume and affords plenty of opportunity for working on technique.

Benefits of the Aerobic Conditioning Zone

Training within the aerobic conditioning zone has many advantages for the endurance athlete and is particularly important for overall training adaptation, which further prepares the body for more intense training. More notable enhancements through O_2 training are as follows:

1. Connective tissue (ligaments and tendons) is strengthened. Supporting muscles gain endurance, and there is increased resistance to muscle cell damage during heavy exercise (Booth and Gould 1975; Tipton et al. 1975).

2. Slow-twitch (ST) muscle fibers gain size and strength. O_2 training effectively stimulates ST motor neurons that contribute to improving exercise economy (Baldwin et al. 1972; Costill et al. 1976; Gollnick et al. 1972; Gollnick et al. 1973).

TABLE 1.1   Training Intensity Zone Continuums

Training intensity zone	Duration/ recovery	Perceived exertion	Heart rate range	Physiological and biological	Workout example
Aerobic conditioning (O_2)	20 minutes to many hours of continuous exercise	Fairly light to somewhat hard	70% to 80% of tested maximal HR per sport—varies with training, fitness, environment, fatigue, hydration, etc.	Endurance and connective tissues	Steady-state distance training of long-duration and low-intensity exercise
Anaerobic conditioning (LVT)	15 to 25 minutes of short rest intervals with rest periods of 5 seconds to 1 minute	Somewhat hard to energetically hard	80% to 90% of tested maximal HR per sport—varies with training, fitness, environment, fatigue, hydration, etc.	Blood volume increases stamina and ST/FT fiber development—specific muscle contractibility	Race pace training simulations: time trials, short-rest interval training; swimming: 4 × 500; cycling: 10 × 1,000 meters; running: 4 × 1 mile
Aerobic capacity ($\dot{V}O_2$)	10 to 21 minutes of exercise time; intervals are 2 to 8 minutes long and the rest interval is the same as the exercise time	Energetically hard to very hard	90% to 95% of tested maximal HR per sport—varies with training, fitness, environment, fatigue, hydration, etc.	Speed and fiber development—increased neurological recruitment and blood buffering	Slightly faster than race pace; swimming: 4 × 200 meters; cycling: 8 × 800 meters; running: 5 × 800 meters
Anaerobic capacity (LAC)	4 to 10 minutes of exercise time; 10-second to 2-minute interval times with rest intervals of twice the interval if less than 1 minute and 3 times the interval if more than 1 minute	Very hard to very, very hard; these are the highest-intensity efforts, yet the duration is short; lactate accumulation is high, and the recovery time is prolonged	±100% of tested maximal HR per sport—varies with training, fitness, environment, fatigue, hydration, etc.; may not reach this HR, as duration of exercise is too short	Speed and strength are developed—neurological recruitment and lactate tolerance are enhanced	Short duration of high intensity: 12 repetitions of 20 seconds followed by 40 seconds of recovery time

3. Increased blood volume carries more hemoglobin (oxygen-carrying molecules) to the working muscles (Kjellberg, Rudhe, and Sjostrand 1949; Oscai, Williams, and Hertig 1968).

4. O_2 training generates a larger capacity for storage of muscle glycogen reserves (carbohydrates and water) (Gollnick et al. 1972; Gollnick et al. 1973).

5. Increases capillary development. (Capillaries, the smallest blood vessels, are where oxygen is passed from the blood to the working muscles.) Training increases the number of capillaries surrounding each muscle fiber, thus expanding the aerobic capacity (Andersen 1975; Andersen and Henriksson 1977; Brodal, Inger, and Hermansen 1977; Hermansen and Wachtlova 1971; Inger 1979).

6. Increases mitochondria, structures within the muscle cells that produce ATP (Costill et al. 1976; Gollnick and King 1969; Holloszy 1967; Howald 1975; Kiessling, Piehl, and Lundquist 1971).

7. Decreases resting heart rate (Morganroth et al. 1975; Zeldis, Morganroth, and Rubler 1978).

8. Increases stroke volume (amount of blood pumped by one contraction of the heart) (Bevegard, Holmgren, and Jonsson 1963; Morganroth et al. 1975; Peripargkul and Scheuer 1970; Rtizer, Bove, and Carey 1980).

9. Improves temperature regulation (heat tolerance via circulatory adaptations).

10. Increases respiratory endurance (lung ventilation ability).

11. Improves free fatty acid (FFA) oxidation (spares muscle glycogen) (Borensztajn et al. 1975; Costill et al. 1977; Gollnick 1977; Hickson et al. 1977; Mole, Oscai, and Holloszy 1971; Oscai, Williams, and Hertig 1968).

12. Increases muscle glycogen storage capacity (Gollnick et al. 1972; Gollnick et al. 1973).

13. Decreases body fat (Barr et al. 1991; Boileau et al. 1971; Pollock, Cureton, and Greninger 1969; Pollock et al. 1975; Wilmore et al. 1970).

Anaerobic Conditioning Zone (LVT)

> Heart rate: 80 to 90 percent of maximum
> RPE: Somewhat hard to energetically hard

This training improves the ability to race consistently at the LVT level, which is the anaerobic or lactate threshold described earlier. I will use the term *race pace* to indicate this intensity zone. Because we can determine this anaerobic threshold accurately, the LVT zone is the intensity level that can be most closely targeted in training. The intensity pace charts (IPCs) in chapters 3, 4, and 5 begin with the LVT pace. The aerobic conditioning (O_2) zone does not have pace charts, as this zone is for recovery and aerobic endurance.

The anaerobic threshold is the point at which lactate production and lactate removal are equal. At intensity levels beyond this steady state, the effects are noticed very quickly as

ANAEROBIC THRESHOLD

Physiologists, coaches, and athletes all talk about the importance of the anaerobic threshold for endurance athletes. Researchers have defined the anaerobic threshold in several different ways, but they are all after the same thing—the balance point where lactic acid or lactate (by-product of anaerobic metabolism) is being produced as fast as it can be cleared. For our purposes, the anaerobic threshold is the maximum sustainable pace or intensity.

The concept of threshold will help you understand the importance of training at the right intensity. The two energy systems, anaerobic and aerobic, operate simultaneously to meet the body's energy demands. At low intensity, such as an easy jog, the aerobic system can supply most of the energy your muscles need. The anaerobic system is operating, but at a lower level, and the lactic acid it produces is easily recycled by the body. At higher speeds and longer durations, the aerobic system can't keep up with the energy demand, and the anaerobic system must supply more of the energy needed. This means more lactic acid is produced.

There is a precise pace at which lactic acid is being produced by the anaerobic system exactly as fast as the body can recycle it. This pace is known as the anaerobic threshold. Speeds above this threshold can only be maintained for a short time, because the lactic acid accumulates quickly and reaches unbearable levels, forcing you to slow down or stop. An endurance athlete may exceed this threshold occasionally during a race but must then slow down to recover. Sometimes exceeding the threshold may be worthwhile from a tactical standpoint, but the best race times will result from holding a steady pace right at the anaerobic threshold and increasing pace only over the last few minutes.

This threshold can be determined in the laboratory or by estimations made in the field. A maximal oxygen consumption ($\dot{V}O_2$max) laboratory test will determine the maximum amount of oxygen being used by the body (transport of oxygen through the heart, lungs, blood vessels, and blood) during a specific period. Blood gathers oxygen in the lungs and takes it to the muscles. Carbon dioxide (CO_2), a waste product of metabolism, is collected from the muscles and returned to the heart and lungs via the blood. The lungs then release the CO_2 in exhaled air and breathe new oxygen. As you exercise or push for a $\dot{V}O_2$max, your heart beats faster to supply the muscles with more blood and oxygen and remove the CO_2. The body cannot store much, if any, oxygen, thus the amount being consumed during exercise can be measured immediately. The amount is expressed in milliliters of oxygen per kilogram of body weight per minute of exercise ($ml \cdot kg^{-1} \cdot min^{-1}$). The greater this amount, the more energy an athlete is capable of producing.

To determine one's anaerobic threshold, another laboratory test is needed in which the blood is taken from an athlete working at different intensities and analyzed for blood lactate concentration. Endurance training improves the anaerobic threshold by delaying increases in blood lactates. The trained endurance athlete will attain higher velocities before the onset of lactates, thus increasing the ability and use of the percentage of maximal oxygen uptake ($\dot{V}O_2$max). Another familiar method for determining the anaerobic threshold is the Conconi test, but this uses heart rate as the measure of intensity and may not be as reliable as laboratory tests. Questions remain regarding the efficacy of this method, as heart rates (more on this later) are not clearly identifiable with exertion.

More important, these methods simply are not practical for most athletes. In certain instances, such as for Olympic and world-class athletes, these tests may be needed when combined with a comprehensive periodization training program, but generally I believe they are unnecessary. Instead, for many years I have advocated using a rating of perceived exertion (RPE), rather than heart rate, and periodic time trials (in each discipline) to determine theoretical anaerobic thresholds or whether $\dot{V}O_2$max has increased.

To illustrate, faster times over regularly repeated time-trial distances indicate improvements in the anaerobic threshold and perhaps $\dot{V}O_2$max. Moreover, in training, as the anaerobic threshold shifts to the right, an athlete will notice a reduced perceived exertion for a particular training pace. The basis of needing to know this is to judge training adaptation. In other words, are the workouts working? Is the training program working and the anaerobic threshold shifting more rightward? Time trials in each discipline performed on the same courses every four to eight weeks are the most practical gauge of this development. These time trials should be between 15 and 25 minutes in duration in each discipline and completed on separate days. Go for time and measure the distance covered, or select a distance on a familiar course and record the time. Then gauge your times against the anaerobic conditioning zone (lactate ventilatory threshold—LVT) paces on the intensity pace charts to adjust your training accordingly.

lactate accumulates in the muscles and the blood. Increased lactate concentration is probably responsible for the burning sensation that comes with extended high-intensity exercise. Several other factors can affect how fast an athlete can go at this critical threshold. Mechanical efficiency of the running stride, swim stroke, or pedal stroke is important. Obviously, the efficiency of the aerobic system is important, because the more energy we can get from the aerobic system, the less we need from the lactate-producing anaerobic system, and training the anaerobic system may also increase the threshold through improved buffering and removal of lactate. The drills and workouts presented in this book aim to improve the overall efficiency of the aerobic system and sport mechanics to improve one's threshold and thus one's ability to go faster for longer distances.

Training in the Anaerobic Conditioning Zone

LVT workouts require between 15 and 25 minutes of LVT pace work to be of benefit within a workout. Exercise durations of less than 15 minutes permit a higher level of energy and oxygen usage. LVT workouts longer than 25 minutes are unnecessary, as the training benefits have already been achieved during this time. The LVTs are a portion of a workout and can be performed along with work at other intensities. In certain instances, a training session might include two or more LVT workouts, depending on the periodization and volume of training. Ordinarily, LVT workouts are longer-duration intervals with short rest periods rather than continuous efforts. Longer intervals with short rest cycles maintain the necessary physiological training intensity and correspond to the race pace. Time trials or race simulations are regularly included in the training program as periodic tests to determine or reevaluate the pace at which the athlete is working the LVT.

Benefits of the Anaerobic Conditioning Zone

Numerous physiological and biological adaptations and improvements can be gained from training in the LVT zone. The more notable enhancements are as follows:

1. Improves exercise technique and biomechanics.

2. Increases mitochondrial accumulation (Costill et al. 1976; Gollnick and King 1969; Holloszy 1967; Howald 1975; Kiessling, Piehl, and Lundquist 1971).

3. Increases myoglobin content (Mole, Oscai, and Holloszy 1971).

4. Increases carbohydrate oxidation enzymes (Hendricksson and Reitman, 1977; Holloszy 1967).

5. Increases lactate threshold.

6. Enhances glycogen storage capacity.

7. Increases race-specific neuromuscular recruitment.

8. Increases stamina (endurance training that stimulates sustained endurance capacity).

9. Slow- and fast-twitch fiber types remain unchanged because of training. However, metabolic capacities of these fiber types increase through training (Baldwin et al. 1972; Costill et al. 1976; Gollnick et al. 1972; Gollnick et al. 1973).

10. Increases blood volume due to increases in plasma and hemoglobin volume (iron pigment in red blood cells having high propensity for oxygen) (Kjellberg, Rudhe, and Sjostrand 1949; Oscai, Williams, and Hertig 1968).

Aerobic Capacity Zone (VO_2)

Heart rate: 90 to 95 percent of maximum
RPE: Energetically hard to very hard

To improve your $\dot{V}O_2$max and lactate threshold, training in the aerobic capacity zone is necessary. $\dot{V}O_2$max is an athlete's capacity for aerobic power, maximum oxygen consumption, and cardiovascular endurance. At a given point in training, this level is no longer increased, but further increases in pace and efficiency are possible with improved oxidative enzymes and biomechanics. The quantity and intensity of this training make it the most strenuous type of training for the endurance athlete. VO_2 workouts are performed at the intensity zone just above race pace and improve both the aerobic and anaerobic metabolic abilities of the athlete. This is achieved by increases in the body's ability to use greater amounts of oxygen for exercise.

Training in the Aerobic Capacity Zone

VO_2 training intensity is approximately 5 percent faster than race pace (swimming 1,500 meters, cycling 40 kilometers, running 10 kilometers). Again, the intensity pace charts (IPCs) in chapters 3, 4, and 5 define the time goals for this intensity training zone. Importantly, each interval lasts between 2 and 8 minutes. The rest interval between repeats is the same time as the interval (1:1 work-to-rest ratio). For example, eight repetitions of 2-minute efforts at 5 percent above LVT pace plus 2 minutes of rest is a VO_2 workout. Within this system, total VO_2 workout time is 10 to 21 minutes of exercise time. In other words, the actual amount of time you'll be working at this intensity in any one workout is 10 to 21 minutes. The rest interval (exercise) is to be done at a "fairly light" intensity to assist full recovery (gentle swimming, spinning, or walking/jogging).

Again, the IPCs provide the distance and time goals for the interval distance based on the LVT or race pace goal times you have selected and are capable of training for. For example, VO_2 training of 2,000 meters of running would have an interval time of 7:36 for an athlete targeting a 40-minute, 10-kilometer goal time. Using the pace charts, an intelligent increase in pace can be accomplished by targeting reasonable goal paces. If an athlete wishes to improve his 10K to 39:00, he must be able to complete the corresponding times indicated in the IPCs within the appropriate recovery times and training volume. If this is accomplished, the athlete will likely be able to race the faster time. Again, successful performances are reached by applying the rule of right intensity.

The Benefits of Aerobic Capacity Training

Numerous physiological and biological adaptations and improvements can be derived from VO_2 training. The more notable enhancements are as follows:

1. Suprathreshold speed workouts enhance anaerobic power.

2. Improves nervous system patterning. Some motor neurons have a high energy threshold so the muscle fibers they enervate are only recruited at higher intensity levels.

3. Increases blood buffering—development of substances in the blood that maintain a constant acid-base pH balance.

4. $\dot{V}O_2$max increases up to an individual limit, probably genetically determined. This maximum value can be maintained but not improved upon (Ekblom et al. 1968; Fox 1975; Fox et al. 1977; Frick et al. 1970; Pollock 1973; Rubal, Resentswieg, and Hamerly 1981; Saltin et al. 1976).

5. Improves cardiovascular response to intense exercise.

6. Enhances glycogen storage and capacity (Gollnick et al. 1972; Gollnick et al. 1973).

7. Increases muscular strength.

Anaerobic Capacity Zone (LAC)

> Heart rate: Approaching 100 percent of maximum
>
> RPE: Very hard to very, very hard

LAC workouts are somewhat like weight training for power. They are of short duration and very high intensity. Yet one important difference is that LAC workouts apply the rule of specific practice. Although training with weights has benefits for the multisport athlete, nothing compares with actually doing the sport to be used in competition. So with LAC sets, an athlete will gain power and strength and will also train higher metabolic and cardiorespiratory systems. LAC efforts are of short duration (10 seconds to 2 minutes) and have rest intervals of two to three times the exercise time. They develop strength, power, and speed.

As with each of the other intensity zones, LAC training is included in the program throughout the season. Yet, also as with each training intensity zone, every cycle in the training season has different training volumes. I believe this is necessary to develop specific, continual muscular and cardiovascular benefits. The LAC intensity zone trains power, strength, and neuromuscular coordination (brain-to-muscle memory response). Each training intensity zone does the same, but with varying degrees of endurance, strength, power, neuromuscular benefit, and anaerobic capacity improvement.

© Jeffrey Dow

Training in the Anaerobic Capacity Zone

LAC training is high-intensity, short-duration training and for any exercise or sport might look something like this: 20 repeats of 20-second intervals plus 40-second recovery times (total exercise time of 6:40). Of course, there are countless ways of expressing workouts in time and distance. Remember, the total exercise time for training this intensity zone is between 4 and 10 minutes. The IPC workout guidelines for an LAC workout geared toward running a 40-minute 10K might be 4 × 400 meters in 1:26 with rest of three times the run interval (+4 minutes of rest).

Lactate: Training for Speed and Strength

Among the endurance athletes I train, the LAC training sets are quite popular for giving the athlete the feeling of speed and fluidness of motion. Another reason for their popularity is that the duration of the training interval is short and the rest is two to three times the interval, quite unlike the LVT training of race pace workloads and very short rest. Heart rate is a less useful indicator for LAC intensity because the heart rate response lags behind actual effort. With the short intervals used here, a maximal heart rate may not be achieved, even with maximum effort. Toward the final repetitions, athletes will sometimes achieve target heart rates, but usually they will not. Training within the correct intensity zone is more reliably determined by following RPE protocol or applying the IPCs. Even though the heart rate often does not reach the top levels, these workouts are physically and cardiovascularly intense. If you go by heart rate, you'll likely be disappointed, but in fact you've probably done the right training. Finally, it is important to have an adequate warm-up period followed by at least 5 minutes of stretching the primary muscle groups involved in this training.

The Benefits of Anaerobic Capacity Training

Numerous physiological and biological adaptations and improvements can be derived from LAC training, including the following:

1. Power, strength, and speed are enhanced to optimum capacities.

2. Increases slow- and fast-twitch muscle fiber contractibility (Costill et al. 1976; Gollnick et al. 1972; Gollnick et al. 1973).

3. Enzymes change to increase ATP-PC conversion (Pollock 1973; Smith and El-Hage 1978; Thorstensson, Sjodin, and Karlsson 1975).

4. Increases glycolytic ability (supply of ATP for muscular effort) (Erikson, Gollnick, and Saltin 1973; Fournier et al. 1982; Gillespie et al. 1976; Saubert et al. 1973; Staudte, Exner, and Pette 1973).

5. Increases neurological recruitment (neuromuscular muscle memory coordination).

6. Increases and improves blood buffering.

7. Maximizes lactate tolerance (acidosis). Acidosis increases unbuffered acids in the blood or reduces the capacity for removal of lactate.

8. Increases muscular strength (muscular capacity to perform repetitive contractions).

GAUGING INTENSITY

In coaching endurance athletes for more than 16 years, I've used just about every method in trying to determine intensity accurately: lactate analyzers, heart rate monitors, time, pace, stroke count, gait, rpms, and perceived exertion (RPE). The two most popular methods of gauging exercise intensity are heart rate monitoring and perceived exertion (RPE). Heart rate may seem a more accurate and objective measure of exercise intensity because one is able to associate quantitative data (number of heart beats per minute) with an intensity level. Be aware, though, that individual heart rate responses vary and there are several problems with trying to ascribe a definite heart rate range to any desired intensity. Perceived exertion, on the other hand is a subjective scale of physical exertion, proven remarkably consistent with other physiological indicators. With practice, I believe perceived exertion to be a more reliable method of gauging intensity.

Training With a Heart Rate Monitor

Although according to a researcher at the U.S. Olympic Training Center, athletes like heart rate monitors (HRMs) because "they have a little solid number to identify intensity with," it is important for athletes to understand that heart rate monitors may not show as reliable a picture of training intensity as many people think.

Many physical factors can affect heart rate, and the monitors themselves may have an error of 5 to 15 beats per minute. Thus the number of beats per minute may be misleading to athletes who do not factor in other variables that affect heart rate such as fitness changes, dehydration, overtraining, fuel reserves, and others.

Heart rate provides useful information, but it is not an exact indicator of exercise intensity. It may not even be the best single indicator. Recent research studies suggest that blood lactate response is a more sensitive measure of exercise stress.

Some athletes will have narrow fluctuations in heart rate even with considerable changes in pace. When this is true, heart rate is not the best indicator of effort. The point is that no single indicator is perfect for determining exercise intensity. I prefer perceived exertion (RPE) because it actually combines many factors like heart rate, ventilation rate, and lactate in the muscles. Training with a heart rate monitor (HRM) may help to develop or refine this sense of RPE, and that's very helpful, but if you use a HRM, use it in combination with RPE and pace references to determine intensity more accurately.

One example will help to illustrate this point. Keep in mind that an important change that comes from training is a higher anaerobic threshold. Athletes often begin base preparation training with a reduced threshold. For example, 80 percent of $\dot{V}O_2$max may improve to 82 percent after a few weeks. However, perceived exertion does not change, but speed and heart rate both will likely be greater at this same level of intensity. If you use RPE as your primary guide to intensity, you will automatically adjust the speed of your intervals to maintain the correct intensity. Athletes who rely primarily on heart rate need to test maximal heart rates in each discipline regularly (at least after each periodization phase). This permits target rates to be adjusted for changes in fitness and heart rate.

Assigning Target Heart Rates

If you use an HRM, you need to understand how to assign target heart rates correctly. Most exercise programs that offer heart rate guidelines simply specify a percentage of the theoretical maximum (HRmax). Ideally, the percentages given in table 1.1 and in the descriptions of the intensity zones should be calculated as a percentage of heart rate reserve (HRR), the difference between resting HR and HRmax. This is known as the Karvonen method. Using this method, the percentage figure closely reflects effort, with 100 percent being as hard as you can go and 0 percent equal to lying down at rest. With percentage of HRmax, 100 percent is still full effort, but 0 percent would be a nonbeating heart—a corpse.

Be aware that HRmax can be a source of error too. The standard formula of 220 minus your age is not very accurate. In addition, your maximum heart rate is most likely different for each sport. Triathletes typically have lower maximum heart rates on the bike than on the run, for example, although there are exceptions. Mike Pigg is one well-known athlete who in 1988 tested a higher maximal heart rate on the bike than on the run. Does this mean his exercise economy was better on the bike than while running? It's an interesting question and suggests this may have been true in his case.

Thus, you need to determine your own HRmax for each sport. Refer to the maximal heart rate field assessment for an easy way to measure maximal heart rate in the field. Once you have accurate numbers for HRmax, use the Karvonen formula (see table 1.2; table A.1) to determine the correct HR for each intensity level.

Other Uses for the Heart Rate Monitor

Noting the time it takes for the heart rate to recover between repetitions is one effective way to use a monitor. A reduction in the time needed for complete recovery is a true indicator of improved fitness.

TABLE 1.2   Heart Rate Zone Template

1.   Subtract your resting heart rate (RHR) from your maximum heart rate (HRmax).

2.   Multiply by the percentage for each intensity zone.

3.   Add your RHR.

4.   Enter your training HR for the zone.

Percentage MHR	Your training intensity zone HR		Intensity zone
± 100	(	)	LAC
95	(	)	VO_2
90	(	)	LVT
85	(	)	LVT
80	(	)	O_2
75	(	)	O_2
70	(	)	O_2

220 - (   ) age = _____ - (   ) RHR = _____ × (%) = _____ + (   ) RHR = _____ training HR

MAXIMAL HEART RATE FIELD ASSESSMENT

For those who use heart rate to gauge intensity, the field test is an effective way to measure the heart rate maximum regularly. Heart rates are different for each sport, indicating the need for the multisport athlete to test in each discipline.

The test is relatively easy to perform (other than that the intensity is very hard), and it takes little time to complete. Here's what you need to do:

1. Warm up for at least 15 minutes, then stretch for 5 minutes. Follow this with another 5-minute warm-up, increasing the effort slightly as you go; then stretch again.

2. After warming up, run, ride, or swim at least 15 minutes. Then, for the next 6 minutes, increase your intensity to what you perceive to be your best effort, knowing the length of effort is only 6 minutes.

3. After 6 minutes, run, ride, or swim the next 30 seconds *all out*.

4. Immediately after completing the final 30 seconds, record your heart rate from the monitor. That's all there is to it. Use this number in the heart rate zone template (table 1.2) to calculate your target HR for each intensity zone. As a backup, immediately take your radial pulse (at the wrist) for 15 seconds and multiply the result by 4.

Remember, however, that athletes should consider ranges and not specific HR targets. HRs vary with fitness level, fatigue, age, gender, environmental conditions, and for each discipline. For more accuracy, you'll want to check this every six weeks or so for training adaptations. The HR monitor can provide a framework for establishing exercise intensity zones and is best used in combination with other methods such as perceived exertion and the intensity pace charts.

There is another important reason for using an HRM—to guard against overtraining! The following are two examples of why I believe this is the most valuable and useful benefit of the HRM. First, when running or cycling, an athlete's heart rate may not increase to "normal" levels; the pace is slowed and RPE is increased. When this happens, it is a good sign that the athlete needs rest and should be consuming fluids and nutritious foods. Second, there is an increase in the time necessary for the heart rate to return to an aerobic (O_2) range after intervals or workouts such as hill climbs. In both instances, the abnormal heart rate response indicates the athlete needs something. I look at recovery time to aerobic (O_2) range first and foremost from my athletes' charts and tables of heart rate workouts.

Perceived Exertion

Perceived exertion is a tried-and-true method for recognizing and determining the intensity of exercise. How an athlete feels psychologically about training intensity is closely linked to effort. It is by far my preferred way of coaching an athlete to use the right intensity in training and competition. The intensity pace charts in the respective swimming, cycling, and running chapters were developed using a combination of RPE and heart rate. To evaluate perceived exertion accurately, you need to get in touch with your feelings about differing levels of effort.

RPE is personal. Your perception of effort is unlike anyone else's, yet there are ways to determine a pace that most everyone can use. RPE is an unconstrained way of looking at physical and emotional boundaries for stamina. RPE does not limit performance or push you beyond your desired intensity training the way targeting a specific heart rate or time might do. RPE can relate to physical and environmental conditions more accurately than a heart rate monitor can.

An athlete's personal perception of the intensity of exercise effort is a reliable way to measure effort. Fine-tuning speed according to the way you feel psychologically allows for modifications in intensity to hit the correct intensity zone. Training using scales of perceived exertion effectively adjusts to the body's signals and requirements.

Although this method doesn't require special equipment, it does have its limitations. Primarily, to certain individuals, RPE may seem harder than the actual intensity. Review the intensity training continuums (table 1.1) and become familiar with the conditions for each intensity zone. Even though you may perceive an intensity is too great to maintain, it may be that you lack psychological and physiological experience. Some athletes have a lower tolerance for the higher psychological (pain) thresholds associated with training and competition. Learning RPE is a matter of recognizing the feelings of exertion and matching them with the right training zone.

Perhaps the most effective way to learn RPE is by applying the training intensity zones. Using the perceived exertion indications such as very hard to very, very hard (LAC), an athlete can best learn RPE. For example, warm up running very easily for 15 to 20 minutes and stretch for 5 minutes. Next, run for 15 seconds with the mental RPE described above. Mark the distance covered. Do this 12 times, resting for 30 seconds after each run. If you run too fast, you won't recover for the next interval; if you run too slow, the distance won't be similar.

Using the training intensity zone continuum (table 1.1) rules for duration and recovery and perceived exertion, the above method can be tested with each intensity zone. In a short time, the athlete will begin to apply the correct pace

MORNING HEART RATE: RECOGNIZING OVERTRAINING

Overtraining can bring about reductions in fitness as a result of ongoing cardiac, musculoskeletal, and physical stresses brought on by too much exercise. There is a gradual falloff in performance, and often muscles are sore and emotions become out of sorts (anxiety, depression, anger). Obviously, these things are not good for the endurance athlete to experience.

Athletes can monitor the morning HR and psychological feelings to check for signs and symptoms of this common training problem. Actually, psychological symptoms are likely to precede an increase in HR response to overtraining. The heart rate training manager (appendix table A.2) is an effective and simple training management tool for monitoring this very important training component.

The HR (morning pulse) taken each morning before getting out of bed should be entered on the appropriate date and location on table A.2. When the trend is upward by more than eight beats, a reduction in training is prescribed. More important, psychological symptoms reveal themselves prior to an increase in morning resting pulse. Thus, by paying close attention to such feelings, you may be able to catch overtraining problems early on. Research has shown these same findings, and mood changes are reported more often in athletes presenting symptoms of staleness and overtraining.

TABLE 1.3   Perceived Exertion

Percentage of HRmax	Training intensity zone	Perceived exertion (RPE)	Numerical rating of RPE	Training pace comparison
± 100 95	LAC	Very hard to very, very hard	10	Lactate sprint training; workout intervals with long rest periods
95 90	VO$_2$	Very hard	8-9	Faster than race pace but not all out; high intensity; rest intervals match work time
90 80	LVT	Energetically hard	4-7	Race pace (RP) training from intervals (starting 10 percent below RP), fartleking, and competition simulation; short rest intervals
80 70	O$_2$	Fairly light	2-3	Distance training at conversation pace; recovery and endurance development types of low-intensity workouts

to the intensity zone as a result of knowing the duration of the effort and the perceived exertion. The longer the exercise, the less intensity or perceived exertion applied.

The hypothesis of psychological pain thresholds is interesting. You see, those with more experience braving certain psychological discomfort due to physical exertion are, in fact, training this barrier. Athletes, especially less experienced ones, will have more difficulty managing these pain barriers at first. They simply have nothing against which to gauge their effort. Also, the cardiovascular and musculoskeletal systems may need adaptation to unfamiliar physical stress. So practice and guidance using the parameters I have laid out will help you make these feelings more readily understood.

How do you learn to understand these feelings? It's simply a matter of a few practice sessions and applying the intended pace and RPE. Tables 1.1 and 1.3 are good places to start. In particular, table 1.3 lists the intensity zones, heart rate, descriptive words for the RPE level, and a numerical rating of RPE. These should

help you understand how to gauge the intensity needed in each zone. Table 1.1 includes a bit more detail and shows workout illustrations applicable for each zone.

Remember, there are specific intensities, durations, and rest intervals for each of the four training intensity zones. Tables 1.1 and 1.3 outline those rules for the right training practice. Make a copy to keep handy, as these rules will help you make the change to RPE training. Finally, because HR is variable to many physiological and environmental conditions, RPE will be the more effective means of determining pace and intensity.

Pace Charts

Pace charts provide an accurate way to gauge intensity as long as wind is not a factor and the course is flat. When training on a track or in a pool, pace charts are a great tool for measuring intensity. The IPCs detail the distance and time for the interval. These are divided according to the sport (swimming, cycling, and running). The athlete simply refers to the chart for the intensity zone desired and reads across from the LVT pace corresponding to his or her own best performance or realistic goal time to find the chosen interval distance and the goal time for that distance. The IPCs for each sport are an originally developed part of this training system and provide specific information for designing workouts with the right intensity. The charts also provide the athlete and coach with the goal development tools needed to achieve even higher levels of endurance performance. In other words, when a faster race pace is desired, the pace charts furnish the workout times for given distances the athlete must achieve to race at this particular intensity. Once the athlete meets these levels in training, the results of competition should not be surprising.

The IPCs are not absolute or infallible. As with perceived exertion and heart rate, these are ranges and are yet another training intensity guide. Again, the charts were developed in conjunction with perceived exertion, heart rate percentages, and each respective training intensity zone. Use the IPCs as a framework for training intensity.

The training intensity zones are the cornerstone of this training system. In use, they provide the athlete with an accurate way to measure intensity in training. This is a significant step in the development of an endurance training program. As the following chapter details, training volume and periodization utilize the four training intensity zones, providing a comprehensive and successful training structure for measuring intensity in each discipline.

© Terry Wild Studio

2

TRAINING VOLUME AND PERIODIZATION

In every training program, the training schedule must fit the needs of the athlete. Designing a complete multisport endurance training program requires thoughtful planning. Managing all the elements of training is complicated, but anything worth achieving is worth the effort. As Euripides wrote in 421 BC: "Much effort, much prosperity."

You'll need to set aside one to three hours to get started, but this is necessary to develop and individualize a training program. This chapter will lead you through the initial steps of putting together your training schedule.

I have coached endurance athletes and designed training programs for 16 years. During this time, I've asked myself many questions, including: What particular workouts should be

done at what time in the season? What overall training volume is best for a particular athlete? What percentage of the total training volume should be O_2 training, LAC training, VO_2 training, and LVT training? How much time should be spent in each training intensity zone? What work-to-rest ratios are best? What are the periodization strategies or cycles? Finally, what is the periodic adjustment of training volume, intensity, and program emphasis?

I have been able to answer many of these questions for myself by creating a systematic training program that can be individualized to the athlete. This chapter guides you through the first steps of this systematic program to help you define your training and competitive goals and develop your program periodization and

TABLE 2.1 Training Program Summary

Step 1: Make a copy of the program overview manager (POM); see table A.3.

Step 2: Determine the dates of your training season and write them onto the POM.

Step 3: Set and rank your training and competition goals.

    a. Enter competition goals onto the POM (rank by importance).

    b. Consolidate your calendars (personal, competition, and business).

    c. Review your previous season's training journal (enter monthly volumes onto table).

Step 4: Determine your season training volume.

Step 5: Determine your periodization cycles (enter appropriate period onto POM).

    a. Base preparation (bp)

    b. Base transition (bt)

TABLE 2.1 *(continued)*

   c. Race preparation (rp)

   d. Peak transition (pt)

   e. Restoration (r)

Step 6: Make a copy of the sport-specific program managers.

Step 7: Determine your periodization cycle volume (percentage of season volume).

   a. Number of cycle weeks (total weeks in each periodization cycle)

   b. Percentage of total weeks (divide 7a by total number of weeks in season)

   c. Percentage of cycle (total season volume multiplied by 7b)

   d. Weekly training volume (table 2.5)

volume. Table 2.1 outlines each of the important steps you'll develop in this chapter. Refer to this table after you've read the chapter for help with keeping the steps in order.

Also, you'll learn how to use the several program managers and then custom build them to suit your personal goals. The program managers for swimming, cycling, and running contain the training intensity zone and weekly training volumes based on the periodization cycles and competitions developed in the program overview manager (POM). Chapter 7 will then provide the information for devising daily workouts based on these principles as well as the techniques and drill ideas discussed in chapters 3, 4, 5, and 6.

STEP 1:
Make a Copy of the Program Overview Manager

The program overview manager (POM) in the appendix (table A.3) and the completed sample illustrated in table 2.2 provide the basic organization for the multisport training program. Later in this chapter, I will detail how this manager is used. Make a copy of the blank POM from the appendix now before going on to the next step. Use the sample POM in table 2.2 as a reference.

STEP 2:
Determine the Dates of Your Training Season

Beginning with your first week of training through the concluding week of the season, enter the dates onto the POM.

STEP 3:
Set and Rank Your Training and Competition Goals

Without doubt, the first consideration when planning a training program should be establishing your competitive goals. Goals provide the motivation behind a training program by pinpointing events you want to focus on and train for. By knowing what competitive events you will be striving for, you can plan your training periodization. Your training program should be unique to your ability and goals. Chapter 9 describes goal setting and mental preparation in more detail, but we'll begin this chapter by discussing goal setting as it relates to planning your training program. That is, what are the competitions and events in which you wish to compete? Will you be participating in events that serve as qualifying competitions for later events? Write all of those events onto the POM now.

In athletics, specific, challenging, but sufficiently difficult goals produce the best results. For example, finishing a marathon or open-water swim, cycling 100 miles, or climbing a mountain are specific goals. Likewise, having shorter-term step-by-step targets en route to these goals help athletes remain focused along the way by providing regular training and competition milestones for periodic testing and gaining confidence in fitness. The POM will help you establish your training and competition goals. Each week, the POM summarizes the training goals for each respective sport. These short-term goals provide directly measurable training markers such as distance workouts, time-trial tests, or technique workouts. Chapter 7 will show you how to arrange these weekly workout goals.

Alongside each competition—duathlon, triathlon, marathon, century, open-water swim, or other athletic event—rank the importance of each. I use two ranking levels: one for events

TABLE 2.2   Program Overview Manager

Athlete_____

Wk	Monday	Competition (rank)	Program emphasis/ Interval	SP	Swim week target (m)	BP	Bike week target (mi)	RP	Run week target (mi)	CAL	ISK	IST
1	1-6-97	Start program	bp/1	bp18	1,000 O_2	bp18	20 O_2	bp18	5 O_2	Wk1	Wk1	Wk1
2	1-13-97		bp/1	bp 17	1,100 O_2	bp 17	25 O_2	bp 17	6 O_2	Wk2	Wk2	Wk2
3	1-20-97		bp/1	bp 16	1,000 trial	bp 16	30 O_2; break; 3 mi.	bp 16	7 O_2	Wk3	Wk3	Wk3
4	1-27-97	Restoration	r/1	r	700 TF	r	Roller TF	r	4 O_2	Off	Off	Off
5	2-3-97		bp/1	bp 15	1,200 O_2	bp 15	30 O_2	bp 15	10 tempo	Wk1	Wk1	Wk1
6	2-10-97		bp/1	bp 14	1,300 O_2	bp 14	10-mi. trial	bp 14	9 O_2	Wk2	Wk2	Wk2
7	2-17-97		bp/1	bp 13	1,000 trial	bp 13	35 O_2; break; 4 mi.	bp 13	10 O_2	Wk3	Wk3	Wk3
8	2-24-97	Restoration	r/1	r	1,000 TF	r	Roller TF	r	5 O_2	Off	Off	Off
9	3-3-97	10K road race (2)	bp/1	bp 12	1,500 O_2	bp 12	40 O_2	bp 12	10K race	Off	Wk1	Wk1
10	3-10-97		bp/1	bp 11	2,000 TF	bp 11	45 O_2	bp 11	11 O_2	Wk2	Wk2	Wk2
11	3-17-97	5K, 30, 5K duathlon (2)	bp/1	bp 10	1,500 O_2	bp 10	Duathlon	bp 10	Duathlon	Off	Off	Off
12	3-24-97	Restoration	r/1	r	Break	r	Break	r	Break	Off	Off	Off
13	3-31-97		bp/1	bp 9	1,000 trial	bp 9	35 O_2	bp 9	12 O_2	Wk1	Off	Wk1
14	4-7-97		bp/1	bp 8	1,600 O_2	bp 8	40 O_2	bp 8	10 tempo	Wk2	Wk2	Wk2
15	4-14-97		bp/1	bp 7	1,700 O_2	bp 7	50 O_2; break; 5 mi.	bp 7	8 O_2	Wk3	Wk3	Wk3
16	4-21-97	Restoration	r/1	r	1,500 TF	r	10-mi. trial	r	12 O_2	Off	Off	Off
17	4-28-97	5K, 30, 5K duathlon (2)	bp/1	bp 6	1,000 O_2	bp 6	Duathlon	bp 6	Duathlon	Off	Off	Off
18	5-5-97		bp/1	bp 5	1,500 TF	bp 5	35 O_2	bp 5	8 O_2	Off	Off	Off
19	5-12-97	21K road race-run (2)	bp/1	bp 4	1,000 trial	bp 4	40 O_2	bp 4	21K race	Off	Off	Off
20	5-19-97	Restoration	r/1	r	Break	r	Break	r	Break	Off	Off	Off
21	5-26-97		bp/1	bp 3	2,000 O_2	bp 3	10-mi. trial	bp 3	8 O_2	Wk1	Wk1	Wk1
22	6-2-97	5K road race (2)	bp/1	bp 2	1,500 TF	bp 2	35 O_2	bp 2	5K race	Wk2	Wk2	Wk2
23	6-9-97		bp/1	bp 1	1,000 O_2	bp 1	50 O_2	bp 1	9 O_2	Wk3	Wk3	Wk3
24	6-16-97	1K, 20, 5K triathlon (2)	r/1	r	Trirace 1K	r	Trirace 20K	r	Trirace 5K	Off	Off	Off

TABLE 2.2   Program Overview Manager

Year_____

Wk	Monday	Competition (rank)	Program emphasis/ Interval	SP	Swim week target (m)	BP	Bike week target (mi)	RP	Run week target (mi)	CAL	ISK	IST
25	6-23-97	Restoration	bt/2	bt6	800 TF	bt6	20 TF	bt6	5 O_2	Off	Off	Off
26	6-30-97		bt/2	bt5	1,200 O_2	bt5	60 O_2	bt5	8 O_2	Wk1	Wk1	Wk1
27	7-7-97		bt/2	bt4	1,500 O_2	bt4	50 O_2	bt4	10 O_2	Wk2	Wk2	Wk2
28	7-14-97	Vacation/holiday	r/2	r	Break	r	Break	r	Break	Off	Off	Off
29	7-21-97		bt/2	bt3	1,000 trial	bt3	10-mi. trial	bt3	8 O_2+5K	Wk1	Wk1	Wk1
30	7-28-97		bt/2	bt2	1,600 O_2	bt2	40 O_2	bt2	9 O_2	Wk2	Wk2	Wk2
31	8-4-97		bt/2	bt1	1,000 O_2	bt1	35 O_2	bt1	6 O_2	Off	Wk1	Off
32	8-11-97	1.5, 40, 10K triathlon (2)	r/2	r	Trirace 1.5K	r	Trirace 40K	r	Trirace 10K	Off	Off	Off
33	8-18-97		rp/3	rp3	1,800 TF drill	rp3	40 O_2	rp3	8 O_2	Off	Off	Off
34	8-25-97		rp/3	rp2	1,600 O_2	rp2	10-mi. trial	rp2	10 O_2	Wk1	Wk1	Wk1
35	9-1-97		rp/3	rp1	1,000 O_2	rp1	35 O_2	rp1	6 O_2	Off	Wk1	Off
36	9-8-97	1.5, 40, 10K triathlon (1)	pt/1	pt1	Trirace 1.5K	pt1	Trirace 40K	pt1	Trirace 10K	Off	Off	Off
37	9-15-97		rp/4	rp3	1,500 O_2	rp3	40 O_2	rp3	8 O_2	Wk1	Wk1	Wk1
38	9-22-97		rp/4	rp2	1,000 O_2	rp2	10-mi. trial	rp2	6 O_2	Off	Off	Off
39	9-29-97		rp/4	rp1	800 O_2	rp1	30 O_2	rp1	4 O_2	Off	Off	Off
40	10-6-97	1.5, 40, 10K triathlon (1)	pt/1		Trirace 1.5K	pt1	Trirace 40K	pt1	Trirace 10K	Off	Off	Off
41	10-13-97		rp/5	rp3	1,200 O_2	rp3	30 O_2	rp3	7 O_2	Off	Off	Off
42	10-20-97		rp/5	rp2	800 O_2	rp2	25 O_2	rp2	6 O_2	Off	Off	Off
43	10-27-97		rp/5	rp1	800 O_2	rp1	20 O_2	rp1	4 O_2	Off	Off	Off
44	11-3-97	1.5, 40, 10K triathlon (1)		pt1	Trirace 1.5K	pt1	Trirace 40K	pt1	Trirace 10K	Off	Off	Off
45	11-10-97	Off-season										
46	11-17-97	Off-season										
47	11-24-97	Off-season										
48	12-1-97	Off-season										
49	12-8-97	Off-season										
50	12-15-97	Off-season										
51	12-22-97	Off-season										
52	12-29-97	Off-season										

I believe are highly important and one for less significant events. Having more than two ranking levels is probably unnecessary. Place a 1 after events that are most important for you, those competitions where you wish to perform your best. Place a 2 next to all "nontaper" events, those competitions that are less important in terms of results but play an important role in overall season outcome. These are training competitions that keep the athlete used to competing while continuing periodization through preparatory training events.

Consolidate Your Calendars

Using two calendars is an excellent way to begin this process. The first is your family/personal/business calendar and the second is a competition calendar. Consolidate these calendars to determine any potential conflicts. For those with families and complex schedules, it is especially important to compare your calendars to determine the most realistic training program that takes into account all that is going on in your life.

When planning your competition calendar and selecting events, be sure to consider travel time, expenses, whether qualifying standards are necessary, and the competitive distances. For now, enter each of your personal, business, and competitive dates onto the POM. This will require time and research, but it is a necessary step in devising your most effective training program. Take some time to collect race, personal, and business calendars, talk with the family about vacations, and write down all intended competitions, events, and holiday dates and enter them onto the POM (table A.3), under "Competition."

Reviewing Your Previous Season's Training Journal

Information about the amounts of training you have done in the past is especially helpful in developing your new training program. Begin by collecting data for the preceding season's total training volume (distance or hours) for each respective sport in which you trained. This information is meaningful because you should

avoid increasing training volume by too much in a single year. Increases greater than 15 percent can lead to injury and overtraining.

Enter your previous season's training volumes by month onto the annual volume worksheet (table A.4). If you have not kept a journal, estimate the previous season's training volume. I recommend a conservative estimation, including all sport-specific training and competitions. This will prevent you from unknowingly increasing your annual volume by more than 15 percent over the previous year. If you are new to endurance or multisport training, it is especially important that you begin training at a low volume and gradually increase the volume as your body adapts.

STEP 4:
Determine Your Season Training Volume

This program's unique implementation of the training intensity zones works exceptionally well with lower training volumes. Athletes often believe that maintaining more distance is the only pathway to success. But high training volume does not always equate to better performance. Rather, training programs should use an integration of training intensities and volume. Training volume is the distance (mileage) or duration (hours) of training necessary to achieve competitive goals. The following paragraphs review several important considerations in determining the right training volume. You will not be entering any data here. The training volume will be organized onto separate program managers for each discipline later in chapter 7.

Your current season training volume is determined by your competitive goals, your prior season's training, and the recommended volumes for respective competitive distances given in table 2.3. I developed this table while working with athletes over the years. Although 15 percent is often given as the upper limit for increases in training volume from one season to the next, I recommend no more than a 10 percent increase in total training volume (for each discipline). That is, your total volume should be no more than 10 percent greater than the previous season's total.

However, an athlete need not necessarily increase volume each season. Rather, consistency in training over multiple seasons without injury is more important for endurance performance. Injury is often the result of inconsistency in training and excessive increases in training volume or intensity. Whether or not an athlete should increase training volume depends on their musculoskeletal health status. First, has training been regularly interrupted by chronic or multiple overuse injury? Following injury, have you suffered from a cycle of reinjury or further overuse-related injuries? If so, the volume and/or intensity of your training program may be too great. Before returning to regular training, an athlete should have full range of motion, strength, and flexibility. If not, I advise continuing rehabilitation of the injured site under qualified medical supervision. Second, are further increases in volume necessary for achievement of a competitive goal? Table 2.3 will help you decide. Answering these personal questions is essential before making the decision to increase training volume.

Table 2.3 lists training volumes needed to compete at several multisport competitive distances. The duathlete and single-sport athlete can use those areas applicable to them. It is important to remember that an athlete may increase or decrease training volume in each sport independent of the other sports. For example, an individual who is stronger at running and weaker at swimming may benefit by increasing swimming volume while decreasing running volume. The purpose, of course, is to allow more time in the weaker discipline. Many athletes do exactly the opposite and spend more time in sports at which they already excel, for reasons that are as diverse as the nature of each personality. Multisport endurance athletes should try to equalize each discipline to their best ability.

How much to increase and decrease volume in any one or more sports is a difficult question to answer. Obviously, there are vast differences in ability and experience that make giving specific guidelines here nearly impossible. For example, a sub-2:30 marathoner with an equally competent cycling background who has never been in the water is going to need some schedule adjustments to become a competitive triathlete.

The distances shown in the swimming, cycling, and running columns of table 2.3 are recommended ranges (low to high) for training

TABLE 2.3   Recommended Training Volume

Event/distance		Swimming Week (m)	Years	Cycling Week (miles)	Year	Running Week (miles)	Year
Sprint	Low	1,500	67,500	15	720	6	288
1K, 20K, 5K	High	9,000	405,000	75	3,375	24	1,080
Olympic triathlon	Low	2,500	112,500	25	1,125	10	450
1.5K, 40K, 10K	High	13,000	585,000	155	6,975	33	1,485
Long course	Low	3,000	144,000	56	2,520	17	765
2K, 90K, 21K	High	16,500	742,500	208	9,360	42	1,890
Ultra/Ironman	Low	4,000	192,000	65	3,120	18	864
4K, 180K, 42K	High	27,500	1,237,500	345	15,525	65	2,925

Note: Based on 48 training weeks and highest or lowest season training weeks volume per season (based on a 48-week season). Athletes often have one or more competitive distance goals and competitions. In these cases, the recommended ranges for longer events are used from the table. The volume recommendations for duathletes apply to similar competitive distance events without the swimming.

The lowest volumes on the table are the minimum training amounts needed to compete successfully at those distances. These recommendations are based on my experiences in developing training programs for endurance athletes over the years. Basically, the volumes are approximate ranges of training needed and are not absolute. It is particularly important for every athlete to work up to the higher ranges gradually. Without sufficient training preparation, injury is almost certainly in the forecast.

STEP 5:
Determine Your
Periodization Cycles

Periodization in athletic training programs refers to how training volume, intensity, and frequency are divided into "periods" or cycles over the course of a training season. In this program, these cycles continue from 1 to 20 weeks. Importantly, the cycles vary the training intensity zone (chapter 1) volumes in any period of training. This method is what sets this program apart from others. Not only is the weekly total volume adjusted, but each training intensity zone volume adjusts with the periodization cycle.

The ensuing periods are what you'll use to organize the periodization of the season. This becomes quite important, as each of these periodization cycles contains percentages of the total season volume. After reading the next section, you'll be able to apply the appropriate period to your program. Now let's review the periods of training to be applied to your program. There are five training periods or cycles of periodization within this system:

1. Base preparation (bp)
2. Base transition (bt)

3. Race preparation (rp)
4. Peak transition (pt)
5. Restoration (r)

Enter the period that fits with your schedule under "Program emphasis" on the POM (table A.3).

Cycles in Training

The training season begins with the base preparation phase, then moves into the base transition, race preparation, and peak transition phases. Each of these periodization cycles represents a phase of training and percentage of total season volume.

Base Preparation

Training in the base preparation phase lasts between 4 and 20 weeks. During this time, the athlete develops a physical foundation for fur-

MASSAGE THERAPY

Massage treatment presents the endurance athlete with several therapeutic, physiological, and psychological benefits. Massage can be used in training for recovery and muscle stimulation and as a precompetition treatment. The use of massage warms the extremities; reduces muscle spasm, swelling, and soreness; is relaxing; and promotes healing and recovery. Use massage therapy cautiously, particularly prior to competitions (chapter 10), as application of a particular technique may cause unnecessary soreness or injury.

ther aerobic and anaerobic conditioning. Generally, the emphasis is on training in the O_2 intensity zone (long and easy aerobic endurance training), but as with each phase all training intensity zones are used in varying amounts. During the base preparation phase, you'll also want to work on correcting any technical skills such as body posture and footstrike while running, spinning efficiently while cycling, or using long strokes, a curvilinear stroke path, and high elbow recovery during swims.

Period: Base preparation (bp)

Length: 4 to 20 weeks

General benefits and phase objectives:

- Endurance and connective tissue development
- Development of general aerobic endurance (long workouts of less intensity, but still including each of the training intensity zones)
- Development of strength, flexibility, mobility, coordination, with emphasis on technical (biomechanical) improvements and corrections
- Development of psychological strategies and practice
- Gradual increase in training volume and intensity as guided by the table of periodization
- Periodic standard tests (time trials)
- Restoration period for one full week after every four weeks

Base Transition

The base transition phase follows the bp phase, continuing from one to six weeks depending on one's overall goals and the number of weeks in the total training season. This cycle can additionally follow an rp phase for a one- to three-week transition, before another rp cycle. As the name implies, this phase serves as a transition period to prepare the athlete for the next phase of training. This is accomplished by reductions in O_2 and increases in LVT, VO_2, and LAC training intensity zones.

Period: Base transition (bt)

Length: One to six weeks

General benefits and phase objectives:

- Further endurance and connective tissue development
- Increase in training volume and intensity
- Further strength, flexibility, mobility, and coordination work
- Narrowed focus on technical skill training (one primary skill, or drill, per sport)
- Focus on psychological strategies (narrow the areas of focus)
- Gradual reduction in aerobic training
- Increased LVT, VO_2, and LAC training volume and intensity
- Periodic standard tests (time trials)
- Restoration period for one full week after every four weeks

PEAKING AND TAPERING

This is the time for athletes to reach their peak athletic performance. It is not the time to make sudden changes in training, nutrition, or tactics for competition. Such changes should have been planned and practiced previously. Having the athlete feel psychologically good about themselves and their fitness is perhaps more important than any other physiological or training aspect.

Top performances occur after maximum conditioning has been achieved. The potential for an athlete suddenly to perform above workout levels without having shown a significant ability increase in training is low. In other words, training typically indicates how an athlete will perform in competition. Of course, there are those who rise above and surprise everyone, but if their program is reviewed in detail, certain indicators of this peak performance potential will likely be evident.

Race Preparation

The race preparation phase has three to eight cycles. This period is used before important competitions and is followed by tapering from one to three weeks (depending on the competitive distance) described below.

Period: Race preparation (rp)

Length: Three to eight weeks (several rp phases can be included over the season)

General benefits and phase objectives:

- More race-specific types of training
- Precedes tapering events (no. 1 rank)
- Reduction in overall training volume
- Further increases in LVT, VO_2, and LAC volume and intensity
- Includes several competitions
- Restoration period every four weeks for one full week

Peak Transition

The peak transition phase includes up to three cycles and is used for fine-tuning the competitive edge (tapering). The first pt week is used when tapering for a multisport event of fewer than three hours. The second week of pt is used for competitions of more than three hours and

fewer than six. The third week of pt is applied to competitions longer than six hours.

Period: Peak transition (pt)

Length: One to three weeks

General benefits and phase objectives:

- Reduce training volume for the purpose of tapering
- Increase potential and feel of speed and fluidity
- Promote recovery and restoration
- Realize peak conditioning by increases in VO_2 and LAC percentage of weekly volume
- Fine-tune psychological strategies (see chapter 9)

Restoration

Restoration consists of recovery or rest weeks strategically placed every four weeks during the training season. Training volume is reduced up to 40 percent of the previous phase's highest week. There is no high-intensity training during these weeks, but longer-distance workouts are often included. These weeks are important, as an athlete can look forward to the reduction in total workout volume and intensity, receiving a much-deserved physiological and psychological break.

Period: Restoration (r)

Length: One week

General benefits and phase objectives:

- Restore physiologically
- Revive psychologically
- Increase adaptation of physical stress (preceding training periodization cycles)
- Prevent overtraining

STEP 6:
Make a Copy of the Sport-Specific Program Managers

The respective swimming, cycling, and running program managers located in the appendix and the completed samples shown in table 2.4, a through c, detail the total training volume and training intensity zone volumes for each periodization cycle and week. Make copies of the blank sport-specific program managers (table A.5, a-c) for your training plan now before going on to the next step.

STEP 7:
Determine Your Periodization Cycle Volume

After the periodization cycles and new season volume have been determined for each respective sport, the weekly volume for each cycle needs to be calculated. This is the amount of volume for each periodization cycle based on a percentage of the total season volume. To do this, the number of weeks in each periodization cycle are divided by the total weeks in the training season.

1. Number of cycle weeks: Determine the number of weeks in each training cycle in your schedule. These are the consecutive bp, bt, and rp cycles, including the restoration weeks but not the pt weeks. They must be in groups of at least four weeks, the last of which is an r week. In other words, all of the consecutive bp weeks (including any r weeks) are counted as a cycle. The bp and bt phases can be linked together (counted as the same cycle), as shown in the program overview manager (table 2.2), with a number designation going through week 12.

2. Percentage of total weeks: Divide the number of weeks in each periodization cycle by the total number of weeks in the season. The result is the periodization cycle's percent of the season.

3. Percentage of cycle: Multiply the total season volume of each sport by the percentage of each periodization cycle. This results in the total training volume for the week and is entered onto the respective program managers (swimming, cycling, and running) under "Volume." This result is used to determine the weekly training volume.

4. Weekly training volume: From table 2.5, select a weekly increase of 2, 4, 6, and 0.6 percent; 10, 10, 10, and 0.6 percent; or 3, 5, 7, and 0.6 percent. These percentages represent the amounts of augmentation applied to each four consecutive weeks. Specifically, week 2 is 1.04 percent of week 1, week 3 is 1.06 percent of week 2, and so on. The percentage step-ups or week 4 step-downs are relative to the previous week's training volume. A different periodization cycle step-up may be applied to each respective discipline.

   a. If you have a 4-, 8-, 12-, 16-, or 20-week periodization cycle, use the respective multipliers furnished in table 2.5.

   b. Divide the total periodization cycle volume by the number of weeks in the cycle.

   c. Multiply this by the multiplier. In table 2.5, find the appropriate number of weeks in the cycle. Begin with the first factor for week 1, using each subsequent factor until you reach the end of the cycle.

   d. Enter this into the volume column on each of the program managers (table A.5, a-c).

Training note: The "rule of pt" must be followed when calculating the periodization

TABLE 2.4a
Swimming Program Manager   Athlete_____

Week	Monday	Competition (rank)	Program emphasis	Period	Week target	Volume (meters)	Pct.	O$_2$	LVT (meters)	VO$_2$	LAC
1	1-6-97	Start program	bp	bp18	1,000 O$_2$	6,525	0.82	4,875	1,350	200	100
2	1-13-97		bp	bp17	1,100 O$_2$	6,775	0.85	5,025	1,425	225	100
3	1-20-97		bp	bp16	1,000 trial	7,200	0.90	5,300	1,525	250	125
4	1-27-97	Restoration	r	r	700 TF	4,325	0.54	4,325			
5	2-3-97		bp	bp15	1,200 O$_2$	7,350	0.92	5,375	1,575	250	125
6	2-10-97		bp	bp14	1,300 O$_2$	7,625	0.96	5,550	1,650	275	150
7	2-17-97		bp	bp13	1,000 trial	8,100	1.02	5,850	1,800	300	150
8	2-24-97	Restoration	r	r	1,000 TF	4,850	0.61	4,850			
9	3-3-97	10K road race (2)	bp	bp12	1,500 O$_2$	8,250	1.04	5,925	1,850	325	925
10	3-10-97		bp	bp11	2,000 TF	8,575	1.07	6,100	1,950	325	175
11	3-17-97	5K, 30, 5K duathlon (2)	bp	bp10	1,500 O$_2$	9,100	1.14	6,450	2,100	375	200
12	3-24-97	Restoration	r	r	Break	5,450	0.68	5,450			
13	3-31-97		bp	bp9	1,000 trial	9,275	1.16	6,525	2,150	375	225
14	4-7-97		bp	bp8	1,600 O$_2$	9,650	1.21	6,725	2,275	400	225
15	4-14-97		bp	bp7	1,700 O$_2$	10,225	1.29	7,075	2,450	450	250
16	4-21-97	Restoration	r	r	1,500 TF	6,125	0.77	6,125			
17	4-28-97	5K, 30, 5K duathlon (2)	bp	bp6	1,000 O$_2$	10,425	1.31	7,175	2,525	450	275
18	5-5-97		bp	bp5	1,500 TF	10,850	1.36	7,400	2,650	500	300
19	5-12-97	21K road race-run (2)	bp	bp4	1,000 trial	11,500	1.45	7,800	2,850	525	325
20	5-19-97	Restoration	r	r	Break	6,900	0.87	6,900			
21	5-26-97		bp	bp3	2,000 O$_2$	7,875	0.99	5,300	1,975	375	225
22	6-2-97	5K road race (2)	bp	bp2	1,500 TF	8,200	1.03	5,475	2,075	400	250
23	6-9-97		bp	bp1	1,000 O$_2$	8,675	1.09	5,750	2,225	425	275
24	6-16-97	1K, 20, 5K triathlon (2)	r	r	Trirace 1K	5,200	0.65	5,200			
25	6-23-97	Restoration	bt	bt6	800 TF	8,850	1.11	5,600	2,450	475	300
26	6-30-97		bt	bt5	1,200 O$_2$	9,200	1.16	5,775	2,575	525	325

Season volume 350,000　　　　　PI volume 7,955

Week	Monday	Competition (rank)	Program emphasis	Period	Week target	Volume (meters)	Pct.	O_2	LVT (meters)	VO_2	LAC
27	7-7-97		bt	bt4	1,500 O_2	9,750	1.23	6,075	2,775	550	350
28	7-14-97	Vacation/ holiday	r	r	Break	5,850	0.73	5,850			
29	7-21-97		bt	bt3	1,000 trial	8,375	1.05	5,175	2,400	475	325
30	7-28-97		bt	bt2	1,600 O_2	8,700	1.09	5,325	2,525	525	350
31	8-4-97		bt	bt1	1,000 O_2	9,225	1.16	5,600	2,700	550	375
32	8-11-97	1.5, 40, 10K triathlon (2)	r	r	Trirace 1.5K	5,525	0.70	5,525			
33	8-18-97		rp	rp3	1,800 TF drill	8,375	1.05	5,075	2,650	425	250
34	8-25-97		rp	rp2	1,600 O_2	8,700	1.09	5,225	2,775	450	275
35	9-1-97		rp	rp1	1,000 O_2	9,225	1.16	5,500	2,950	475	300
36	9-8-97	1.5, 40, 10K triathlon (1)	pt	pt1	Trirace 1.5K	4,175	0.53	3,125	600	300	150
37	9-15-97		rp	rp3	1,500 O_2	8,375	1.05	5,075	2,650	425	250
38	9-22-97		rp	rp2	1,000 O_2	8,700	1.09	5,225	2,775	450	275
39	9-29-97		rp	rp1	800 O_2	9,225	1.16	5,500	2,950	475	300
40	10-6-97	1.5, 40, 10K triathlon (1)	pt	pt1	Trirace 1.5K	4,175	0.53	3,125	600	300	150
41	10-13-97		rp	rp3	1,200 O_2	8,375	1.05	5,075	2,650	425	250
42	10-20-97		rp	rp2	800 O_2	8,700	1.09	5,225	2,775	450	275
43	10-27-97		rp	rp1	800 O_2	9,225	1.15	5,500	2,950	475	300
44	11-3-97	1.5, 40, 10K triathlon (1)	pt	pt1	Trirace 1.5K	4,175	0.53	3,125	600	300	150
45	11-10-97	Off-season									
46	11-17-97	Off-season									
47	11-24-97	Off-season									
48	12-1-97	Off-season									
49	12-8-97	Off-season									
50	12-15-97	Off-season									
51	12-22-97	Off-season									
52	12-29-97	Off-season									

TABLE   2.4b
Cycling Program Manager   Athlete_____

Week	Monday	Competition (rank)	Program emphasis	Period	Week target	Volume (miles)	Pct.	O$_2$	LVT (miles)	VO$_2$	LAC
1	1-6-97	Start program	bp	bp18	20 O$_2$	56	0.82	51.00	3.50	1.25	0.50
2	1-13-97		bp	bp17	25 O$_2$	59	0.85	53.50	3.75	1.25	0.50
3	1-20-97		bp	bp16	30 O$_2$; break; 3 mi.	62	0.90	55.75	4.25	1.50	0.50
4	1-27-97	Restoration	r	r	Roller TF	37	0.54	37.00			
5	2-3-97		bp	bp15	30 O$_2$	64	0.92	57.25	4.50	1.50	0.75
6	2-10-97		bp	bp14	10-mi. trial	66	0.96	58.75	4.75	1.75	0.75
7	2-17-97		bp	bp13	35 O$_2$ break; 4 mi.	70	1.02	62.00	5.25	2.00	0.75
8	2-24-97	Restoration	r	r	Roller TF	42	0.61	42.00			
9	3-3-97	10K road race (2)	bp	bp12	40 O$_2$	71	1.04	62.50	5.50	2.00	1.00
10	3-10-97		bp	bp11	45 O$_2$	74	1.08	64.75	6.00	2.25	1.00
11	3-17-97	5K, 30, 5K duathlon (2)	bp	bp10	Duathlon	79	1.14	68.75	6.75	2.25	1.25
12	3-24-97	Restoration	r	r	Break	47	0.69	47.00			
13	3-31-97		bp	bp9	35 O$_2$	80	1.17	69.25	7.00	2.50	1.25
14	4-7-97		bp	bp8	40 O$_2$	84	1.21	72.25	7.75	2.75	1.50
15	4-14-97		bp	bp7	50 O$_2$; break; 5 mi.	89	1.29	76.00	8.25	3.00	1.50
16	4-21-97	Restoration	r	r	10-mi. trial	53	0.77	53.00			
17	4-28-97	5K, 30, 5K duathlon (2)	bp	bp6	Duathlon	90	1.31	76.50	8.75	3.00	1.75
18	5-5-97		bp	bp5	35 O$_2$	94	1.36	79.50	9.50	3.25	2.00
19	5-14-97	21K road race-run (2)	bp	bp4	40 O$_2$	100	1.45	84.00	10.25	3.50	2.00
20	5-19-97	Restoration	r	r	Break	60	0.87	60.00			
21	5-26-97		bp	bp3	10-mi. trial	68	0.99	56.75	7.25	2.50	1.50
22	6-2-97	5K road race (2)	bp	bp2	35 O$_2$	71	1.03	59.00	7.75	2.75	1.75
23	6-9-97		bp	bp1	50 O$_2$	75	1.09	62.00	8.50	3.00	1.75
24	6-16-97	1K, 20, 5K triathalon (2)	r	r	Trirace 20K	45	0.65	45.00			
25	6-23-97	Restoration	bt	bt6	20 TF	77	1.11	61.25	10.50	4.25	1.25

Season volume 3,030   PI volume 69

Week	Monday	Competition (rank)	Program emphasis	Period	Week target	Volume (miles)	Pct.	O_2	LVT (miles)	VO_2	LAC
26	6-30-97		bt	bt5	60 O_2	80	1.16	63.25	11.00	4.50	1.25
27	7-7-97		bt	bt4	50 O_2	85	1.23	66.75	12.00	4.75	1.50
28	7-14-97	Vacation/ holiday	r	r	Break	51	0.74	51.00			
29	7-21-97		bt	bt3	10-mi. trial	72	1.05	56.25	10.25	4.25	1.25
30	7-28-97		bt	bt2	40 O_2	75	1.09	58.25	11.00	4.50	1.50
31	8-4-97		bt	bt1	35 O_2	80	1.16	61.50	12.00	4.75	1.50
32	8-11-97	1.5, 40, 10K triathlon (2)	r	r	Trirace 40K	48	0.70	48.00			
33	8-18-97		rp	rp3	40 O_2	72	1.05	55.00	13.00	2.50	1.50
34	8-25-97		rp	rp2	10-mi. trial	75	1.09	57.00	13.75	2.75	1.50
35	9-1-97		rp	rp1	35 O_2	80	1.16	60.50	15.00	3.00	1.75
36	9-8-97	1.5, 40, 10K triathlon (1)	pt	pt1	Trirace 40K	36	0.53	30.00	2.25	3.00	1.00
37	9-15-97		rp	rp3	40 O_2	72	1.05	55.00	13.00	2.50	1.50
38	9-22-97		rp	rp2	10-mi. trial	75	1.09	57.00	13.75	2.75	1.50
39	9-29-97		rp	rp1	30 O_2	80	1.16	60.50	15.00	3.00	1.75
40	10-6-97	1.5, 40, 10K triathlon (1)	pt	pt1	Trirace 40K	36	0.53	30.00	2.25	3.00	1.00
41	10-13-97		rp	rp3	30 O_2	72	1.05	55.00	13.00	2.50	1.50
42	10-20-97		rp	rp2	25 O_2	75	1.09	57.00	13.75	2.75	1.50
43	10-27-97		rp	rp1	20 O_2	80	1.16	60.50	15.00	3.00	1.75
44	11-3-97	1.5, 40, 10K triathlon (1)	pt	pt1	Trirace 40K	36	0.53	30.00	2.25	3.00	1.00
45	11-10-97	Off-season									
46	11-17-97	Off-season									
47	11-24-97	Off-season									
48	12-1-97	Off-season									
49	12-8-97	Off-season									
50	12-15-97	Off-season									
51	12-22-97	Off-season									
52	12-29-97	Off-season									

TABLE   2.4c
Running Program Manager   Athlete_____

Week	Monday	Competition (rank)	Program emphasis	Period	Weekly target	Volume (miles)	Pct.	O_2 (miles)	LVT	VO_2	LAC
1	1-6-97	Start program	bp	bp18	5 O_2	15	0.82	14	0.50	0.25	0.25
2	1-13-97		bp	bp17	6 O_2	15	0.85	14	0.75	0.25	0.25
3	1-20-97		bp	bp16	7 O_2	16	0.90	15	0.75	0.25	0.25
4	1-27-97	Restoration	r	r	4 O_2	10	0.54	10			
5	2-3-97		bp	bp15	10 tempo	16	0.92	15	0.75	0.25	0.25
6	2-10-97		bp	bp14	9 O_2	17	0.96	15	1.00	0.25	0.25
7	2-17-97		bp	bp13	10 O_2	18	1.02	16	1.00	0.50	0.25
8	2-24-97	Restoration	r	r	5 O_2	11	0.61	11			
9	3-3-97	10K road race (2)	bp	bp12	10K race	18	1.04	16	1.00	0.50	0.25
10	3-10-97		bp	bp11	11 O_2	19	1.08	17	1.25	0.50	0.25
11	3-17-97	5K, 30, 5K duathlon (2)	bp	bp10	Duathlon	20	1.14	18	1.25	0.50	0.50
12	3-24-97	Restoration	r	r	Break	12	0.69	12			
13	3-31-97		bp	bp9	12 O_2	21	1.17	19	1.50	0.50	0.50
14	4-7-97		bp	bp8	10 tempo	22	1.21	19	1.50	0.50	0.50
15	4-14-97		bp	bp7	8 O_2	23	1.29	20	1.75	0.75	0.50
16	4-21-97	Restoration	r	r	12 O_2	14	0.77	14			
17	4-28-97	5K, 30, 5K duathlon (2)	bp	bp6	Duathlon	23	1.31	20	1.75	0.75	0.50
18	5-5-97		bp	bp5	8 O_2	24	1.36	21	2.00	0.75	0.50
19	5-12-97	21K road race-run (2)	bp	bp4	21K race	26	1.45	22	2.25	0.75	0.75
20	5-19-97	Restoration	r	r	Break	15	0.87	15			
21	5-26-97		bp	bp3	8 O_2	18	0.99	15	1.50	0.50	0.50
22	6-2-97	5K road race (2)	bp	bp2	5K race	18	1.03	15	1.50	0.50	0.50
23	6-9-97		bp	bp1	9 O_2	19	1.09	16	1.75	0.75	0.50
24	6-16-97	1K, 20, 5K triathlon (2)	r	r	Trirace 5K	12	0.65	12			
25	6-23-97	Restoration	bt	bt6	5 O_2	20	1.11	17	2.00	1.00	0.50

Season volume 780   PI volume 18

Week	Monday	Competition (rank)	Program emphasis	Period	Weekly target	Volume (miles)	Pct.	O$_2$ (miles)	LVT	VO$_2$	LAC
26	6-30-97		bt	bt5	8 O$_2$	21	1.16	17	2.25	1.00	0.50
27	7-7-97		bt	bt4	10 O$_2$	22	1.23	18	2.50	1.00	0.50
28	7-14-97	Vacation/ holiday	r	r	Break	13	0.74	13			
29	7-21-97		bt	bt3	8 O$_2$+5K	19	1.05	15	2.00	1.00	0.50
30	7-28-97		bt	bt2	9 O$_2$	19	1.09	15	2.25	1.00	0.50
31	8-4-97		bt	bt1	6 O$_2$	21	1.16	17	2.50	1.00	0.50
32	8-11-97	1.5, 40, 10K triathlon (2)	r	r	Trirace 10K	12	0.70	12			
33	8-18-97		rp	rp3	8 O$_2$	19	1.05	15	2.75	1.00	0.50
34	8-25-97		rp	rp2	10 O$_2$	19	1.09	15	2.75	1.00	0.50
35	9-1-97		rp	rp1	6 O$_2$	21	1.16	16	3.25	1.00	0.50
36	9-8-97	1.5, 40, 10K triathlon (1)	pt	pt1	Trirace 10K	9	0.53	7	0.50	0.75	0.25
37	9-15-97		rp	rp3	8 O$_2$	19	1.05	15	2.75	1.00	0.50
38	9-22-97		rp	rp2	6 O$_2$	19	1.09	15	2.75	1.00	0.50
39	9-29-97		rp	rp1	4 O$_2$	21	1.16	16	3.25	1.00	0.50
40	10-6-97	1.5, 40, 10K triathlon (1)	pt	pt1	Trirace 10K	9	0.53	7	0.50	0.75	0.25
41	10-13-97		rp	rp3	7 O$_2$	19	1.05	15	2.75	1.00	0.50
42	10-20-97		rp	rp2	6 O$_2$	19	1.09	15	2.75	1.00	0.50
43	10-27-97		rp	rp1	4 O$_2$	21	1.16	16	3.25	1.00	0.50
44	11-3-97	1.5, 40, 10K triathlon (1)	pt	pt1	Trirace 10K	9	0.53	7	0.50	0.75	0.25
45	11-10-97	Off-season									
46	11-17-97	Off-season									
47	11-24-97	Off-season									
48	12-1-97	Off-season									
49	12-8-97	Off-season									
50	12-15-97	Off-season									
51	12-22-97	Off-season									
52	12-29-97	Off-season									

cycle step-ups. These have their own separate multipliers. For example, pt1 is 0.5 percent of rp1, pt2 is 0.7 percent of rp1, and pt3 is 0.8 percent of rp1, respectively. In other words, pt1 is 0.50 percent of the volume of rp1, pt2 is 0.70 percent of rp1, and pt3 is 0.80 percent of rp1. Second, race volumes are not included in the week. The volume of a pt week is only applied to the training preceding the event.

USING THE PROGRAM OVERVIEW MANAGER

The POM is a summary worksheet that highlights the cycles, periodization, and volumes of each training intensity zone necessary for the entire training season. It details the season competitions, program emphasis, general and specific weekly goals, periodization cycles, and

TABLE 2.5 Periodization Interval Step-Up

Group	#	Step 2/4/6/0.6 Multiplier	Step 10/10/10/0.6 Multiplier	Step 3/5/7/0.6 Multiplier
4	1	1.0515689	0.9910803	1.0396091
	2	1.0936317	1.0901883	1.0915896
	3	1.1592496	1.1992071	1.1680008
	4	0.6955498	0.7195243	0.7008005
8	1	0.9899691	0.8503477	0.9638482
	2	1.0295679	0.9353825	1.0120406
	3	1.0913419	1.0289208	1.0828835
	4	0.6548052	0.6173525	0.6497301
	5	1.1131688	1.1318128	1.11537
	6	1.1576955	1.2449941	1.1711385
	7	1.2271573	1.3694935	1.2531182
	8	0.7362944	0.8216961	0.7518709
12	1	0.9309129	0.729882	0.8920293
	2	0.9681494	0.8028702	0.9366307
	3	1.0262384	0.8831573	1.0021949
	4	0.615743	0.5298944	0.6013169
	5	1.0467632	0.971473	1.0322607
	6	1.0886337	1.0686203	1.0838738
	7	1.153917	1.1754823	1.1597449
	8	0.692371	0.7052894	0.695847
	9	1.1770307	1.2930305	1.1945373
	10	1.224112	1.4223336	1.2542642
	11	1.2975587	1.5645669	1.3420627
	12	0.7785352	0.8534002	0.8052376
16	1	0.874383	0.6163877	0.8241106
	2	0.9093583	0.6780264	0.8653162
	3	0.9639198	0.7458291	0.9258883
	4	0.5783519	0.4474974	0.555533
	5	0.9831982	0.820412	0.9536649
	6	1.0225261	0.9024532	1.0013482
	7	1.0838777	0.9926985	1.0714426
	8	0.6503266	0.5956191	0.6428655
	9	1.1055552	1.0919684	1.1035858
	10	1.1497774	1.2011652	1.1587651
	11	1.2187641	1.3212817	1.2398787
	12	0.7312585	0.7206991	0.7439272
	13	1.2431394	1.4534099	1.277075
	14	1.2928649	1.5987509	1.3409288
	15	1.3704368	1.7586259	1.4347938
	16	0.8222621	1.0551756	0.8608763
20	1	0.8203552	0.5178076	0.7600348
	2	0.8531694	0.5695883	0.7980366
	3	0.9043595	0.6265472	0.8538991
	4	0.5426157	0.3759283	0.5123395
	5	0.9224467	0.6892019	0.8795161
	6	0.9593446	0.7581221	0.9234919
	7	1.0169053	0.8339343	0.9881363
	8	0.6101432	0.5003606	0.5928818
	9	1.0372434	0.9173277	1.0177804
	10	1.0787331	1.0090605	1.0686694
	11	1.1434571	1.1099665	1.1434763
	12	0.6860743	0.6054363	0.6860858
	13	1.1663262	1.2209632	1.1777806
	14	1.2129793	1.3430595	1.2366696
	15	1.285758	1.4773654	1.3232365
	16	0.7714548	0.8864193	0.7939419
	17	1.3114732	1.625102	1.3629336
	18	1.3639321	1.7876122	1.4310803
	19	1.4457681	1.9663734	1.5312559
	20	0.8674608	1.179824	0.9187535

HOW TO USE THE TABLE OF PERIODIZATION

The table of periodization (table 2.6) displays percentage multipliers for the training intensity zones indicated in each swim, bike, and run column. Using this system, you can effectively manage the volume and intensity of your weekly training. The table applies to single- and multiple-sport endurance athletes. To train more or less in any one sport, an athlete may choose to have different periodization cycles in each sport. On the table you will note different multipliers that are used to calculate the training intensity zones for each week's volume. For example, "bp20/swim O_2" indicates 75.75 percent of the week's total volume is to be done in the aerobic conditioning training intensity zone. However, an athlete may wish to begin with bp17 on the bike and bp15 on the run, choosing to train at differing intensities to serve their needs more adequately.

Chapter 7 shows you how to develop workouts from these results. These multipliers are calculated with the weekly training volume you've determined in the previous section. Note that for each sport (swim, bike, run), there are specific columns for each of the four training intensity zones: O_2, LVT, VO_2, and LAC.

1. Acronyms are used for each training intensity zone and sport: swim, bike, and run O_2, LVT, VO_2, and LAC. Under each training intensity zone column are percentages or multipliers used for determining the amount of weekly training to be done in a particular training intensity zone. The multipliers change for any particular training period and for each sport.

2. Under "Period" are listed bp20, bp19, bp18, . . . through pt1 and r. The rows from left to right are training intensity zone multipliers for each sport. Multiply these by the training volume of each week in your program.

For example, if the training volume for a cycling week is 100 miles and the period you selected is bp7, the calculations work as follows:

Period: bp7 (go to the bp7 row)
Sport (column): Bike (go to the Bike LVT column)
Training volume (week): 100
Multiplier: 9.4 (taken from row bp7 and column Bike LVT.)

Now multiply week volume (100) by 9.4 percent (0.094)
100 miles × 9.4 percent (0.094) = 9.4 miles of LVT training for the week
(Chapter 7 will discuss how this is applied to the training week.)

supplemental training. Table 2.2 shows a sample POM. A blank POM is provided in the appendix. The following define the columns (left to right) on the blank POM.

1. Week: The week number of the season (up to 52 weeks).

2. Monday: Monday date of the week and year.

3. Competition: Competitions and important personal and work-related dates (vacations, etc.). Rank: Rank of competitions and events (1 = taper, 2 = nontaper).

4. Program emphasis: The periodization

TABLE 2.6 Table of Periodization

Period	Swim O$_2$%	Swim LVT%	Swim VO$_2$%	Swim LAC%	Bike O$_2$%	Bike LVT%	Bike VO$_2$%	Bike LAC%	Run O$_2$%	Run LVT%	Run VO$_2$%	Run LAC%
bp20	75.75	20.00	3.00	1.25	92.00	5.50	2.00	0.50	94.00	3.50	1.50	1.00
bp19	75.25	20.30	3.10	1.35	91.50	5.80	2.10	0.60	93.50	3.80	1.60	1.10
bp18	74.75	20.60	3.20	1.45	91.00	6.10	2.20	0.70	93.00	4.10	1.70	1.20
bp17	74.25	20.90	3.30	1.55	90.50	6.40	2.30	0.80	92.50	4.40	1.80	1.30
bp16	73.75	21.20	3.40	1.65	90.00	6.70	2.40	0.90	92.00	4.70	1.90	1.40
bp15	73.25	21.50	3.50	1.75	89.50	7.00	2.50	1.00	91.50	5.00	2.00	1.50
bp14	72.75	21.80	3.60	1.85	89.00	7.30	2.60	1.10	91.00	5.30	2.10	1.60
bp13	72.25	22.10	3.70	1.95	88.50	7.60	2.70	1.20	90.50	5.60	2.20	1.70
bp12	71.75	22.40	3.80	2.05	88.00	7.90	2.80	1.30	90.00	5.90	2.30	1.80
bp11	71.25	22.70	3.90	2.15	87.50	8.20	2.90	1.40	89.50	6.20	2.40	1.90
bp10	70.75	23.00	4.00	2.25	87.00	8.50	3.00	1.50	89.00	6.50	2.50	2.00
bp9	70.25	23.30	4.10	2.35	86.50	8.80	3.10	1.60	88.50	6.80	2.60	2.10
bp8	69.75	23.60	4.20	2.45	86.00	9.10	3.20	1.70	88.00	7.10	2.70	2.20
bp7	69.25	23.90	4.30	2.55	85.50	9.40	3.30	1.80	87.50	7.40	2.80	2.30
bp6	68.75	24.20	4.40	2.65	85.00	9.70	3.40	1.90	87.00	7.70	2.90	2.40
bp5	68.25	24.50	4.50	2.75	84.50	10.00	3.50	2.00	86.50	8.00	3.00	2.50
bp4	67.75	24.80	4.60	2.85	84.00	10.30	3.60	2.10	86.00	8.30	3.10	2.60
bp3	67.25	25.10	4.70	2.95	83.50	10.60	3.70	2.20	85.50	8.60	3.20	2.70
bp2	66.75	25.40	4.80	3.05	83.00	10.90	3.80	2.30	85.00	8.90	3.30	2.80
bp1	66.25	25.70	4.90	3.15	82.50	11.20	3.90	2.40	84.50	9.20	3.40	2.90
bt6	63.25	27.75	5.50	3.50	79.50	13.50	5.50	1.50	83.00	10.25	4.50	2.25
bt5	62.75	28.05	5.60	3.60	79.00	13.80	5.60	1.60	82.50	10.55	4.60	2.35
bt4	62.25	28.35	5.70	3.70	78.50	14.10	5.70	1.70	82.00	10.85	4.70	2.45
bt3	61.75	28.65	5.80	3.80	78.00	14.40	5.80	1.80	81.50	11.15	4.80	2.55
bt2	61.25	28.95	5.90	3.90	77.50	14.70	5.90	1.90	81.00	11.45	4.90	2.65
bt1	60.75	29.25	6.00	4.00	77.00	15.00	6.00	2.00	80.50	11.75	5.00	2.75
rp8	63.00	30.00	4.50	2.50	79.00	16.50	3.00	1.50	80.50	13.00	4.25	2.25
rp7	62.50	30.30	4.60	2.60	78.50	16.80	3.10	1.60	80.00	13.30	4.35	2.35
rp6	62.00	30.60	4.70	2.70	78.00	17.10	3.20	1.70	79.50	13.60	4.45	2.45
rp5	61.50	30.90	4.80	2.80	77.50	17.40	3.30	1.80	79.00	13.90	4.55	2.55
rp4	61.00	31.20	4.90	2.90	77.00	17.70	3.40	1.90	78.50	14.20	4.65	2.65
rp3	60.50	31.50	5.00	3.00	76.50	18.00	3.50	2.00	78.00	14.50	4.75	2.75
rp2	60.00	31.80	5.10	3.10	76.00	18.30	3.60	2.10	77.50	14.80	4.85	2.85
rp1	59.50	32.10	5.20	3.20	75.50	18.60	3.70	2.20	77.00	15.10	4.95	2.95
pt3	64.00	24.00	8.00	4.00	77.50	13.00	7.00	2.50	80.00	10.00	7.00	3.00
pt2	65.00	21.00	9.00	5.00	79.00	10.00	8.00	3.50	83.00	7.00	9.00	2.50
pt1	75.00	14.50	7.00	3.50	83.00	6.00	8.00	3.00	82.50	6.00	8.00	3.50
r	100.00	0.00	0.00	0.00	100.00	0.00	0.00	0.00	100.00	0.00	0.00	0.00

cycle designation (base preparation, base transition, race preparation, peak transition, or restoration).

5. Interval: The periodization cycle. All consecutive base preparation, base transition, and race preparation weeks are assigned a week number. These are later totaled and used to determine the volume of each cycle in relation to the season volume. (Placing bp and bt in the same cycle for continuity is fine. Additionally, a bt cycle of one or more weeks after an rp phase is reasonable too.)

6. SP, BP, and RP: The periodization acronyms from the table of periodization (table 2.6). This is a chart of multipliers from which to determine the volume of each training intensity zone. The multipliers correspond with the number of weeks in each periodization cycle. For example, cycle 1 has 12 weeks and contains 7 bp, 2 bt, and 3 r weeks. Because bp has 7 weeks, begin with bp7 to bp1 and bt2 to bt1 with the r weeks.

> *Training Note:* The last week in any periodization cycle always ends with bp1, bt1, or rp1. Again, bp and bt are often linked within the same cycle for continuity, as shown in the example (table 2.2). These will then be followed by a restoration week or peak transition weeks. Keep in mind that every fourth week is a restoration week or the beginning of a one- to three-week taper (peak transition) period. Enter your periods onto each of the program managers, beginning with the POM.

7. Swim, bike, and run week: The swim, bike, and run week targets are reviewed in chapter 7.

8. CAL, ISK, and IST: These columns refer to the respective supplemental training exercises in chapter 6,—calisthenics, isokinetics, and isotonics. Refer to chapter 6 for more information on this training.

THE IMPORTANCE OF RECOVERY

Multiple-sport endurance athletes need periodic recovery periods. More important, I recommend these periods be scheduled in advance and planned into the training program. We've included these in the program managers designed so far.

However, restoration and recovery are prescribed not only for specific weeks, but also during each week. The endurance athlete needs to blend the relationship between frequency, volume, and the training intensity zone continuums into every workout each week. Chapter 7 will describe how to organize the data into weekly schedules of training. This will ensure enhancement, progression, and optimal performance.

Recovery is particularly important from a psychological perspective as well, more so if the restoration period is a planned one; that is, if the athlete knows in advance when those periods of recovery will occur. During more difficult weeks of intense effort and volume, athletes can look forward to the time when the intensity and volume will lessen. That's important for psychological (emotional) and physiological reasons.

You now have the framework for developing your endurance plan. Chapter 7 will complete the training program process, but first more sport-specific training information is needed. This is covered in chapters 3, 4, 5, and 6—the swimming, cycling, running, and supplemental training sections of the book. In these chapters, you will learn the essential components of training techniques, biomechanics, and workout design—information necessary to complete your program.

PART II

TECHNIQUE AND TRAINING

3

SWIMMING

Unlike cycling and running, swimming is technically more difficult to learn. For this reason, triathletes should emphasize the right kinds of swim training before putting in lap after lap of hard work. The triathlete is not likely to attain the speed and technical skill of the single-sport distance swimmer, just as the decathlete will probably not have the 1,500 speed that a 1,500-meter specialist would have. Both race the same discipline but in different competitive arenas. Moreover, for many triathletes, swimming continues to be the most complicated of the three sports to master. By nature, swimming is a sport that requires technique in an environment that is unfamiliar to a majority of endurance athletes. Yet with capable coaching and concentration, your swimming speed and skill can be improved predictably and fast.

In this chapter, I will provide you with swimming techniques that work. These techniques will not only fine-tune your freestyle swimming, they will also bolster your confidence and make you faster—you only need apply yourself and stay committed and focused.

This chapter begins by discussing the characteristics of water and forces that affect speed, propulsion, and buoyancy. I won't bore you with a lot of scientific facts, but I will outline the basics of flow and drag to help you understand why body position and technique are so important. Following that, I will divide the stroke into phases and discuss specific training tips and drills for improving your swimming stroke by focusing on these phases. Remember, you must work on technique every time you get in the water. If you consistently integrate the technique drills into your workouts, you will improve your swimming speed and endurance.

Next, developing the right training intensity zones in the appropriate amounts will give your swimming the right physiological focus. The intensity pace charts work within the guidelines of the training intensity zones discussed in chapter 1. With this strategy, the swimmer will be training with both the right technique and the right intensity.

FIGHTING THE ELEMENTS

It is fundamentally important to move through the water in the most streamlined manner possible. To do this, the swimmer must rotate about an axis through the center of the body. The better this is performed, the less frontal surface area there is meeting with oncoming water. I like my swimmers to "move off" the flat part of their chests quickly while the streamline is maintained. Likewise, finishing the pull of the stroke past the hip and toward the thigh improves the streamline, permitting more appropriate body roll (rotation). According to Jane Cappaert, PhD, chief biomechanist with the United States Swimming Center for Aquatic Research, "Streamlining can do more for forward propulsion than improving stroke mechanics in many cases." For that reason, reducing the water's resistance against the body is an important consideration for the swimmer.

Because water is much denser than air, there is far more drag on bodies moving through it. This is why good technique and a streamlined body position are so important to fast swimming. In addition to the density of water, both laminar and turbulent flow affect swimming speed. The best technique will minimize turbulent flow so that less energy is expended overcoming drag.

Later in the chapter, I'll review some excellent drills and stroke tips for doing just that. For now, as you read the next section, I'd like you to take into account how water moves over, around, beneath, and behind you when you are swimming. Those differentiating properties are the result of laminar and turbulent flow.

Laminar (Smooth) and Turbulent Flows

Laminar flow is like the water pouring from a teakettle. The flow is smooth and essentially unrestricted, moving freely in the same continuous direction. Most fluids are relatively smooth-flowing with laminar qualities, unless they encounter a substance that alters their flow. Obviously, laminar flows have the least amount of resistance.

Turbulent flows are what results when pouring water from a teakettle into a cup. The flow of the liquid is now jumbled and disorderly, changing to a drag-induced flow as the water thrashes and churns in numerous indiscriminate directions. Drag is present whenever you swim simply as a result of your body taking up space in and trying to move through the water. When a swimmer moves or engages the water in a turbulent way, as with a forceful entry, drag is further increased. The swimmer whose hands, arms, feet, body position, and movements are more skilled reduces this drag, resulting in a more laminar, less turbulent flow in and around the body. Obviously, this condition will increase swimming speed.

Drag

Drag produces resistance to the swimmer's motion or progress. Swimmers face three types of drag and flow resistance: form drag, wave drag, and frictional drag. Drag is caused by the amount of space occupied by a swimmer's body (form), waves (oncoming flow), and skin in contact with the water (friction). Drag works to pull the swimmer in the opposite direction of travel.

Form Drag: Streamlined Versus Broad

To paint a picture of form drag, let's compare the shape and movements of two ordinary

DRAFTING AND OPEN-WATER SWIMMING

Following another swimmer's feet reduces the oncoming flow of water, potentially allowing the trailing swimmer to maintain the pace of the lead swimmer without expending as much effort. This has advantages in terms of conserving energy and possibly increasing swimming speed. But you should be aware that this technique has disadvantages as well. First, by following another swimmer, you also swim the same course, which may not be the correct one. You need to be sure you know where you are going to stay on course. Sight the course before the start of the swim, and during the race, raise your head occasionally (every 10 to 15 strokes) for sighting. Second, swimming behind a swimmer who is slower than you are can lead to longer swim times. Be sure the person you are drafting is faster than you are by checking your perceived exertion. You should feel close to race pace, otherwise you may be following the wrong feet.

water vessels. The first, a sailboat, cuts smoothly through the waves opposite the second, a slowly moving barge carrying heavy cargo (fig. 3.1). The waves encounter the broad front of the barge as the water churns and splashes (turbulence) in different directions.

The sailboat is streamlined, as its shape allows the water to slide easily by it (laminar flow).

Wave Drag

Open-water swimming produces more drag than swimming in lane pools, where the lane-

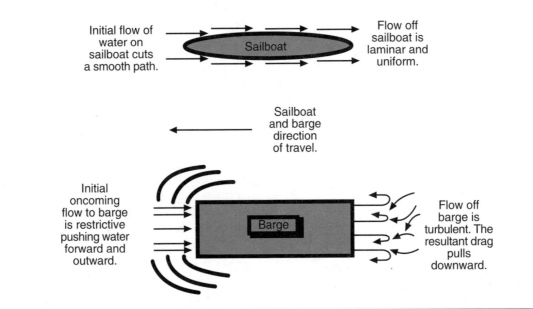

FIGURE 3.1   Form drag: Laminar and turbulent flows.

FIGURE 3.2   Wave drag: Turbulent entry.

ARE OPEN-WATER SWIM TIMES THE SAME AS POOL TIMES?

No! Open-water swimming presents many obstacles not encountered in pool swimming. Temperatures are likely to be cooler, distances inaccurate, conditions rougher (turbulence), and sighting is essential (no pool lines here). Colder temperatures reduce the oxygen capacity of the swimmer and minimize the coordination of the limbs for taking long, fast, smooth strokes. Open water is often rougher than pool water, thus increasing the oncoming flow and lateral turbulence on the swimmer. Finally, sighting is necessary, requiring the swimmer's head to come out of the water and causing the legs to lower, which increases surface drag and reduces swimming speed. Also, each time the swimmer pushes off the pool wall, the time is improved over open-water swimming times.

marker and gutter systems reduce the wave action of the water. A swimmer causes additional wave drag when making a turbulent entry by splashing down on the water, curling the wrists, or pushing water forward (fig. 3.2). In effect, wave drag causes turbulence and thus reduces speed by increasing drag.

Friction or Surface Drag

Surface drag is the result of what is on the surface of the body: namely, body hair and a swimsuit. Each causes friction to occur between the water and skin or suit surface. Anything that alters the streamlined shape of the body will influence how water flows around it, resulting in more turbulence and increased drag. This is a good reason for shaving body hair before competitions.

BODY POSITION AND ALIGNMENT

Swimming speed depends greatly on the body position carried in the water. The horizontal and lateral positions affect lift and drag, but buoyancy often makes the difference. Individuals vary in body density and buoyancy. Certain swimmers simply float higher in the water. Unless wearing a wet suit, swimmers can

do little about buoyancy without putting on or taking off a considerable amount of body fat.

Horizontal Fine-Tuning

In many respects, a good horizontal body position is a consequence of the swimmer's natural buoyancy (fig. 3.3). Yet there are techniques the swimmer can use to decrease the amount of drag. Remember laminar and turbulent flows and what causes drag? Think of these concepts relative to the amount of space occupied from the surface of the water to the highest points on your body. The more vertical space your body occupies, the more resistive drag you will encounter. So a swimmer riding higher in the water occupies less space and therefore encounters fewer molecules of water to impede speed.

The following technique makes for better streamlining and flow awareness in swimming. Push off from the wall, body outstretched, with your hands touching back to back. Stay in the most streamlined position possible, with your hands and arms stretched out front and your head between your arms (eyes looking forward). This position is much like the sailboat's shape as it cuts through the water. You should feel the water flow over your palms and under your forearms, upper arms, and armpits.

Some techniques for improving your horizontal body position are as follows:

• Keep your head in a natural position—don't try to hold it higher or lower than normal. The water line should be at about the middle of your forehead.

• Keep your back reasonably straight—don't arch it.

• Roll your head to the side when breathing rather than lifting it and then turning to the side. Move your face just far enough to the side to get the "bite" of air needed.

• The kicking motion of your feet should range from just below the water's surface on the upbeat to just slightly below your body on the downbeat.

• Kick on your back with your arms outstretched overhead and your hands atop one another. Tilt your head back until the water is at eyebrow level. You should notice how changing this position to the middle of your head slows you down (increasing drag by altering the surface area).

Lateral Fine-Tuning

Lateral or side-to-side body movements in swimming increase surface area and drag because your body effectively takes up a larger area in the water. Imagine that the lower half of your body is in a cylinder just wide enough for your hips. The cylinder's purpose is to limit your lateral motion. Let's further suppose this flume runs the length of the pool. For the entire distance in either direction, your hips and legs cannot move sideways, but your swimming motion is not hindered. This would be the optimal position to decrease lateral rotation and thus decrease drag (fig. 3.4).

To create this optimal position, you need to swim within this imaginary tunnel. To do so,

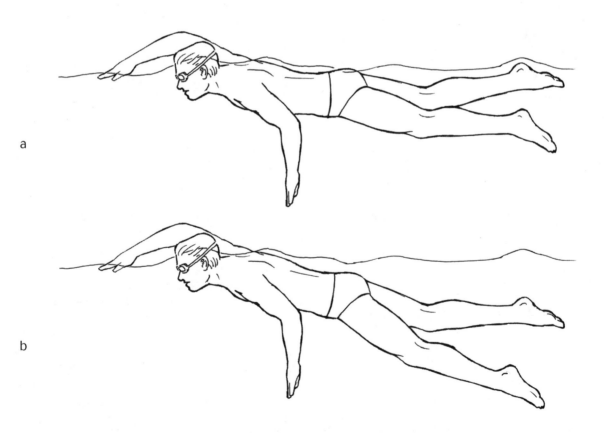

a

b

FIGURE 3.3 *a,b* Correct (*a*) and incorrect (*b*) horizontal body alignment.

Adapted, by permission, from G. Town and T. Kearney, 1994, *Swim, Bike, Run* (Champaign, IL: Human Kinetics), 56.

you must allow for and attain rotation within the cylinder's area, sort of like spinning in a semirotation from one side to the other. In other words, the length of the stroke should be fully completed (not shortened). Be sure to finish the stroke completely past the thigh and achieve a fully outstretched entry (see figure 3.6). This should maintain your movement within the cylinder.

FIGURE 3.4 Lateral rotation.

The Key to Streamlining

Streamlining is optimizing the position and motion of the body as it encounters the oncoming flow of water while swimming. A more streamlined body reduces drag and is fundamentally important in learning to swim efficiently. Streamlining is enhanced by a long, stretched glide through the water with a fluid, rotational movement along the axis of the body—rotating from one side to the other and moving off the chest area smoothly yet rapidly.

Without body roll and rotation, the chest, hips, and shoulders further impede forward movement, reducing the streamline. The longer a swimmer is flat on top of the water, the more surface resistance the body needs to overcome.

As a streamlining drill, swim 10×50 meters at light (O_2) intensity with 15 seconds of rest between each interval. For the first 25 meters, divert the oncoming flow of water by placing the hand entry at a 45-degree angle (index finger enters first, the thumb is closest to the water). Stretch your arm out fully (bring the shoulder of the outstretched arm to the chin), maximizing the length of glide and making sure your hand and arm enter cleanly. Rotate your hips (in your cylinder) with each arm stroke. Feel the flow of water moving onto the palm of your hand and your forearm and along the sides of your body. For the second 25 meters of the 50, swim freestyle except breathe every fourth stroke and decrease the number of strokes taken from the previous 25 meters.

THE WHOLE STROKE

One problem with learning new techniques is being taught too many tips at once. Have your coach point out one or two things to work on and then apply those techniques toward improving the skill. Practice the techniques until you can do them when swimming fast (race pace) intervals. You'll master the skills, but you must be patient and give your nerves and muscles time to develop.

Too many swimmers wallop their hands and arms into the water and start pulling immediately with all their might. This could not be further from the correct technique. After the entry, the downsweep phase of the pull, the intensity should be low and the emphasis on technique high. During the pulling phases, the hand changes angle and speed throughout the stroke. Hand speed increases after each phase but decreases slightly during the transition from one phase to the next. The fastest hand speed occurs during the final portion of the pull, the upsweep. Experienced swimmers do this instinctively, knowing that this type of approach generates lift and speed. The less experienced swimmer engages the water too forcefully, forgets to keep the elbow flexed, and does not put the hand in at the right angle due to hurrying the stroke.

Perhaps, the most important swimming technique is the curvilinear stroke path of the arm pull, the S-shaped sculling motion of the hand as it moves throughout the stroke. To maximize propelling efficiency, the swimmer needs to sweep the hand in different directions. However, many swimmers pull their hands straight backward, trying to muscle through the stroke. It is a misconception that strength (propulsive force) is the predominate factor in swimming. Rather, efficiency of the stroke, or what is specified as propelling efficiency, makes a faster swimmer. Not only does pulling straight back increase the propulsive drag but this mistake is often negatively reinforced by using flat or oversized hand training paddles that straighten the stroke.

Endurance Sports Technology Group, Inc., has developed the SwimFoil, a swimming paddle that uses an airfoil design to account for the combinations of lift and drag forces acting on the hand (fig. 3.6). These patented paddles, licensed by Speedo USA, reinforce a swimming stroke which optimizes propelling efficiency not propulsive force.

Swimming research boasts volumes of sport science and biomechanical information. This information, when applied in practice, can result in improved performance. Swimming is much more than working hard—you've got to work smart too! The rest of this chapter is directed toward helping the swimmer do just that—work smart. First, we'll look at the entire stroke from start to finish, then at each phase by itself.

The upper body action of freestyle swimming can be divided into six arm stroke phases:

1. The entry: The hand enters the water, stretching forward, reaching for the greatest length possible. The hips and shoulders should be allowed to move rotating on an axis freely from side to side (fig. 3.5).

2. The downsweep and catch: The hand traps water as the wrist is flexed outward and downward, with the fingertips pointed toward the bottom of the pool. The fingers should be spread slightly apart to increase the surface area of the hand. The forearm and hand continue

FIGURE 3.5   Endurance Sports Technology Group, Inc., developmental prototype of the patented SPEEDO SwimFoil.

pulling downward, deflecting water away from the hand (the leading edge is the thumb, pitched slightly to divert water to the outside, away from the body). The elbow is flexed and higher than the hand. The bottommost point of the downsweep is called the catch (fig. 3.7).

3. The insweep: The hand is pitched at 40 degrees and rounds off, sweeping inward and upward to at least the midline of the body (fig. 3.8).

4. The upsweep: This final sweep produces maximum propulsion as the hand now presses from the midline upward, outward, and backward. The fingertips are kept pointing downward and press to a nearly full extension to the thigh (fig. 3.9).

5. The release: This occurs as the hand reaches the thigh and the little finger follows the elbow out of the water (the opposite arm is now beginning the downsweep; fig. 3.10).

6. The recovery: The elbow leads and is higher than the hand. The palm of the hand faces the body during the first two-thirds of the

recovery. The recovery is exactly that, a time for the arm and shoulder muscles to relax. The elbow is high, working in coordination with the natural body roll of 45 degrees (fig. 3.11).

Now that you have the general idea, let's break down the stroke further into separate parts so the swimmer can apply these techniques individually during swim workouts and stroke drill sets. Remember, the swimmer only needs to work on one part of the stroke at a time. Trying to link all of the technical aspects together can be confusing unless the athlete works at mastering one skill at a time. For that matter, it may take an entire season to see signs of improvement, but this is the slow, determined type of training I recommend. Once these skills are neuromuscularly ingrained, they'll hold up when the intensity increases.

Entry

The initial placement of the hand and forearm into the water at the entry is important for efficient swimming. With proper technique, the swimmer can potentially generate more lift, reduce turbulent drag, and make a more efficient and smooth entry. The entering hands are used to move water away from the front of the body to lessen the resistance of the oncoming flow.

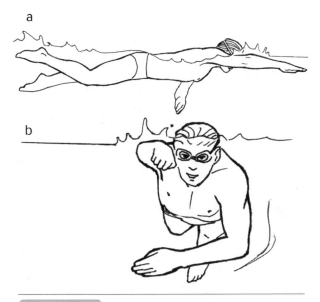

FIGURE 3.6   Entry.

Entry of the hand into the water is made with the thumb and index finger first at a point slightly inside the shoulder and about half an arm's length in front ahead of the shoulder. The hand now enters the water at a 40-degree angle, cutting a smooth pathway.

To reduce drag, the arm entry must be smooth. The fingertips, hand, forearm, elbow, and shoulder follow one another in a streamline. Don't be one of those swimmers who engages the water with a straight-arm landing on top of the water. The wave drag resulting from this technique is significant, and the hand and arm are not in a good position for making the downsweep.

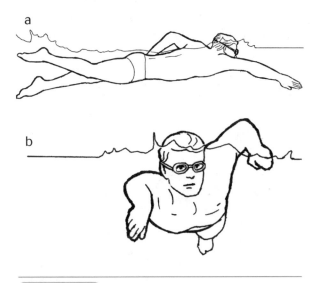

FIGURE 3.7   Downsweep and catch.

Downsweep and Catch

The next movement after the hand enters the water is the downsweep. This term may be misleading, as the swimmer really shouldn't apply downward force here. Rather, the movement should be a gentle sweep of the forearm and hand as the elbow remains high (above the hand) and slightly flexed. Its primary purpose is to position the hand and arm for the insweep and upsweep phases of the stroke.

What is the correct way to do the downsweep and catch? First, the direction of the hand and arm is forward and downward, with the wrist flexed as the sweep is initiated. At this point, the elbow flexes as the forearm and hand move slightly downward, outward, and backward. Keep in mind that this is where the least force is applied. The whole purpose is to set the hand to make the catch. The catch occurs at the end of the entry, and the elbow flexes higher up due to the pressure (lift) on the hand. The hand is now ready to begin the insweep, as the pitch and angle of attack now change (sweep and round off) toward the midline of the body.

Insweep (Inward Scull)

When the downsweep and catch have ended, the insweep begins. At this point, there is a natural tendency for the hand to begin moving inward, upward, and backward toward the midline of the body. The insweep is the first larger propulsive part of the stroke. The swimmer will feel lift and considerable hand pressure from the water during this move.

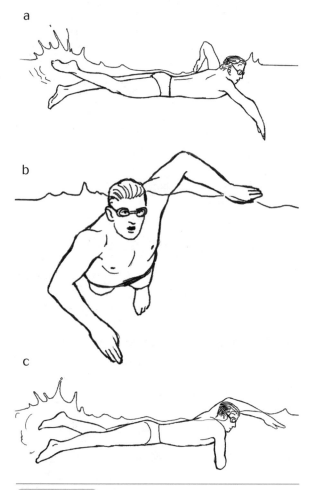

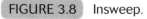

FIGURE 3.8   Insweep.

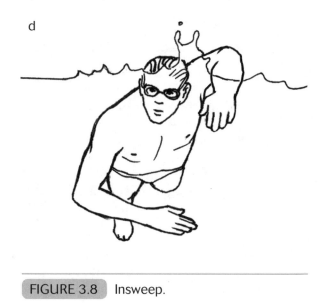

FIGURE 3.8   Insweep.

Upsweep (Outward Scull)

This is where the greatest power is generated, which is then translated to propelling efficiency for the swimmer. The efficient swimmer will engage the water with more effective hand positioning (angles of attack). During the upsweep, the hand rotates outward, upward, and backward toward the thigh (fingertips down); that is, the sweeping motion is backward and away from the midline of the body. Remember that each of these sweeps is in effect a diagonal sideways sculling motion, not straight backward. Incidentally, when taking a longer stroke, it should be thought of as a motion that enhances this length by sculling in a sweeping curvilinear manner.

Thinking of the hand as an airfoil moving through the water may help you move the hand and arm in a curvilinear pathway (S-shaped stroke path). To generate lift, the foil (hand) needs to be positioned so as to optimize lift and propulsion. This is done by changing the pitch of the hand during the stroke. By pitch, I am referring to the inclination of the thumb and little fingers of the hand. The thumb should be above or below the little finger throughout the stroke as the hand moves into and out of each phase of the underwater stroke. By changing this pitch (angle of attack), the swimmer will generate greater propulsive forces.

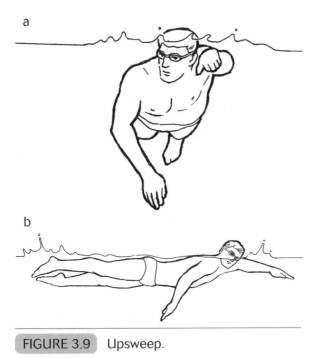

FIGURE 3.9   Upsweep.

Release

The release, the last phase of underwater hand and arm sweeping movements, is a phase of the freestyle stroke that many swimmers do incorrectly. The correct movement is for the little finger to exit the water first (following the tip of the elbow). In the most efficient technique, once the hand reaches the thigh (during the upsweep), the release begins as the palm

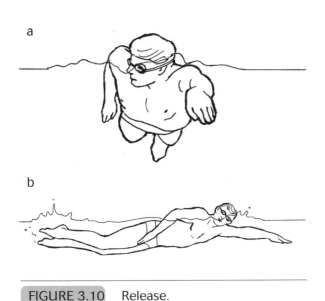

FIGURE 3.10   Release.

rotates toward the side of the thigh. This puts the little finger closest to the surface, and after the elbow, this finger is next to exit the water.

Many swimmers make the mistake of not rotating the palm toward the thigh. In fact, the palm presses up toward the water's surface (pushing upward against the water). The result is an opposite reaction of the hips that forces the hips and legs deeper into the water. Remember, the more water above the body, the greater the amount of drag.

Recovery

The recovery phase starts when the elbow exits the water on completion of the upsweep and release. As stated above, the elbow is the first body part to exit the water—not the hand or little finger, which exit (palm facing the body) after the elbow. The arm is brought forward by flexing at the elbow (elbow high and leading the hand). It helps to begin this movement by lifting the elbow out of the water with the aid of the shoulder. When the elbow is in line with the shoulder, the palm turns away from the body (the thumb is pointing down, palm out), ready to make its entry. To reduce excessive lateral body movement, hold your elbow above and in front of your hand during the first two-thirds of the recovery phase.

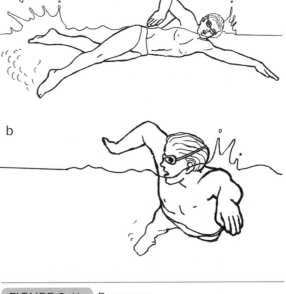

FIGURE 3.11   Recovery.

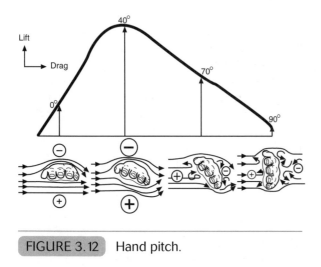

FIGURE 3.12   Hand pitch.

STROKE TRAINING DRILLS

In *Swimming into the 21st Century*, author Cecil Colwin (1992) recommends drills to improve sweeping technique and hand and palm sensitization. The sweeping motions have been described in detail above and relate to the curvilinear sculling motions (downsweep, insweep, and upsweep). Palm-sensitizing drills are used to increase the acuity of the hand in performing these lateral and diagonal sweeping motions. I have outlined and modified these three techniques in the drills that follow. However, these are not the only technical skill training drills the swimmer can practice. Following this brief section, I will describe about a dozen stroke-enhancing techniques I use. As you will see later in the model sets, these drills are used in nearly every workout. I don't believe a swimmer can get enough of drill and skill training.

Palm-Sensitizing Drills

Fist Closed FC

Swim the first 100 to 200 meters of a workout with your fists closed. This activates nerve end-

ings in your palms, making them more sensitive to water flow when your hand is opened. Start the stroke (entry) with your wrist turned outward and your thumb downward. This will place more emphasis on forearm rotation and help place the elbow in the high position.

Funnel Flow or A-Okay! FF

This drill will teach the swimmer much about flow as the hand direction changes during the stroke. Typically, I design sets that include 25 meters of drill followed by the same distance or more of recovery while working the similar motion. Press the thumb and index fingers lightly together and hold this position throughout the stroke. The object of the drill is to make the water go through the circle formed by the thumb and index finger, as through a funnel. The water must pass through during the downsweep, insweep, and upsweep (fig. 3.12). This drill forces the elbow to flex and remain above the hand during the underwater pull, a position that places the hand in the most dynamic position for sculling in a curvilinear pathway.

According to Colwin (1992), this drill "grooves" the stroke pathway (the sweeping patterns) almost automatically. In other words, it helps teach the curvilinear, S-shaped pulling motions discussed earlier by keeping the elbow high above the hand and forcing the hand to change angles of attack to generate lift. If the

FIGURE 3.13   Funnel flow (A-Okay).

elbow drops below the hand, the water flow will not pass through the funnel.

Fingertip Pressing FP

This series of drills can be done anytime, anywhere, perhaps even during a dry-land training session: (1) Press each fingertip in turn against the thumb; (2) press the fingertips of both hands, one against the other, hard and quickly; (3) press each fingertip of one hand against its counterpart on the other hand; (4) scrape the fingertips, rubbing them firmly against a coarse surface or while resting before the next swim interval (fig. 3.13).

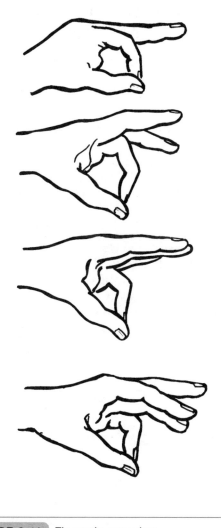

FIGURE 3.14 Fingertip pressing.

Stroke Phase Drills

Stroke Drill SD

This training technique consists of drills in which the swimmer isolates and emphasizes a particular component of the swimming technique. A recognized technique is using three left-arm pulls and then three right-arm pulls while focusing, for example, on the entry. Each of the three strokes works specifically on the entry (thumb down, palm out, index finger first into the water). Another common technique is doing single-arm pulls for the length of the pool followed by a regular swim. I like to use these drills whenever instructing a swimmer on the finer points of stroke biomechanics.

Catch-Up Freestyle CU

This is an exceptional drill for developing the full stroke, from the entry to the kick. Begin by touching both hands (at entry) before making the next stroke. From the release at the thigh (after the upsweep), the swimmer drags the fingertips slowly alongside the body during recovery (high elbow). While alternating arms, the swimmer should breathe on the pulling arm side and keep the idle arm out in front of the head until touched by the entry arm. I use this drill to teach swimmers the proper feel of their mechanics, such as the catch, shoulder roll, or downsweep. This is a particularly effective drill for the downsweep, as the elbow flexes correctly following the natural flexion of the wrist.

Bilateral Breathing BB

During the base preparatory phase of the season, I have my athletes breathe every third stroke. This technique promotes a smooth, rolling motion, clean entry, low water disturbance, and trains the O_2 system. The technique also amplifies breathing capacity by encouraging the swimmer to take fuller breaths, expel air completely, and most important, breathe as efficiently as possible. Generally, the air should be expelled slowly, gently, and fully. Bilateral breathing is an excellent way to balance the stroke mechanics of both sides of the body, something many triathletes should work on during the off-season. In competition, most swimmers will breathe to one side, but by improving the range of flexibility, coordination, strength, and sculling efficiency of the weak side, overall swimming is improved.

Sculling SC

Sculling is the lateral motion of the hands and feet during the stroke. How these extremities articulate depends on an individual's anatomy. Sculling drills help increase the swimmer's hand sensitivity to the inward and outward deflection of water and increase essential muscle strength. For the inexperienced swimmer, sculling is a fundamental drill and principal component of learning how to deflect water and generate propulsive lift.

Wide-Arm Sculling WAS

Kicking (freestyle) in the prone position, with or without fins, push off from the wall in a fully streamlined position (hands together, arms straight overhead, with biceps covering the ears). Rotate your hands in small outward and downward sculling motions, kicking just enough to maintain momentum, if necessary. As you progress across the pool, move your arms farther and farther apart, continuing to scull (making small figure-eights). Once your arms are about 8 inches farther apart than your shoulders, return inwardly, continuing sculling until your hands are at the beginning streamlined position. The feeling should be one of deflecting water to propel the body forward. Some swimmers need very little kick to move quite well using this technique.

Pike Sculling PS

Float on your back with your toes pointed and legs kicking gently. Your hands should be externally rotated even with your shoulders and your elbows close to the sides of your chest (torso). Scull with your hands by moving them outward and inward by leading with the thumb then change directions by leading with the little finger. Bring your knees toward your chest and hold them there briefly, continuing

to scull, then extend your knees and feet to the beginning position. You should do this drill for the length of the pool. You can also change the position of your hands by extending your elbows farther toward your thigh and sculling in this or any position in between.

Shoulder-to-Thigh Sculling STS

While kicking freestyle (without a board), move your hands from the streamlined position to your hips, then to your thighs, sculling (figure-eights) momentarily at each position. With your feet, try to deflect the water in a similar sculling manner (outward) as you make a downward beat.

Vertical Sculling VS

Scull in a diving pool or in water deep enough to maintain a vertical position. Your elbows should be close to the sides of your body and your hands in front of your body. Make small figure-eights with your hands, sculling with quick deflection of the still water. Don't kick in this drill (cross your legs). You can move your hands down toward your hips, sculling and deflecting water using slightly different muscles. If you are a more skilled swimmer (sculler), place a weight (up to 10 pounds) between your knees and do the same drills.

Stroke Accelerators SA

These drill sets are like buildups during each swim. Over the distance, you should constantly but gradually increase the speed of the swim. Try to maximize the length of the stroke and speed of each upsweep. Take long and fast strokes, accelerating the pull throughout each arm stroke. I usually recommend doing these drills for 25 and 50 meters with moderate amounts of rest (20 seconds).

Peripheral Drills: Horizontal, Vertical, and Lateral PD

These drills refer to the three sweeping planes of the arm stroke. Horizontal refers to the length of the stroke, which begins when the swimmer makes the entry and extends the arm and fully rotates the torso and hips. Vertical relates to the depth of the stroke (deepest point in the pull), and lateral is the width of the stroke describing the diagonal (side-to-side sculling) motions while swimming. In effect, the PDs are the downward, lateral inward and outward, and upward motions of the hand and forearm (downsweep, insweep, and upsweep).

This drill is used for isolating each of the pulling phases. In other words, the swimmer emphasizes each of these sections (downsweep, insweep, and upsweep) separately during a technical drill training session. For example, a set of 3 (4 × 50) has the swimmer working the downsweep, insweep, and upsweep separately during each subset of four.

Distance per Stroke DPS

The purpose of distance-per-stroke drills is to encourage a long, full stroke. By taking fewer strokes, the swimmer actually increases the propelling efficiency. This occurs as a result of delaying the beginning of the downsweep momentarily. Obviously, this permits the most propulsive sweep to finish completely and powerfully. Counting the number of strokes for a given distance and subsequently reducing the number taken will result in considerable improvement in stroke efficiency.

Good swimmers take long, fast, and powerful strokes, prolonging momentum. Fewer strokes result in greater efficiency and a faster pace. The drill consists of three sets of 4 × 50 with a send-off interval of 15 seconds. Decreasing the number of strokes taken by one each set provides an ideal DPS set. For example, for the first 4 × 50 meters, the stroke count is 24, 23, 22, and 21, and the next set of four should start at 23 and decrease from there. Do the same for the last set of four, beginning with the stroke count of the second swim.

Kicking Drills

Kicking is propulsive and will help reduce water resistance. For years I've said, "A good kick won't make the swimmer much faster, but a bad one slows the swimmer down." It's true,

and I am living proof, having lost significant ankle flexibility and neuromuscular control due to several ankle operations. Poor flexibility in the ankle decreases the lift (propulsion) of an efficient kick and increases drag (taking up more space in the water). Those with poor kicks should work on strengthening and improving flexibility of the ankles through supplemental training (chapter 6) as well as doing a reasonable number of kicking drills.

The knees should be slightly bent (about 15 degrees) on the downbeat, and the depth of the kick should be equivalent to the width of the body. The ankles should not come out of the water, and the swimmer should try to deflect water downward with the foot. Kick frequencies of 2, 4, 6, and 10 beats are used by all types of swimmers; however, the 2-, 4-, and 6-beat frequencies seem to be the most common. The distance swimmer typically uses fewer beats per arm pulling cycle, with the norm being a 2-beat crossover, 2-beat straight, and 4-beat kick, respectively.

As a general rule, I prefer the triathlete to kick mostly without the use of a kickboard. The reason is that the lower back is in a hyperflexed position when using a kickboard. This places the swimmer into an unnatural position that is unlike freestyle swimming. Also, when not using a kickboard, the swimmer can scull the hands and generally get a better cardiovascular workout.

The following paragraphs describe the various types of kicks I use.

Freestyle KF Prone, on Stomach

This kick is done without the arm motions of freestyle swimming. After pushing off from the wall in the streamlined position and with hands together out front, the swimmer works the freestyle kick. This is somewhat different from what is done in full swimming because the kick is constant. For breathing, use a breaststroke pull, raising the head and taking a breath. The swimmer can vary the pace and intensity of this or any of the following kicks by increasing or decreasing the send-off interval. The benefits of this kicking drill are increased ankle flexion and improved circulatory capacity in the legs.

Backstroke `KB` *Supine, on Back*

For this drill, the hands are outstretched overhead, on top of one another, with the biceps covering the ears. Maintain a horizontal position in the water by keeping the head tilted backward (water line at the eyebrows). The eyebrow water line helps the swimmer's hips to come up (reducing drag), and more important, when swimming freestyle, a higher water-line position is more easily held because of the overexaggerated head position training in backstroke kicking. Point the toes slightly, and work the kick from the hips with a relaxed but rapid up-and-down kicking motion. A more challenging addition is to work the sculling motion (figure-eights) while on the back. In this case, the swimmer will scull just below the water's surface and not in the same manner as for WAS. The hands are at the sides, just above the hips. This drill helps teach the swimmer how to deflect water with the feet and improves ankle flexibility. It also leads to a better streamlined position.

Lateral `KL`

The lateral kick is done with the swimmer in a side-lying position on either side of the body. Again, the hands are clasped together and outstretched overhead. To breathe, the swimmer needs to rotate slightly onto his or her back. Kick on one side, then rotate to the other side for several seconds or kick counts. This kick improves streamlining, flexibility, and hip rotation.

Butterfly Prone `KBP`

After pushing off from the wall, the dolphin/butterfly kick is begun, with the swimmer arching the legs and hips and kicking upward and downward. The feet and legs should be together while making each dolphinlike motion. The swimmer should do two to four kicks before each breath. This drill improves ankle flexion and strengthens the quadriceps and hip flexors.

Butterfly Supine `KBS`

This is a slightly more challenging kick and mirrors the prone butterfly kick. The hands are outstretched overhead after pushing off onto the back. The butterfly kick is performed swiftly and more shallow than when prone. Keep the head tilted back. Some athletes may need to use fins for this kicking drill. Again, the benefits are flexibility, strength, and coordination.

Spiral `KS`

I learned this kick from Kerry O'Brien, head coach of the Walnut Creek, California, masters team. Push off the wall onto the back with hands outstretched overhead. Kick for several seconds or counts, then rotate underwater to the left, all the way onto the back. Kick again for several counts, then rotate to the right, returning to the back. Keep repeating this for the length of the pool. Follow this leg with a normal swim of 25 to 50 meters, then do another set, and so on. The swimmer should notice that the body rides higher in the water, perhaps due to spinning and kicking throughout the spiral. To be honest, I don't know why this is so, but it works! If you want to feel higher in the water, try this drill.

Incorporating the Drills Into Workouts

One way I make sure to get stroke technique drills into my workouts is to designate certain swim and kick sets as technical form (TF) swim sets. TF is a method of working specifically and regularly on stroke mechanics.

An example of broken TF swim training is three sets of 600-meter swims. The first 600 is broken into 6 × 100 freestyle with a 1:40 send-off time, the second 600 is broken into 3 × 200 freestyle with a 3:10 send-off time, and the third 600 is broken into 2(4 × 75) technical form drills with a 1:20 send-off. You'll need to make the send-off interval times match your ability, so allow for about 10 to 20 seconds of rest and remember to do these swims at a fairly light intensity (O_2).

Included within each of these sets are predetermined technique drills or stroke emphasis points. For example, for the 6 × 100, you'll work on rotating the chest, torso, and hips in an efficient lateral motion. For the second 600

(3 × 200), you'll count your strokes (see DPS) for the last 50 of each 200. Add the stroke count to the swim time and decrease this sum for each successive 200. For the third broken 600 consisting of 2(4 × 75), swim the first set as follows: 25 meters backstroke; 25 meters freestyle, pulling with the left arm for three strokes, then the right arm for three strokes, and so on; and 25 meters kicking without a kickboard. For the second set, do 25 meters sculling, 25 meters breaststroke, and 25 meters lateral kicking, right and left side.

The above workout (or portion of a longer set) shows how 1,800 meters can be smoothly organized into a quality technical form training session. You're not just training technique, either. There are physiological conditioning benefits as well, and depending on the intensity and rest interval allowed, the drills provide the swimmer with any number of training positives.

Additional Training Methods

Pulling (P)—I recommend using a conventional pull buoy, paddles, and swim tubes for no more than 20 percent of the total workout. The primary reason is that swimming with these aids is too unlike freestyle swimming, thus using these devices too much can cause technique to suffer. Another misconception is that using the paddles will increase strength. In reality, propelling efficiency is more important than propulsive force (strength).

Nonetheless, there are a few advantages to including some pulling sets. In particular, the pull buoy places the swimmer higher in the water in a horizontal position similar to wearing a wet suit. For the weaker swimmer, this is a distinct advantage, as drag is reduced. The more experienced swimmer, who already has a higher horizontal position in the water, does not achieve the same benefits. However, if you will be competing in a wet suit, you should practice in open water occasionally with the wet suit to rehearse mechanics and the changes of stroke.

Negative Split (NS) and Descended Swims (DS)—Negative splits are swims where the second half of the distance is swum faster than the first half. They are an effective means of training the distance swimmer. Essentially, the swimmer learns to make even splits (not going out too fast) and how to finish strong. I like all my triathletes to negative split the swims in workouts and competitions. At a minimum, they must do even splits for LVT sets. Descending swim sets are similar to negative split swims in terms of training benefits; they involve a series of decreasing swim and send-off times. The following four sets of 4 × 100 meters are examples of descending swim sets:

- Set 1: Decrease swim time by 1 second for swims 1 through 4, with a send-off of 1:30. Swim 1 is 1:24, swim 2 is 1:23, and so on.
- Set 2: Negative split—send-off of 1:25. The second 50 of each 100 meters is faster than the first 50.
- Set 3: Negative split—send-off of 1:20. Same as set 2, but the send-off interval is 5 seconds faster.
- Set 4: Decrease (nonfreestyle 50 backstroke, 50 breaststroke) 1 through 4 on 2:00 send-off.

Note: Adjust your send-off times to allow for a 15-second rest interval before decreasing send-off time.

SWIMMING INTENSITY PACE CHARTS

Now that we've covered the biomechanics, this chapter wouldn't be complete without the swimming intensity pace charts (IPCs). These charts show the distance of the interval (in meters) and designate a time for each training intensity zone based on your goal or (multisport) test time. The chart times are based on the intensity training zone guidelines in chapter 1. If you are swimming in a pool measured in yards, you can easily convert the paces by multiplying the number of yards by 0.91 to determine the times for meters.

Shortly, I'll show you how to use these charts to zero in on the right training intensities whenever you train. Again, the training intensity zones are O_2 (aerobic conditioning), LVT swim-

OVERDISTANCE SWIM TRAINING

Just as with cycling and running, regular, long-distance, continuous swimming sessions are necessary. Most of my athletes perform weekly continuous swims that are determined by the periodization being applied. I like to increase this distance by approximately 10 percent per week to 10 percent over the intended race distance. These workouts are aerobic, and the intensity is fairly light to somewhat hard. This long-distance training is best done in open water and 50-meter pools. Keep the intensity down, and work on one or two technique areas the entire time.

ming, VO_2 swimming, and LAC swimming. O_2 training is not included because it is longer-duration aerobic conditioning where intervals are not used. Swimming energy system training is based on anticipated, actual, or goal times for 1,500-meter multisport competition—in other words, the best time the swimmer can swim 1,500 (LVT) meters during a race.

• O_2 (aerobic conditioning) = Long and gradual continuous aerobic training.

• LVT (anaerobic conditioning) = Short send-off intervals (5 to 60 seconds). *Note:* Sets are a minimum of 15 minutes to a maximum of 25 minutes, and occasionally up to two sets are used (depending on training volume).

• VO_2 (aerobic capacity) = The rest time is equal to the interval time, or double the swim time. *Note:* Sets are 15 to 21 minutes long, with each swim interval lasting from 2 to 8 minutes.

• LAC (anaerobic capacity) = Rest is two times the interval if less than 1 minute of swim time and three times the interval if more than 1 minute. *Note:* Sets are 4 to 10 minutes, with swim times from 10 seconds to 1:20.

Training Note: Each intensity training zone has required durations of exercise time. These durations are necessary to achieve the correct physiological training effect. In the VO_2 and LAC training intensity zones, the minimum exercise time (distance) requirements sometimes are not met. This usually occurs during base preparatory phases when the volume of training is low. If this is the case, it is appropriate to complete less than the minimum VO_2 or LAC workout times within any training session.

Locate your appropriate swim time under the "Split 1,500" column. This is your best 1,500-meter time. The LVT pace per 100 meters is displayed in the third column from the left. This is the average pace per 100 meters during the swim at race pace. LVT refers to a 1,500-meter race pace.

For example, an LVT section of a workout is 1,000 meters and the 1,500-meter pace time is 24:00. Read across the rows from left to right for goal times for the LVT swim distance. In this case, the goal times are 48 seconds for 50 meters, 1:36 for 100 meters, and 8:00 for 500 meters, respectively. If the distance you are swimming is not displayed, add distances from the chart to equal the sum of your desired distance.

The shorter the LVT training distance, the shorter the rest interval (5 to 15 seconds). For swims of 300 meters and more, the rest interval time should range from 20 to 60 seconds. It's best to use a pace clock for determining the send-off interval for each swim. For example, a set of 8 × 200 meters swam in 2:40 (LVT 1,500 pace of 20:00 from the IPC) would have a send-off interval of either 2:45, 2:50, or 2:55. Additionally, the swimmer could make the first four of eight on the 2:55 and the last four swims on the 2:45 (descending send-off interval time). As a reminder, if the intensity training zone is VO_2 or LAC, go to those respective charts and read from left to right to get the time goals for given distances.

In the above example, a set of 5×200 VO_2 would be swum with an average time of 2:32 and a rest interval of ±2:32. These times are taken from the swimming IPCs (tables 3.1, 3.2, and 3.3) for the respective training intensity zone based on the above 20:00 for the 1,500. For LAC training, a set of 8×50 has a swim time goal of 30 seconds and a rest interval of 60 seconds, or the swimmer leaves every 90 seconds for the next swim.

It is important to remember that the swimmer must be able to complete the total distance in the time prescribed to have a successful workout. An LVT set of 15×100 with a send-off of 1:30 means the swimmer must swim each 100 meters with enough time for recovery and leaving on the 1:30. If the swimmer can't make the total swimming volume, rest interval, or goal time for any of the training intensity zones, she may have started out too ambitiously. To get the most out of this workout, it is important to repeat intervals with a send-off time matching your ability.

MODEL SWIMMING SETS

The following organized models of swim training workouts are arranged within the training intensity zones described in chapter 1. There are four examples: one for each of the LVT, VO_2, and LAC training intensity zones and one combining several intensity training zones. Aerobic (O_2) swim training, an important component of training, can be accomplished each week by swimming one continuous swim up to or over the race distance. During this aerobic swim, the focus is often on specific technical form components (sometimes two or more but broken by certain distances for each TF) such as 2,000 meters, and each 500 meters has a particular TF highlight. Two things are accomplished with this type of swimming. First, the oxygen system is trained by way of low-intensity exercise, and second, there is an opportunity to focus specifically on technique.

LVT Model Set

Anaerobic conditioning (LVT) training increases race pace endurance using the perceived exertion of somewhat hard to energetically hard. LVT sets are workouts done at or near 1,500-meter race pace. Send-off intervals are short, with rest periods of 5 to 15 seconds for swims between 25 and 300 meters. LVT sets often total 1,000 to 3,000 meters and are completed as broken sets. These sets will include several distances, ranging from 50 to 500 meters. Generally, the send-off interval for each distance is your 100-meter average pace for 1,500 meters plus 5 seconds. For example, if you average 1:25 per 100 during a 1,500-meter swim, your send-off time per 100 meters would be 1:30.

Short-rest-interval training permits just enough rest for removal of excess lactic acid. The burning sensation felt in the arms when pushing the pace is caused by oxygen demands being too great for efficient removal of lactate. As fitness gains take place, the cardiorespiratory system improves and the threshold for the onset of lactate increases. The athlete will likely be able to perform a greater volume or distance with lower send-off interval times without accumulating as much lactate. Gradual increases in training volume and intensity and mixing the intensity training zones will improve the LVT.

There are an infinite number of ways to design the LVT, but keep in mind that the swimmer should train the right system for the right amount of time. By this I mean that you can use short, middle, or long distances, or a combination of these, to accomplish the same results. The amount of rest you take between the intervals is what determines the training effect. Of course, the send-off time should be at such a pace that the training intensity zone is right.

The physiological focus of LVT training should be on maintaining pace, decreasing the pace time slightly, or negative splitting the swims as the sets progress. If the swimmer cannot hold pace as the sets progress, the intensity is too high. Thus it is important to keep the rest interval short—this will keep the swim time within the LVT range. Refer to the drill and exercise section for the acronyms used in the following workouts.

I. Warm-up (always done at O_2 pace):

A. Swim 500 meters 2 (150 freestyle, 50 back-stroke, 50 WAS)

B. Kick 200 meters (no board, streamlined position from push-off; kick from hip with feet loose at the ankles (relax after downbeat)

C. Swim 600 meters (TF training): 12 × 50 (plus 10-second send-off; SD, three strokes left and three right; 25 meters SD, 25 meters freestyle swimming)

> 1-4.   FF (elbow high; water passes through hole)
>
> 5-8.   DPS (descend 1-4 on swim back)
>
> 9-12. FC for 25 meters after streamline from pushoff

II. Main set: Swim 6 × 400 LVT (60 seconds between sets)

> 1-2.   400 meters freestyle plus 30-second send-off interval; NS at the 200 for each swim; goal time of 6:24*
>
> 3.   400 IM (individual medley—100 butterfly, 100 backstroke, 100 breast-stroke, and 100 freestyle) broken at each 25 meters for 10 seconds
>
> 4-5.   400 freestyle plus 20-second send-off intervals, DS by 4 seconds from set 2
>
> 6.   400 IM broken at each 50 meters for 15 seconds

Note: Based on 24:00 1,500 time. Go to the IPC to determine your own pace.

III. Warm-down (always done at O_2 pace): Pull 300 meters (4 × 75 meters at DPS O_2 + 10-second send-off)

Note: This is a TF warm-down set; work on diverting oncoming flow and keep finger-tips pointing downward by flexing and extending the wrist (changing angle).

Total workout distance: 4,000 meters

Note: Refer to the swimming IPCs for goal times and pace. The previous times are for illustration only.

VO_2 Model Set

$\dot{V}O_2$max training raises aerobic capacity or maximum oxygen capacity (aerobic power). The efforts are slightly faster than race pace but not all out. The workouts use a perceived exertion of energetically hard to very hard. VO_2 (aerobic capacity) sets are done at workout intensities approximately 5 percent above race pace. This 5 percent increase is not easy to achieve, but with enough rest and selecting the right goal pace, the swimmer should be successful. This, of course, is determined using the intensity pace chart and the swimmer's 1,500-meter trial time. Each swim distance should last between 2 and 8 minutes. In addition, the total time in any one workout for training VO_2 is between 15 and 21 minutes. This amount is determined in the program manager and workout training managers, as described in chapter 2.

I. Warm-up (always done at O_2 pace):

A. Swim 500 meters: 4 × 125 meters at O_2 pace plus 10 seconds; streamline from the push-off plus six relaxed ankle kicks; work on hand pitch change during insweep and upsweep

B. Kick 400 meters: 4 × 100 at O_2 pace, building up to low end of LVT plus 20 seconds; vary type of kick every 25 meters (KL, KBS, KS, KF; no board; fins okay)

C. Swim (TF) 300 meters: 6 × 50 meters; sculling drills, two each of FF, VS, and PS

D. Pull (TF) 900 meters: 6 × 150 plus 15-second send-off at O_2 to low LVT pace

> 1-2.   Straight swims working entry and high elbow recovery
>
> 3.   Alternate by 25 meters freestyle and backstroke
>
> 4.   2 × (25 meters butterfly, 25 back-stroke, 25 breaststroke)
>
> 5.   Straight swim: O_2 hypoxic (breath-holding drill) 3-5-7-9 (if possible); breathe on indicated cycle
>
> 6.   SD swim by 25 meters using three left and three right arm pulls; work on FC 25, freestyle 25

II. Main set: 1,000 meters: 5 × 200 VO$_2$ at swim time of 2:45; equal time rest interval (2:45)

Note: Based on 21:45 for 1,500 meters. Refer to IPC to determine your pace.

III. Warm-down (always done at O$_2$ pace): Swim 250 meters: 10 × 25 meters plus 10 seconds; work on high elbow during downsweep on odd swims and on side-to-side body roll on even swims

Total workout distance: 3,350 meters

Note: Refer to the swimming IPCs for goal times and pace. The above times are for illustration only.

LAC Model Set

LAC (anaerobic capacity) training is the highest-intensity (fastest speeds) training the swimmer will do. The perceived exertion is very hard to very, very hard. The shortest interval time is 10 seconds and the longest time is 2 minutes. These are usually in swims of 25 to 200 meters. The rest periods are twice the swim time for intervals of less than 1 minute and three times the swim time for intervals of more than 1 minute of exercise time. A set of 10 × 50 in 30 seconds has a send-off time of 1:30 (rest of 60 seconds). A set of 4 × 100 in 1:15 has a send-off time of 5:00 (rest of 3:45). The total time for this intensity training zone in any single workout is 4 to 10 minutes. A key point in LAC training is for the final repeat to be the fastest. To do this, the athlete should make sure the previous repetitions are not too fast.

I. Warm-up (always done at O$_2$ pace)

A. Swim 500 meters: 10 × 50 plus 10 seconds at O$_2$ pace; long and loose, streamlined from the push-off; swim the even 50-meter legs nonfreestyle

B. Swim TF 750 meters: 10 × 75 meters plus a 10-second send-off interval

   1.   25 meters streamline from push-off, then kick/SC

   2.   25 meters DPS

   3.   25 meters CU using two left and two right arm pulls

II. Main set: 10 × 50 LAC meters in 30 seconds with 1:30 of rest between each set

Total duration of set is 5 minutes, not including rest time.

III. Warm-down (always done at O$_2$ pace):

A. Swim 300 meters: 10 seconds of rest after each 50 meters; work on smooth entry and recovery

B. Kick 600 meters: 8 × 75 meters plus 15-second send-off interval; alternate KF/KS each 75 meters; no board on 1-4, board on 5-8; 25 easy, 25 moderate, 25 sprint (building up intensity)

Total workout distance: 2,650

Note: Refer to the swimming IPCs for goal times and pace. The above times are for illustration only.

Mixed Training Intensity Zone Model Set

Workouts often include several intensity training zones. Some sections of the previous model sets include multiple intensity training zones, but for clarification, I wanted to provide a specific multiple training intensity workout. This mixing of training intensities adds another important component—variety! Two important things I learned early on in coaching endurance athletes and designing workouts were: (1) keep the workouts interesting, and (2) have the right mix of intensity (I did this by never repeating the same swim, bike, or run workouts). There are endless ways to achieve the same training by adjusting the distance, intensity, and rest interval of a training session.

Mixing the training intensity zones is appropriate, but two general rules apply. First, the highest-intensity training in any workout should come toward the end. I believe this is the best way to train technique, cardiorespiratory endurance, and power, as the swimmer learns to work well when fatigued. In addition, the swimmer will be warmed up well at this point. Second, allow for enough rest between repeats, and make every effort to get the right goal pace.

I. Warm-up (always done at O₂ pace):

A. Swim 400 meters (work on the insweep, changing angle of hand pitch)

B. Kick 400 meters (4 × 100 meters plus 20-second send-off intervals (no board, but fins are okay)

    1-3.   50 meters KF, 50 meters KBP

    2-4.   KF, negative split at 50

Pull 400 meters (breathe on weaker side only and work on high elbow recovery, palm inward, then outward)

II. LVT swim: 1,500 meters: 3(200 meters + 4 × 75 meters) plus 15-second send-off interval

III. O₂ swim: 150 meters nonfreestyle swimming (work on DPS and body roll)

IV. Swim TF: 300 meters: 6 × 50 plus 10-second send-off interval

    1-3.   SD (three left and three right arm pulls; work wrist (catch) flexion at extension

    4-6.   CU (high elbow at downsweep; elbow pointed to side)

V. LAC swim: 300 meters: 12 × 25 meters in 13 seconds + 45-second send-off interval

VI. O₂ swim: 150-meters nonfreestyle swimming

Total workout volume: 3,600 meters

Note: Refer to the swimming IPCs for goal times and pace. The above times are for illustration only.

As you implement the workouts in this chapter, consider swimming on your own or with a few endurance sport and triathlete friends once or twice a week. During these workouts, you can work on the VO₂ and LAC training sets. You won't find many of these in any masters program, so it would be a good idea to do them alone or preferably with others who have the same intentions. In masters workouts, change lanes occasionally for higher or lower intensity (based on your periodization and recovery needs). If you swim with better swimmers, you'll learn more about good mechanics, even though they are faster. Finally, tell your coach about any special training needs you have as well as about upcoming and long-term competitions. Your coach will likely recognize many of the triathletes who are targeting the same events and can alter the workouts in your direction or set aside a lane for you.

TABLE 3.1   Intensity Pace Chart - LVT Swimming*

Split 1,500	Split Ironman	LVT pace per 100	50	100	200	500
0:15:00	0:38:37	01:00	00:30	01:00	02:00	05:00
0:15:30	0:39:54	01:02	00:31	01:02	02:04	05:10
0:16:00	0:41:11	01:04	00:32	01:04	02:08	05:20
0:16:30	0:42:28	01:06	00:33	01:06	02:12	05:30
0:17:00	0:43:45	01:08	00:34	01:08	02:16	05:40
0:17:30	0:45:03	01:10	00:35	01:10	02:20	05:50
0:18:00	0:46:20	01:12	00:36	01:12	02:24	06:00
0:18:30	0:47:37	01:14	00:37	01:14	02:28	06:10
0:19:00	0:48:54	01:16	00:38	01:16	02:32	06:20
0:19:30	0:50:12	01:18	00:39	01:18	02:36	06:30
0:20:00	0:51:29	01:20	00:40	01:20	02:40	06:40
0:20:30	0:52:46	01:22	00:41	01:22	02:44	06:50
0:21:00	0:54:03	01:24	00:42	01:24	02:48	07:00
0:21:30	0:55:20	01:26	00:43	01:26	02:52	07:10
0:22:00	0:56:38	01:28	00:44	01:28	02:56	07:20
0:22:30	0:57:55	01:30	00:45	01:30	03:00	07:30
0:23:00	0:59:12	01:32	00:46	01:32	03:04	07:40
0:23:30	1:00:29	01:34	00:47	01:34	03:08	07:50
0:24:00	1:01:47	01:36	00:48	01:36	03:12	08:00
0:24:30	1:03:04	01:38	00:49	01:38	03:16	08:10
0:25:00	1:04:21	01:40	00:50	01:40	03:20	08:20
0:25:30	1:05:38	01:42	00:51	01:42	03:24	08:30
0:26:00	1:06:55	01:44	00:52	01:44	03:28	08:40
0:26:30	1:08:13	01:46	00:53	01:46	03:32	08:50
0:27:00	1:09:30	01:48	00:54	01:48	03:36	09:00
0:27:30	1:10:47	01:50	00:55	01:50	03:40	09:10
0:28:00	1:12:04	01:52	00:56	01:52	03:44	09:20
0:28:30	1:13:22	01:54	00:57	01:54	03:48	09:30
0:29:00	1:14:39	01:56	00:58	01:56	03:52	09:40
0:29:30	1:15:56	01:58	00:59	01:58	03:56	09:50
0:30:00	1:17:13	02:00	01:00	02:00	04:00	10:00
0:30:30	1:18:30	02:02	01:01	02:02	04:04	10:10
0:31:00	1:19:48	02:04	01:02	02:04	04:08	10:20

TABLE 3.1   *(continued)*

Split 1,500	Split Ironman	LVT pace per 100	50	100	200	500
0:31:30	1:21:05	02:06	01:03	02:06	04:12	10:30
0:32:00	1:22:22	02:08	01:04	02:08	04:16	10:40
0:32:30	1:23:39	02:10	01:05	02:10	04:20	10:50
0:33:00	1:24:57	02:12	01:06	02:12	04:24	11:00
0:33:30	1:26:14	02:14	01:07	02:14	04:28	11:10
0:34:00	1:27:31	02:16	01:08	02:16	04:32	11:20
0:34:30	1:28:48	02:18	01:09	02:18	04:36	11:30
0:35:00	1:30:05	02:20	01:10	02:20	04:40	11:40
0:35:30	1:31:23	02:22	01:11	02:22	04:44	11:50
0:36:00	1:32:40	02:24	01:12	02:24	04:48	12:00
0:36:30	1:33:57	02:26	01:13	02:26	04:52	12:10
0:37:00	1:35:14	02:28	01:14	02:28	04:56	12:20
0:37:30	1:36:31	02:30	01:15	02:30	05:00	12:30
0:38:00	1:37:49	02:32	01:16	02:32	05:04	12:40
0:38:30	1:39:06	02:34	01:17	02:34	05:08	12:50
0:39:00	1:40:23	02:36	01:18	02:36	05:12	13:00
0:39:30	1:41:40	02:38	01:19	02:38	05:16	13:10
0:40:00	1:42:58	02:40	01:20	02:40	05:20	13:20
0:40:30	1:44:15	02:42	01:21	02:42	05:24	13:30
0:41:00	1:45:32	02:44	01:22	02:44	05:28	13:40
0:41:30	1:46:49	02:46	01:23	02:46	05:32	13:50
0:42:00	1:48:06	02:48	01:24	02:48	05:36	14:00

TABLE 3.2 Intensity Pace Chart - VO2 Swimming

Split 1,500	Split Ironman	LVT pace per 100	100	200	300	400	500	700
15:00	0:38:37	01:00			02:51	03:48	04:45	06:39
15:30	0:39:54	01:02			02:57	03:56	04:55	06:52
16:00	0:41:11	01:04		02:02	03:02	04:03	05:04	07:06
16:30	0:42:28	01:06		02:05	03:08	04:11	05:13	07:19
17:00	0:43:45	01:08		02:09	03:14	04:18	05:23	07:32
17:30	0:45:03	01:10		02:13	03:19	04:26	05:32	07:46
18:00	0:46:20	01:12		02:17	03:25	04:34	05:42	07:59
18:30	0:47:37	01:14		02:21	03:31	04:41	05:51	
19:00	0:48:54	01:16		02:24	03:37	04:49	06:01	
19:30	0:50:12	01:18		02:28	03:42	04:56	06:10	
20:00	0:51:29	01:20		02:32	03:48	05:04	06:20	
20:30	0:52:46	01:22		02:36	03:54	05:12	06:29	
21:00	0:54:03	01:24		02:40	03:59	05:19	06:39	
21:30	0:55:20	01:26		02:43	04:05	05:27	06:48	
22:00	0:56:38	01:28		02:47	04:11	05:34	06:58	
22:30	0:57:55	01:30		02:51	04:16	05:42	07:07	
23:00	0:59:12	01:32		02:55	04:22	05:50	07:17	
23:30	1:00:29	01:34		02:59	04:28	05:57	07:26	
24:00	1:01:47	01:36		03:02	04:34	06:05	07:36	
24:30	1:03:04	01:38		03:06	04:39	06:12	07:45	
25:00	1:04:21	01:40		03:10	04:45	06:20	07:55	
25:30	1:05:38	01:42		03:14	04:51	06:28		
26:00	1:06:55	01:44		03:18	04:56	06:35		
26:30	1:08:13	01:46		03:21	05:02	06:43		
27:00	1:09:30	01:48		03:25	05:08	06:50		
27:30	1:10:47	01:50		03:29	05:13	06:58		
28:00	1:12:04	01:52		03:33	05:19	07:06		
28:30	1:13:22	01:54		03:37	05:25	07:13		
29:00	1:14:39	01:56		03:40	05:31	07:21		
29:30	1:15:56	01:58		03:44	05:36	07:28		
30:00	1:17:13	02:00		03:48	05:42	07:36		
30:30	1:18:30	02:02		03:52	05:48	07:44		
31:00	1:19:48	02:04		03:56	05:53	07:51		

(continued)

TABLE 3.2   *(continued)*

Split 1,500	Split Ironman	LVT pace per 100	100	200	300	400	500	700
31:30	1:21:05	02:06	02:00	03:59	05:59	07:59		
32:00	1:22:22	02:08	02:02	04:03	06:05			
32:30	1:23:39	02:10	02:03	04:07	06:10			
33:00	1:24:57	02:12	02:05	04:11	06:16			
33:30	1:26:14	02:14	02:07	04:15	06:22			
34:00	1:27:31	02:16	02:09	04:18	06:28			
34:30	1:28:48	02:18	02:11	04:22	06:33			
35:00	1:30:05	02:20	02:13	04:26	06:39			
35:30	1:31:23	02:22	02:15	04:30	06:45			
36:00	1:32:40	02:24	02:17	04:34	06:50			
36:30	1:33:57	02:26	02:19	04:37	06:56			
37:00	1:35:14	02:28	02:21	04:41	07:02			
37:30	1:36:31	02:30	02:22	04:45	07:07			
38:00	1:37:49	02:32	02:24	04:49	07:13			
38:30	1:39:06	02:34	02:26	04:53	07:19			
39:00	1:40:23	02:36	02:28	04:56	07:25			
39:30	1:41:40	02:38	02:30	05:00	07:30			
40:00	1:42:58	02:40	02:32	05:04	07:36			
40:30	1:44:15	02:42	02:34	05:08	07:42			
41:00	1:45:32	02:44	02:36	05:12	07:47			
41:30	1:46:49	02:46	02:38	05:15	07:53			
42:00	1:48:06	02:48	02:40	05:19	07:59			
42:30	1:49:24	02:50	02:41	05:23				
43:00	1:50:41	02:52	02:43	05:27				
43:30	1:51:58	02:54	02:45	05:31				
44:00	1:53:15	02:56	02:47	05:34				
44:30	1:54:33	02:58	02:49	05:38				
45:00	1:55:50	03:00	02:51	05:42				
45:30	1:57:07	03:02	02:53	05:46				
46:00	1:58:24	03:04	02:55	05:50				
46:30	1:59:41	03:06	02:57	05:53				
47:00	2:00:59	03:08	02:59	05:57				

TABLE 3.3 Intensity Pace Chart - LAC Swimming

Split 1,500	Split Ironman	LVT pace per 100	50	75	100	150	200
15:00	0:38:37	01:00	00:00:23	00:00:35	00:00:48	00:01:12	00:01:36
15:30	0:39:54	01:02	00:00:23	00:00:36	00:00:50	00:01:14	00:01:39
16:00	0:41:11	01:04	00:00:24	00:00:37	00:00:51	00:01:17	00:01:42
16:30	0:42:28	01:06	00:00:25	00:00:39	00:00:53	00:01:19	00:01:46
17:00	0:43:45	01:08	00:00:25	00:00:40	00:00:54	00:01:22	00:01:49
17:30	0:45:03	01:10	00:00:26	00:00:41	00:00:56	00:01:24	00:01:52
18:00	0:46:20	01:12	00:00:27	00:00:42	00:00:58	00:01:26	00:01:55
18:30	0:47:37	01:14	00:00:28	00:00:43	00:00:59	00:01:29	00:01:58
19:00	0:48:54	01:16	00:00:28	00:00:44	00:01:01	00:01:31	
19:30	0:50:12	01:18	00:00:29	00:00:46	00:01:02	00:01:34	
20:00	0:51:29	01:20	00:00:30	00:00:47	00:01:04	00:01:36	
20:30	0:52:46	01:22	00:00:31	00:00:48	00:01:06	00:01:38	
21:00	0:54:03	01:24	00:00:31	00:00:49	00:01:07	00:01:41	
21:30	0:55:20	01:26	00:00:32	00:00:50	00:01:09	00:01:43	
22:00	0:56:38	01:28	00:00:33	00:00:51	00:01:10	00:01:46	
22:30	0:57:55	01:30	00:00:34	00:00:53	00:01:12	00:01:48	
23:00	0:59:12	01:32	00:00:34	00:00:54	00:01:14	00:01:50	
23:30	1:00:29	01:34	00:00:35	00:00:55	00:01:15	00:01:53	
24:00	1:01:47	01:36	00:00:36	00:00:56	00:01:17	00:01:55	
24:30	1:03:04	01:38	00:00:37	00:00:57	00:01:18	00:01:58	
25:00	1:04:21	01:40	00:00:37	00:00:58	00:01:20	00:02:00	
25:30	1:05:38	01:42	00:00:38	00:01:00	00:01:22		
26:00	1:06:55	01:44	00:00:39	00:01:01	00:01:23		
26:30	1:08:13	01:46	00:00:40	00:01:02	00:01:25		
27:00	1:09:30	01:48	00:00:40	00:01:03	00:01:26		
27:30	1:10:47	01:50	00:00:41	00:01:04	00:01:28		
28:00	1:12:04	01:52	00:00:42	00:01:06	00:01:30		
28:30	1:13:22	01:54	00:00:43	00:01:07	00:01:31		
29:00	1:14:39	01:56	00:00:43	00:01:08	00:01:33		
29:30	1:15:56	01:58	00:00:44	00:01:09	00:01:34		
30:00	1:17:13	02:00	00:00:45	00:01:10	00:01:36		
30:30	1:18:30	02:02	00:00:46	00:01:11	00:01:38		
31:00	1:19:48	02:04	00:00:46	00:01:13	00:01:39		

(continued)

TABLE 3.3 *(continued)*

Split 1,500	Split Ironman	LVT pace per 100	50	75	100	150	200
31:30	1:21:05	02:06	00:00:47	00:01:14	00:01:41		
32:00	1:22:22	02:08	00:00:48	00:01:15	00:01:42		
32:30	1:23:39	02:10	00:00:49	00:01:16	00:01:44		
33:00	1:24:57	02:12	00:00:49	00:01:17	00:01:46		
33:30	1:26:14	02:14	00:00:50	00:01:18	00:01:47		
34:00	1:27:31	02:16	00:00:51	00:01:20	00:01:49		
34:30	1:28:48	02:18	00:00:52	00:01:21	00:01:50		
35:00	1:30:05	02:20	00:00:52	00:01:22	00:01:52		
35:30	1:31:23	02:22	00:00:53	00:01:23	00:01:54		
36:00	1:32:40	02:24	00:00:54	00:01:24	00:01:55		
36:30	1:33:57	02:26	00:00:55	00:01:25	00:01:57		
37:00	1:35:14	02:28	00:00:55	00:01:27	00:01:58		
37:30	1:36:31	02:30	00:00:56	00:01:28	00:02:00		
38:00	1:37:49	02:32	00:00:57	00:01:29			
38:30	1:39:06	02:34	00:00:58	00:01:30			
39:00	1:40:23	02:36	00:00:58	00:01:31			
39:30	1:41:40	02:38	00:00:59	00:01:32			
40:00	1:42:58	02:40	00:01:00	00:01:34			
40:30	1:44:15	02:42	00:01:01	00:01:35			
41:00	1:45:32	02:44	00:01:01	00:01:36			
41:30	1:46:49	02:46	00:01:02	00:01:37			
42:00	1:48:06	02:48	00:01:03	00:01:38			
42:30	1:49:24	02:50	00:01:04	00:01:39			
43:00	1:50:41	02:52	00:01:04	00:01:41			
43:30	1:51:58	02:54	00:01:05	00:01:42			
44:00	1:53:15	02:56	00:01:06	00:01:43			
44:30	1:54:33	02:58	00:01:07	00:01:44			
45:00	1:55:50	03:00	00:01:07	00:01:45			
45:30	1:57:07	03:02	00:01:08	00:01:46			
46:00	1:58:24	03:04	00:01:09	00:01:48			
46:30	1:59:41	03:06	00:01:10	00:01:49			
47:00	2:00:59	03:08	00:01:10	00:01:50			

4

CYCLING

"Let's go for a ride! Just a spin, nothing hard, and no hills today. It's a recovery day of spinning!" Surely you've heard or said this many times, but 99.9 percent of the time the intention is hastily forgotten once the wheels begin to turn and the body warms up. Add to this a friend or unknown cyclist some 200 meters in front, and inevitably your pace is elevated. The easiest of rides becomes another hard workout. Wasn't today supposed to be easy?

This time, however, it's going to be different: Your workout today will consist of reading about optimization of technique in cycling. It's a journey I expect you'll find practical, with expert tips and techniques for improving aerodynamics, efficiency, muscle use, aero fitting, pedaling technique, cadence, gearing selection, energy utilization, and cycling drill training.

Cycling is a lot more than pushing on the pedals. It involves a rider/bicycle relationship completely unique to each athlete, and as with swimming, good technique and attention to streamlining are important. In this case, however, the cyclist uses a mechanical device—the bicycle and its various components—for movement. The frame size and shape, wheel type (spoke, disk, aero), tire type and inflation or diameter, rider positioning, crank length, pedal, handlebar type, and many other geometric variables affect efficiency. Combining those elements with environmental conditions such as wind, hills or uneven terrain, surface friction, heat, cold, and altitude also result in changes in efficiency. Efficiency can be defined simply as the amount of body energy used to achieve speed. To improve efficiency, factors associated with both rider and bicycle must be considered for optimum results.

THE RIDER/BICYCLE DYNAMIC

Before getting into the more meaningful parts of this chapter, a few comments on equipment and fitting are in order. First, there are dozens of manufacturers for every component of the endurance athlete's bicycle. And for obvious reasons, all of us are influenced by the "faster, lighter, and sleeker" rationale. However, the endurance athlete cannot buy speed without having trained properly and setting up the bike in the proper manner.

Advances in fitting systems and aerodynamic analysis are changing the way we look at rider/bicycle interaction. Anatomy and biomechanics are so individualized that only a sound fitting system will work to get the right fit. Thus it is wise to seek the guidance of a professional in finding the most efficient bike and riding position.

It's a good idea to keep abreast of developments in aero fitting, even though self-assessment principles are reviewed in detail here. With all due respect to local bike shops and owners, many are not equipped to advise athletes on positioning. This cannot be done using guesswork and arbitrary processes. Subjective or off-the-rack fitting is a mistake for

AERODYNAMICS OF BODY POSITION

Jim Martin is a registered engineer, exercise physiologist, director of Sport Science for Team EDS Cycling, and a doctoral student in neuromuscular function at the University of Texas. In his unpublished paper, "The Aerodynamics of Cycling," he offers the following on the importance of body position:

Although much attention is focused on the aerodynamics of equipment, the most important aerodynamic consideration for a bike and rider combination is the rider. A typical 70-kg rider on a regular bike with standard wheels will have a drag of about 8 lb. at 30 mph. A better position will reduce drag to about 7 lb., and an excellent position will yield a drag of 6 lb. Based on these drag numbers, and the power outputs estimated above, [an equation] can be used to predict the effects of these positions on cycling performance on a flat course with no wind, as shown in table 4.1, *a* and *b*. The differences in performance with no change in power are remarkable, ranging to about six minutes when changing from a typical to an excellent position.

TABLE 4.1*a*:   Predicted 40K time, flat course, calm conditions, three body positions, standard wheels.

Position	Drag at 30 mph	Elite	Well-trained	Trained	Recreational
Typical	8.0	62:49	65:51	70:16	76:01
Good	7.0	60:14	63:07	67:22	72:57
Excellent	6.0	57:23	60:10	64:07	69:47

TABLE 4.1*b*:   Predicted time savings for a 40K based on two body positions compared with a typical position, flat course, calm conditions, standard wheels.

Position	Drag at 30 mph	Elite	Well-trained	Trained	Recreational
Typical	8.0	62:49	65:51	70:16	76:01
Good	7.0	2:35	2:44	2:54	3:04
Excellent	6.0	5:26	5:41	6:09	6:14

The key elements of a good aero position are as follows:

1. A horizontal torso, defined by having your chest or, better yet, your back parallel to the ground, is the most important element, as it can result in large-magnitude changes in aerodynamic drag. Unfortunately, it may be the most difficult to achieve, because as you approach this position, your thighs start to bump against your torso. This interference imposes limits on your body's aerodynamic position but is due to traditional bike geometry (i.e., seat tube angles of 73 to 75 degrees).

The way to overcome this limitation is to go to a more forward position that will allow you to roll your entire body forward. A note of caution: A forward-position seat post and long, steeply dropped stem may allow you to assume a good aero position but will result in a bike that is not well balanced and possibly dangerous to ride. A much better approach is to buy a frame that is designed to be ridden in a forward position.

Be aware, however, that riding in this position may exacerbate the condition of prostatitis (inflammation of the prostate), which is common among male cyclists. Extra seat padding helps but does not eliminate the problem. A truly anatomical saddle that distributes your body weight over the entire seat might help. Some riders try to alleviate this problem by tilting the nose of the saddle down, but this only results in a tendency to slide off the saddle, which strains the shoulders and arm muscles. Also, and to a much lesser degree, riding in the forward position tends to cause a sore neck the first few times you ride; the discomfort lessens with time and can be minimized with stretching and massage. These drawbacks are minimal, though, because you don't have to ride in the forward position daily to keep up a fast speed. My experience with Team EDS, as well as with my own bike, is that you only need to ride in the position once a week (maybe less) to stay adapted to it.

2. Narrowly spaced elbows are an essential detail of an aero position; however, the magnitude of improvement is much less than that achieved by adopting a horizontal torso position. Unpublished research by Boone Lennon conducted at the Texas A&M University wind tunnel has shown that subtle changes in elbow width and aero bar angle may have significant effects on drag. This research was performed on traditional-geometry bikes, with the torso adopting the characteristic cupped shape, and probably illustrates the need to block airflow from the torso area. More recent data on riders in a horizontal torso position show much less effect from these variables. I do not believe these findings are contradictory; rather, they indicate that once the torso is horizontal, you can do little to improve or impair aerodynamic drag.

3. Knee width can change aerodynamic drag by up to a half pound. Pedaling with your knees close to the top tube is essential to good aerodynamics.

4. Is there a tradeoff between position and power output? If done poorly, perhaps, but if done well, no. A recent study by Heil, Wilcox, and Quinn (1995) shows that your cardiovascular stress for a given power is increased by decreasing the trunk-to-femur angle. Therefore, if you lower your elbow position, you may need to move the saddle forward to maintain your trunk-to-femur angle while achieving a lower, more nearly horizontal torso position.

athletes who want to get an edge on the competition. I believe the best fit advice is obtained from businesses or manufacturers who make, sell, or fit time trial bikes. These experts have the experience many local bike shops don't have.

The purpose of the chapter is not to debate opinions about what the best wheel size, top tube length, or bike materials are, but to outline what I feel are suitable and sound fitting principles no matter what type of bike you ride.

Aerodynamics and Air Resistance

Most of a rider's energy goes toward overcoming air resistance. As cycling speeds become faster and faster, energy use increases exponentially. Doubling one's speed produces four times as much wind resistance. The position of the body relative to the oncoming airflow is most crucial for optimum cycling performance, but even the smallest variables such as body hair, clothing, and the type and position of water bottles and cables will make a difference in aerodynamic drag and energy consumption.

It doesn't take a lot of science to understand that aerodynamics is fundamental to cycling speed and efficiency. Obviously, a more streamlined object will travel through the air with less drag. In his book, *Serious Cycling*, Edmund Burke, PhD (1995), points out how aerodynamics make significant contributions to faster speeds. Aero wheels can save 39 seconds, aero handle bars 30 to 60 seconds, an aero helmet 20 to 25 seconds, and two-disk wheels up to 70 seconds over 40 kilometers. Even an aero water bottle and clipless pedals save 9 to 14 seconds over this distance. Long-haired and helmetless athletes must overcome additional resistance and need greater power outputs for given speeds than more aerodynamic competitors.

Aero Fit Fine-Tuning

Let's get right into the first principles of the measurement recommendations for aero fitting. Set up your bike on an indoor trainer, making certain the front wheel is level with the

rear. Then have a partner or professional bike mechanic take measurements and make accurate adjustments. Here is some of the equipment you will need to take these measurements:

Goniometer: A goniometer is a long-arm-angle measuring device (it can be purchased at a medical supply store—you don't need an expensive one). If you like, you can make one using two pieces of wood about the size of a ruler. Attach them at one end with a small bolt, washer, and wing nut. You'll need to measure an angle of about 28 degrees (using a protractor) on the wood, using an intersection to form the angle, then lightly tighten the wing nut.

Plumb line: Made with 24 inches of string with a small weight attached to one end.

Tape measure: Either inches or centimeters (centimeters are more accurate).

Tools: Allen wrench set, sockets, screwdrivers, and other general bicycle adjustment tools to adjust the seat post, saddle, stem, and shoe cleats. Basically, look at these areas and decide which tools you'll need. Often a set of Allen wrenches will do everything.

Marker: A felt-tip, broad-point marker for marking anatomical points. I've also used stick-on dots.

Clothing: Wear a swimsuit and sleeveless top so marking and measurement can be done easily.

Calculator: It will help with making a few quick calculations.

All right! You're all set up and ready to get started, so let's get aero! First, you'll need to have four spots marked on your body. Stand as your partner makes half-inch dots on the following sites (right side of body):

Trochanter: This bony portion on the side of your hip can be felt easily. To locate it, turn your right foot outward and then inward several times while standing. As you do so, place your hand and fingers on the side of your hip. You'll feel the trochanter moving up and down as your ankle turns. Press on this point with your finger and have your partner mark the spot.

Knee: Now, sit in a chair and look for a bony point at the outside front of your right knee, to the front and side of the patella. This is called the lateral epicondyle. Mark this point.

Shoulder: Next, have your partner locate a point on the outside of your right shoulder by following the line of the trapezius out laterally. Mark this point.

Elbow: Finally, cross your right arm over your heart, then run your left hand over your elbow. The bony point you can easily feel is the lateral epicondyle. Mark this point (see fig. 4.1).

FIGURE 4.1   Trochanter, knee, shouder, and elbow markers.

Now you're ready to get aero, so with your partner at your right side and the tools nearby, take a few minutes to spin in the small chain ring on the wind trainer. Once you feel comfortable and are in your normal riding (aero) position, the following measurements can be taken and the necessary adjustments made.

1. *Saddle Height* (hip and knee): This measurement is taken from a relaxed (neutral) riding position. Place a marker on the floor directly under the crank arm (180 degrees), then spin in the aero position (on pads) for a few minutes. Without sliding too far forward onto the tip of the saddle, slowly start to reduce the rpms (stay relaxed) until over the marker. Stop right there! Don't move the ankle! Your partner should now do the following: (1) place the go-

niometer directly on the trochanter (this is vertical 0 degrees), (2) rotate the measuring arm toward the knee (marker), and (3) note the width of the angle from the trochanter to the knee (for most, this will be 25 to 35 degrees; fig. 4.2).

FIGURE 4.2   Saddle height.

A few things need to be considered here. First, the optimum angle is 28 degrees from hip to knee. If the measurement is 3 degrees more or less than 28, first check the elbow and shoulder angle (see item 2 below). This angle should be the same as the hip and knee measurement. Second, plumb the knee and pedal axis (see item 3). If the plumb is vertical, assume everything is fine, and these two measurements ensure that the saddle height is correct. If all three measurements are the same (within 3 degrees) and the athlete is comfortable, you should generally leave the saddle where it is. If you need to change the saddle height, measure all points again in the new saddle position. Make sure you remeasure after every adjustment.

There's another way to determine saddle height. In this method, a measurement is taken from your crotch (pubic symphysis) to the floor

PROPER SEAT HEIGHT

Lower saddle heights result in higher energy or muscle force and obviously higher oxygen consumption. In other words, a seat height in the proper range allows an athlete to pedal most efficiently at high workloads. Inversely, a saddle height that is too high is inefficient, as it causes the leg to stretch, lessening power as the pelvis rocks wildly on the saddle trying to extend the leg to the bottom of the pedal stroke.

(bare feet). The height of the saddle should be 106 to 109 percent of this measurement. This number is then applied to the pedal axis (180 degrees), or when the pedal is at the bottom dead center (BDC) of the stroke and the top of the seat above the seat post. For example, if you measure 34 inches, you would then multiply 34 × 1.09 = 37.06 inches, or 94.13 centimeters (inches × 2.54 = centimeters).

2. *Elbow and Shoulder Angle:* With the cyclist in his or her racing position, place the goniometer on the mark on the outside of the shoulder. Swing the arm of the goniometer to the mark on the lateral epicondyle of the elbow (fig. 4.4). This measurement should be the same as the seat height (see item 1), or near 28 degrees. What do you do if it is not the same? First, ensure that the stem (see item 4) is adjusted correctly. Second, remeasure the seat position (see item 2). If those are correct, go on to the stem extension (item 4) and check the measurement and sizing.

3. *Saddle Position* (front to back): Position the crank arm (foot and pedal) at 90 degrees (3 o'clock). Have your partner hold the plumb line at the lateral epicondyle of your knee. The line should pass through the center of the pedal axle (fig. 4.3). If it passes either forward or backward of the axle, the saddle should move in that direction. The knee should be slightly in front of the pedal axle because it accommodates the forward riding position (aero position) used by the triathlete and duathlete.

4. *Stem Extension:* Hold the plumb line on the bridge above the nose and note where the line falls. It should fall just behind the stem's back edge and aero bar connection (1/4 to 1/2 inch), regardless of the seat tube angle of the bike. If

© Jeffrey Dow

FIGURE 4.3　Saddle position.

the handlebar junction is too far forward or backward, choose a longer or shorter stem.

5. *Foot Position on Pedal:* There are two choices for this position, depending on how far forward the knee is in relation to the pedal axle (item 2). If the knee is over the pedal axle, place the ball of the foot slightly behind the axle. If the knee is ahead of the pedal axle, position the ball of the foot slightly toward the front of the axle. This increases the efficiency of the foot, shoe, and pedal interface.

6. *Stem Height:* The height of the stem is measured from the top front of the saddle to the top of the stem. By placing a level yardstick

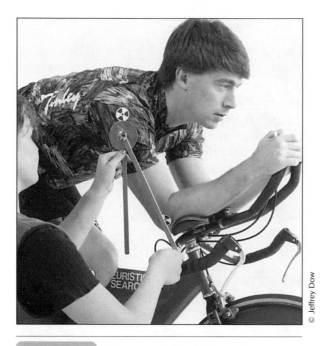

FIGURE 4.4 Elbow and shoulder angle.

over the saddle and stem, you can easily measure this difference. The stem should be lower, but no more than 2 inches, or about 5 centimeters at most. Ideally, this difference should be about 1 inch (2.5 centimeters).

7. *Aero Bar Tilt:* Use the goniometer to measure the angle between the top tube and the aero bars (fig. 4.5). It should be between 18 and 28 degrees. The chin of the athlete should be slightly above the front tip of the aero bar. This position forms a smoother (streamlined) profile, as air is less apt to enter the chest area. To make an adjustment, loosen the stem/bar connection slightly. While remeasuring, move the bars to the appropriate angle.

8. *Seat Tilt:* Angle the front tip of the saddle to balance your weight between your pelvis and elbows on the aero bar pads. You should not feel any discomfort, and you should have a good sense of balance.

9. *Back:* Your back should be relatively flat when in the aero position. This should be easy to obtain with a good fit, but you may need to rotate the top of your pelvis slightly forward. This takes just a bit of practice, but in time both your position and your aerodynamics will improve.

10. *Crank Length:* The crank length is imprinted on the inside of each crank. I have seen crank lengths ranging from 160 to 185 millimeters. The length of the crank arms is important because they affect leg movement and pedaling (cadence) rates. For example, the longer the length, the greater the leg movement for each revolution. Shorter lengths require less leg movement.

Some cyclists change their crank length depending on the conditions of the course. For hilly courses, a slightly longer crank is preferred, as more leverage is obtained. There is an easy way to determine the correct crank length for you. Recall that in item 1, you measured the distance from your crotch (pubic symphysis) to the floor. Let's use the same example of 34 inches. In this case, multiply 34 3 0.20 (20 percent of distance from pubic symphysis to floor) = 6.8 inches. Then multiply 6.8 3 0.254 (to convert from inches to millimeters) = 172.72 millimeters. The closest crank length available is 172.5 millimeters.

FIGURE 4.5 Aero bar tilt.

KEEPING YOUR BIKE CLEAN

The importance of keeping your bike and its integral parts clean and well lubricated is often forgotten. When parts become worn, deteriorated, and soiled, rider/bicycle efficiency decreases. Keep friction to a minimum by regularly replacing revolving parts (bottom bracket, head set, hubs, chain), cleaning, and lubricating your bike. It's kind of like shaving down before the big race, only the friction and drag are being stripped from the parts of your bike.

Riding Posture and Alignment

When riding, comfort is important, but so are efficient aerodynamics, particularly your body position relative to the oncoming air. The more streamlined the frontal area of your body, the greater the reductions in drag. Everything, including clothing type, geometric variables, skin friction, hair, and any number of the bicycle/rider position relationships, affects speed. The cyclist must consider many elements to maximize performance. The following are a few additional considerations in determining your best posture on the bike.

1. *Elbows and Knees:* Place your elbows on the aero pads 1 to 3 inches inside the lateral side of the shoulder. This profile streamlines your position against the airflow (narrower shape). If the elbows are too far apart, you have a broader opening for air to enter the chest area. Keep your arms in the narrowest profile possible to meet the oncoming flow of air without compromising stability. Make an effort to have the inside of your knees angled slightly toward the toptube during the overstroke. This position helps streamline the cyclists and, I believe, improves the position for the downstroke.

2. *Preventing Neck and Back Pain:* Cyclists who experience neck or back pain from cycling may want to consider some of the following adjustments: moving the seat position forward, shortening or raising the stem, and switching hand positions frequently. Also, the problem may be due to a difference in leg length causing either higher or lower pelvis movement on either side. This can be assessed by a podiatrist and corrected through orthotics, inserts, or using a different-sized crank arm on each side.

Bicycle Weight and Mass

Why is bicycle weight such an important consideration? The following scenario offers a simple explanation. When a heavier, larger-muscled cyclist powers along on flat terrain and downwind, it is difficult for most to keep up; however, change the conditions to uphill, and the results are entirely different. Speed is equal to available power, weight, and angle of slope or resistance. The less resistance, the faster a more powerful individual is. With a greater slope or air resistance, the heavier rider/bicycle combination needs more power or energy capacity. Thus, heavier riders need a bicycle light enough to maximize speed and efficiency on hilly courses.

Rolling Resistance

The wider the tire, the greater the hindrance to speed. Tires with a larger cross section have more resistance because they have more surface area. Thus it makes sense to buy thinner tires and to pay attention to the quality of the tire. Tires with a higher profile (amount of tire above the rim) perform better on straight roads, and those with a lower profile are better for cornering. Don't waste your hard training and considerable investment in bike equipment by buying low-quality tires. Get the very best you can afford.

And keep your tires pumped up! Higher tire pressures mean less rolling resistance. Some tires can be inflated up to 180 psi and have tested "bursting points" of as much as 500 psi. However, in talking with several manufacturers, a psi between 115 and 130 is sufficient.

According to in-house studies by manufacturers, tire pressures above 130 psi do not lessen rolling resistance. A properly inflated tire is also more puncture-resistant. For racing, the 19-millimeter tubular tire is preferred over clinchers. Continental and Vittoria make the best ones and have outstanding reputations for quality and performance.

THE TECHNIQUE OF PEDALING

Learning to ride "right" is more than clipping in and letting the circular mechanics of the chain ring and cranks do the work for you. Cyclists need to think and to direct the motion of their feet. In its simplest form, an optimal pedaling stroke works forward and downward. It does not push down and then pull up, but rather has an oval-shaped (elliptical) motion stressing the downstroke—a forward and downward movement of the foot during the downstroke. To illustrate how this feels, find a moderately inclined hill. As you begin the gentle ascent, note how the pedal stroke tends to emphasize the front portion (downstroke); that is, the foot presses with more emphasis on the downstroke than during any other section of the pedal stroke. This is how the downstroke should be performed in nearly all terrain.

I developed and have used sector (phase) training for years in teaching the importance of the downstroke and improving the neuromuscular coordination of the other, less important phases of the pedaling stroke. Sectors refer to the four phases of the pedal stroke, and sector training concentrates on developing each phase separately. The backstroke, upstroke, and overstroke are what I call transitional phases of the pedal stroke. These phases do not play particularly important roles in total power output but lead into and out of the downstroke. Still, practicing these less important sectors improves the movement and efficiency of the entire stroke.

The foot and pedal move circularly, but the force applied to the pedal varies around the 360 degrees of the pedaling revolution. The position of the foot (toe up or down) varies as well according to the technique or preference of the rider. In general, during the 0 to 180 degrees (top dead center to bottom dead center) of the downstroke, the toe tends to point slightly upward, whereas in the 180- to 360-degree range, the toe generally points more downward.

Usually, the backstroke, upstroke, and overstroke are best trained independently in workouts. For example, a cyclist might do 3 × 2 minutes, concentrating on each secondary sector. During those 2 minutes, the other sections of the stroke are diminished. This should be followed by 3 to 6 minutes with emphasis on the downstroke (eliminate focus on other sectors entirely).

1. *Downstroke:* The downstroke begins as the foot and pedal move from 0 to 180 degrees, with the more propulsive section between 45 and 135 degrees (fig. 4.6a). The motion of the foot should be directed *forward* and *downward* during the downstroke. Later, I'll discuss some drills and technical exercises to help you improve this important motion of the foot; however, the single most important pedaling tip I can offer is to maintain constant concentration on pressing the foot forward and downward on the pedal.

In race conditions, the amount of force generated by the downstroke is more than 96 percent of total power. This leaves roughly 4 percent for the rest of the pedaling stroke. Yet many athletes consciously try to pull up on the pedals, which contributes very little to total power output. By pedaling in a rounded or elliptical motion, the cyclist should continually strive to emphasize the forward and downward motion (downstroke).

2. *Backstroke:* The backstroke is the sector immediately following the downstroke in which the transition from the downstroke ends on one side and begins on the other (fig. 4.6b). The backstroke overlaps with the downstroke and upstroke and is made by pulling backward and upward from approximately 120 to 220 degrees (4 to 8 o'clock). While in this sector, the opposite foot and pedal are entering the downstroke. The backstroke is a transitional phase and should be emphasized only in specific technique workouts.

3. *Upstroke:* For upstroke drills, the emphasis is on pulling upward from 270 to 360 degrees (fig. 4.6*c*). Do not pull up when riding normally, as there is little if any power benefit (probably less than 5 percent). You may want to work this aspect when out of the saddle on hills or moderately rolling terrain, however.

4. *Overstroke:* The overstroke is the last transitional movement and precedes the downstroke by pressing *forward* over the top from about 320 to 20 degrees (fig. 4.6*d*). As with any of these sectors, drill exercises are an important part of training. I recommend training sectors regularly as part of the warm-up, during breaks between intervals, when riding with a slower friend, or during the warm-down. There are virtually countless ways to design these workouts: time (8 × 30 seconds at each of the four sectors), distance (4 × 250 meters at each sector), or revolutions (four sets of 2 × 100 revolutions at each sector), and so on.

Later in this chapter, I'll describe particular drills and exercise techniques for improving these four sectors. Training these sectors independently improves the transition from one phase to the next and thereby increases pedaling efficiency. Remember, however, that the most powerful phase of the pedaling stroke is the *downstroke*.

Use of Muscles

The major muscles used in the pedaling motion are the vastus medialis and lateralis, gastrocnemius lateralis, and soleus (fig. 4.7). Although there are variations among individuals due to biomechanics, equipment, pedal and foot interfaces, intensity, and terrain, for the most part, riders use similar muscle groups in cycling. During the downstroke, the rectus femoris (flexor of the hip and knee extensor) is most active when the hip is extending (pushing downward and forward on the pedals). Additionally, the gluteus muscles are highly active during this phase, and the hamstrings and biceps femoris oppose this motion and sta-

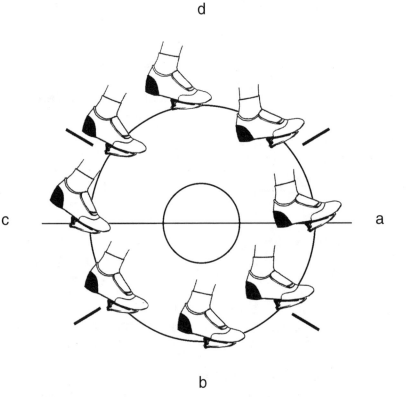

FIGURE 4.6 *a-d*   (*a*) Downstroke, (*b*) backstroke, (*c*) upstroke, and (*d*) overstroke.

Adapted, by permission, from P.R. Cavanagh and D. J. Sanderson, 1986, The Biomechanics of Cycling: Studies of the Pedaling Mechanics and Elite Pursuit Riders. In *The Science of Cycling*, edited by E.R. Burke (Champaign, IL: Human Kinetics), 95.

bilize the movement. Once at the bottom of the stroke, the hamstrings are highly active, driving the pedal backward and upward. Next, the tibialis anterior activates during the upstroke, and the gastrocnemius muscles act to balance ankle movement on the top of the pedal stroke.

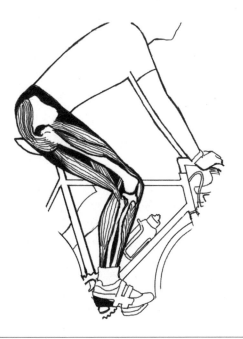

FIGURE 4.7 Major muscles in cycling.

Importance of Cadence

It is important to know that cadence (revolutions per minute of the pedal/crank arm) can be, and is, variable. No cyclist rides at any one set level of rpms due to changes in gear selection, terrain, wind, glycogen and energy reserves, and simply choice. However, experienced cyclists tend to increase their cadence as workload increases, thus reducing their energy expenditure. On the other hand, slower cadences require more energy and higher oxygen consumption ($\dot{V}O_2max$) than faster cadences. Perhaps this is why good climbers tend to spin at faster rates.

Is there an optimum cadence? Yes and no! More correctly, there are ranges of optimum cadences for different types of events, individual physiology and fitness, muscle fibers, gearing, terrain, and other environmental conditions. Cadences vary in relation to energy stores, length of ride, wind conditions, eleva-

tion, and type of terrain (hilly or flat). These variations are not as broad as you may think, yet there are differences, so there is no one set rule—except the shorter the event, the lower the cadence.

The same is true for heart rates, as discussed in chapter 1. There are just too many variables to set yourself into a specific targeted heart rate. Yet using perceived exertion (chapter 1) is one of the best ways to manage cadence and energy. Pedal pressure changes are the first indicator that pedaling rate is either too fast or too slow. As the forces required to press the pedal increase, there is a corresponding mental perception (RPE) that higher intensity is required to maintain a given cadence. When this happens, it's time to shift to a lighter gear to maintain a uniform pace. Conversely, with a lighter pedal force, as the rpms increase, the perceived exertion lessens as the athlete needs to shift into a harder gear ratio. The fact is, cyclists should shift gears frequently on the basis of intensity (perceived exertion). This is an excellent way to manage energy and optimize speed.

The most efficient cadences typically fall between 60 and 120 rpm. On flats, you'll likely be close to 90 rpm, and on hills, about 70 rpm (±10). There will be occasions when the cadence exceeds 120 rpm, for example, downhill and downwind conditions. Additionally, the cadence may fall below 60 rpm when climbing a very steep grade. It depends on the athlete's fitness and the gearing used, but these instances will be infrequent and should not affect performance significantly. However, on courses with particularly hilly or flat and downwind conditions, the athlete is wise to consider gearing choices most suitable for his conditioning and the course.

The Right Gearing: Determining When to Shift

If you shift a car transmission going from first gear to fifth, the engine and transmission wobble and may stop altogether. Or even worse, how does the transmission react when you accidentally shift into *reverse*? Well, needless to say, it just doesn't work right. Your bike's gears are the same, but with one huge difference: To recover from poor shifts, you must use your energy, not step on or off the gas pedal. An efficient cyclist changes gears many times as terrain conditions, energy use, and cadence demand. This is the most effective way to preserve and manage pace.

Gearing selection (where you shift the chain ring) is important and is often thoroughly misunderstood or even ignored by cyclists. It boggles my mind that athletes spend thousands of hours training and large sums of money for equipment, only to overlook one of the most important aspects of efficient cycling—gearing!

Gearing choice goes beyond the number of cogs in the freewheel. It's the shifting sequences that affect performance and energy use. In other words, as with your car, you must select the right gear when speeding up and slowing down. The result of choosing the wrong gear is expending either too much or too little energy.

I coach athletes to shift according to pedal pressure increases or decreases and by using perceived exertion. Beyond this, though, they need to know their shifting pattern and what gears they have. Making the calculations takes about fifteen minutes. Some riders even tape a table of their bike's gears to the handlebar while they are learning the pattern.

Use a gear chart (available at bike shops) or the following formula for calculating the gear ratio: Number of teeth on the chain ring divided by number of teeth on the freewheel cog multiplied by wheel diameter (CR ÷ FW × WD). In the example in table 4.2, gear 1 results in a 47-inch gear. This is the lowest or easiest gear. The highest is gear 16, which is 115 inches. On the chart, you'll notice how I chose to go from gear 6 (78 inches) to gear 12 (81 inches). Although this jump is quite small, it is better than going to gear 7 (84 inches), because then the closest shift would be to gear 13 (92 inches), which is an 8-inch difference and 2 inches over a typical shift. Another reason for charting the sequence like this is that smart riders avoid using the inner chain ring with the outermost cogs. This needlessly puts the chain at too much of an angle and introduces excessive mechanical friction and wear. As you can see from the gearing table, these gears (7 and 8) are nearly duplicates of gears 12 and 13, which have a better chain angle and run more smoothly.

TABLE 4.2   Shifting Sequence Guide—Wheel diameter: 26

Freewheel cogs (number of teeth per cog)	Gear ratio of large chain ring (teeth: 53)	Freewheel cog number (shaded are shift selections)	Gear ratio of small chain ring (teeth: 42)	Freewheel cog number (shaded are shift selections)
12	115	**16**	91	8
13	106	**15**	84	7
14	98	**14**	78	**6**
15	92	**13**	73	**5**
17	81	**12**	64	**4**
19	73	11	57	**3**
21	66	10	52	**2**
23	60	9	47	**1**

Shifting sequence (shaded area): 1, 2, 3, 4, 5, 6, 12, 13, 14, 15, and 16

CLIMBING SHORT HILLS

Knowing your gearing is the key to climbing short hills. As you approach the hill, pedal pressure and cadence slow as more force is applied to the pedal. When this occurs, shift two positions (harder gear) and stand up out of the saddle. Keep the bike tracking straight (no unnecessary lateral movement) and hold onto the top of the brake hoods. When the pedal pressure begins to increase and cadence slows again, shift back one gear (to an easier gear) and sit down in the saddle. Continue this over the hill or, if the grade permits, shift to a harder gear for 5 to 10 pedal strokes, then downshift and sit down the rest of the way. This technique keeps speed and rpms constant and uses cardiovascular and metabolic energy in the most efficient way.

EXERCISE AND DRILL TRAINING

The riding technique of an elite cyclist displays a smooth pedaling action that is relaxed, fluid, elliptical, and appears to be effortless. The body position is aerodynamic and efficient. When someone is really good at something, they make it look easy. This is not true for many triathletes and duathletes, who lack the fluidity of the single-sport cyclist. This is why technique training in each discipline is so crucial.

Keep your shoulders relaxed, your back flat (hips rotated forward), grip lightly, and when you stand out of the saddle, do so without losing forward momentum. When standing, your cadence decreases but your body weight sometimes permits a one- or two-gear increase; therefore, shift up when standing out of the saddle. Ride with single-sport specialized cyclists from time to time to learn important bike-handling skills. Also, use the following drills and exercises in group or single-rider drill sessions.

The following technical form exercises and drills are ones I've used over the past 16 years of coaching the endurance athlete. The TF drills allow athletes to think and train their technique and add variety to the workouts to keep them interesting.

Saddle-Ups SU

These "out of the saddle" combination drills are used in several ways. Essentially, the ath-

lete rides without sitting down. I've had athletes ride out of the saddle for several miles (on the flats) in a large gear ratio. This drill trains hill-climbing technique and muscles without having to work as hard. It's an aerobic way to train those muscles when getting out of the saddle during a climb. The athlete can also use a smaller gear ratio (42 × 21) to do the same thing. In this situation, the length of the interval is less than 2 minutes and the rpms can reach more than 120. Also, riding moderate hills at low-intensity SU is another way to work the muscles used when standing, except the duration is substantially longer. In competitive situations, I advise athletes to get out of the saddle only when the steepness of the grade changes to a point where 10 to 20 pedal strokes will help maintain pace. Each drill can be performed during O$_2$, LVT, VO$_2$, and LAC workouts. For example, an LAC set might be 4(4 × 200) meters with a rest interval equal to two times the interval, and sets 2 and 4 are out of the saddle doing LAC pull-downs (see page 82).

High Revolutions per Minute HRPM

HRPM spin training is a great training exercise. Spinning at high revolutions trains the pedaling motion by improving neuromuscular coordination (brain-to-muscle control). This drill is one of the best for learning how to spin properly. Athletes learn to optimize their stroke with these light-intensity, high-revolution spinning drills. Additionally, they're good cardiorespiratory training, as exertion rates are higher. Practically every training session should have HRPMs as part of the warm-up, warm-down, transition after hard intervals, or a TF drill set alone.

The following are a few examples of how I use this technique (more are given in the model training sets at the end of this chapter). As a TF set after an LVT, for example, the athlete can do 4×3 minutes of HRPM spinning. The pedaling rate for the first set is 100 spins per minute. The rates for the second, third, and fourth sets are 105, 110, and 120, respectively. Another suggestion would be to add sectors to each set, perhaps emphasizing the downstroke (forward and downward press) on sets 2 and 4. Still another would be to add isolated-leg spins (see below) to sets 1 and 3. Do these sets in the small chain ring using the lighter gears, with rpms between 100 and 140.

Isolated-Leg Spins ISO Spins

I have had my clients doing ISO spins since the beginning of my endurance sport coaching career in 1981. Their effectiveness is actually theoretical, but they seem to improve the performance of the spin stroke. Isolating each pedaling stroke develops neuromuscular (brain-to-muscle) coordination, especially during the forward and downward motions of the downstroke. If I want an athlete to know what a good stroke feels like, I have them do ISO spins. They immediately feel the emphasis on pressing forward and downward, then pulling back. Ordinarily, the drill is completed using a low gear ratio (42×21), as this causes the pedal stroke to work the most important aspect, the downstroke. This lighter gear encourages the cyclist to maintain a constant pressure on the downstroke to hold a constant rpm rate (no lower than 85 and as high as 130).

ISOs are easy to execute by isolating one leg from the other. For example, an ISO spin with the right leg leads the left. The left leg simply trails behind the right and does not apply pressure on the pedal. Some example ISO spin workouts are: 16 minutes of ISO spins broken into four sets of 4 minutes. Sets 1 and 3 alternate the left and right legs on 30-second cycles, and sets 2 and 4 work the left and right legs on 15-second cycles. Or, on a gently rising uphill (long and moderate grade), work the ISO for 12 minutes as follows: Do 10 spins with the left leg followed by one with the right leg, then 9 with the left leg and 2 with the right. Continue to do one less spin with the left leg and one more spin with the right leg each cycle until you've reached 1 and 10 for the opposite leg, then begin again for 12 minutes.

Down-Spins DS

These are done on a downhill using the small chain ring and gear ratio. The goal is to spin as

---

DESCENDING LONG HILLS ON THE BIKE

One of the things I tell my athletes is to keep the legs moving in situations where the descent is several miles long, even when out of gearing. It is important to keep the blood flowing to the muscles. You don't need to spin more than 30 revolutions per minute, but where circumstances such as gentle switchback descents call for more stability, you should move your legs. When you are descending a long, straight section, your legs shouldn't move. You want to maximize aerodynamics here, so tuck your legs in next to the top tube, slide forward on the saddle, and "let 'em go!"

For steep descents and turns, hold the bars gently and, when turning, kick the inside knee toward the turn while gently tilting your head in the same direction. This is probably not the time to be outstretched on the aero bars, either. Hold the bars on the brake hoods or in another secure position.

long and fast as possible without shifting to a higher gear ratio while keeping the buttocks from bouncing off the saddle. I've seen athletes reach rpms as high as 150 doing this exercise. Generally, the exercise is done for no more than 30 seconds followed by a rest spin, then several repetitions. The benefit of this drill is that it trains the muscular coordination of the spinning stroke. It works!

LAC Pull-Downs LPD

LPDs are short-duration intervals of LAC training (up to 20 seconds) repeated for from 4 to 10 minutes of total exercise time. They are done on short (100- to 300-meter), gradual climbs. The LPD is executed at high intensity (LAC) but with the addition of pulling down on the aero bar with the opposite arm on each downstroke. This should be an exaggerated effort of both the leg and arm. Pulling down on the arm helps apply more force on the downstroke.

Sectors S

Sector training divides the pedaling stroke into four sectors—downstroke, backstroke, upstroke, and overstroke—which are then trained independently during this exercise. For instance, 12 minutes of S training might be broken into three sets of 4 × 1 minute. Work on one sector each minute, beginning with the backstroke. During this time, work both the left and right legs and emphasize only the backstroke section.

Breathing B

Coordinate your exhalation with the downstroke of your right leg for 5 minutes. Then do the same with your left leg. Count the number of crank revolutions you take between each breath, and strive to make the number the same for your right and left legs. Try to inhale fully as well.

Hill Shifts HS

For this drill, you need to know your gear ratios (shifting sequence), which were detailed earlier in this chapter. This drill is actually a riding technique that I have all my clients do on short hills. It is an excellent way to keep and even gain momentum, use energy correctly, and work most efficiently. The sequence is as follows: (1) Select a 100- to 200-meter hill with a moderate grade; (2) approach the hill from an additional 200 meters back; (3) ride toward the hill in the saddle at an LVT perceived pace; (4) when the pedal pressure starts to become slightly harder, shift up two gears (harder); (5) immediately after the shift, stand and do 5 to 10 powerful strokes; and (6) simultaneously, shift down one gear (easier) and sit in the saddle and spin over the top of the hill.

Descending ISO Spins DISO

I especially like this exercise I thought up 13 years ago. The purpose is to isolate the legs, improving the muscular coordination of each leg separately. Some athletes, particularly those recovering from injury, seem to have one leg that is stronger than the other. This drill helps balance those differences and improve performance. Start ISO spinning with the left leg and do 10 revolutions. Switch over to the right and do another 10. Then do 9 with the left leg and 9 with the right, and so on, down to 1 with the left leg and 1 with the right. Again, you can do as many of these as you like, but I like to hold the total at 10 in order to switch back and forth between legs frequently.

Pace Line Roll-Through PL

This is an excellent bike-handling, wheel balance, and tracking exercise that you can do with two riders, but three to five is best. Ride single file, with each rider following the wheel of the rider in front. Try to maintain a distance of 6 to 12 inches between your front wheel and the rear wheel of the rider in front of you. Notice that as the gap widens, there is more wind resistance. The rider in the first position leads, pushing the pace and using a higher gear ratio. Riders 2, 3, and so on, are in lower gear ratios and spinning a bit faster than the leader. The leader should try to keep a constant pace and should not stand up out of the saddle, as this will slow the pace momentarily and the

CLIMBING LONG HILLS ON THE BIKE

With the right gearing and a keen understanding of shift sequences, long climbs will be less formidable. On climbs longer than 1 mile, the best technique is to ride 95 percent of the time in the saddle. This permits several things to occur. First, the tracking or side-to-side movement of the bike is decreased. Second, sliding back slightly in the saddle makes the forward press and upward pull phases more powerful. Third, breathing is more controlled because standing uses more energy and requires more oxygen consumption. Fourth, sitting while climbing (seated back) allows you to use your arms during the press. As one foot enters the press phase, pull up on the handlebars to apply more downward pressure. After the press phase, relax your arms momentarily, then begin pulling up on the handlebars again as the other foot enters the press phase.

pace line will collapse, potentially causing an accident. After the leading cyclist has ridden in front for an interval of, say, 1 minute, the leader moves a foot or two toward the left and allows the pace line to surge ahead. When the last rider's front wheel comes in view, the leader moves into drafting position (6 to 12 inches behind), and the next person in line takes the lead.

Off the Front OTF

This drill works much like the PL, but one person is selected to go out ahead of the pace line and is given a head start of, say, 20 seconds. However, this rider must stay in the small chain ring (42 × 14) for the entire time, or in an easier gear ratio if the terrain changes. The rest of the line is timed after the head start is given and tries to catch the rider "off the front." The time is marked once the last person of the PL has gone past the OTF rider. This exercise makes the team PL work together, and the OTF rider spins like there's no tomorrow because of the limited gear ratio.

Hill Over and Down HOD

The goal of this exercise is to maintain the same intensity on the downhill as on the uphill climb. Lots of time can be gained on the downhill by simply working at or near the intensity used on the climb. Perceived exertion is a great way to monitor and maintain this form, as you must pay close attention to the intensity. Although

downhill time trials can be dangerous because of the speeds reached, I think this drill is an often-overlooked training exercise that pays big dividends for cornering technique and maintaining pace intensity.

Figure-Eights FE

This exercise is excellent for developing better bike-handling skills. Frankly, many triathletes and duathletes could stand to learn a bit more finesse on the bike. On a safe street (cul de sac) or in the corner of a parking lot (where no cars park), start by making a figure-eight in an imaginary box 15 feet wide and 30 feet long. Mark the box corners with chalk or tape, if you like. Repeat the movement several times until you can do the figure well. If you're feeling ambitious, narrow the box. Some athletes can do a track stand figure-eight and hardly move at all!

Motor Pacing MP

First, a word or two of caution: Never motor pace (car or motorcycle) in busy traffic areas, on rough roads, or when the driver and cyclists have no motor pace experience. It's dangerous enough. Check with local authorities before doing so, as there may be a law against motor pacing behind a car or motorcycle.

Motor pacing is an effective training tool for several reasons. First, the car or motorcycle is always faster than the cyclist, thus high-intensity interval sessions are guaranteed. Second, the cyclist learns aerodynamic aspects that transfer to time-trial tactics. As the pacer pulls away ever so slightly, the cyclist will immediately lower their profile to avoid losing any more slipstream. Third, speeds of 35 to 40 miles per hour can be maintained for some time when motor pacing a good course. The athlete gets the feeling of going fast aerodynamically, learns to spin with high revolutions, and keeps the tracking (side-to-side) motions of the wheel smooth.

Uphill Downstroke UD

This drill is done on moderate hills. The cyclist concentrates on the forward and downward movement of the pedal stroke during the downstroke. As mentioned earlier, cycling moderate hills already emphasizes this motion, but here the cyclist will further concentrate on this pedal motion. Again, this is perhaps the single best technique for improving the movement of the pedal stroke.

Look-Back Drill LBD

I use this exercise between other drills or training intensity zone intervals for teaching stability and safety. The idea is for the cyclist to "look back" over the left shoulder touching the chin to the shoulder (when conditions are safe), then return to looking forward. This is repeated 5 to 10 times before moving to the right shoulder. Cyclists tend to zigzag when looking back, and this exercise will help correct this tendency and improve stability.

Low-Tire Rollers LTR

I haven't yet mentioned rollers or wind trainers, but I am a strong advocate of both. I like athletes to use both, because rollers are great for working on pedaling technique and stability and wind trainers are good for doing harder training intensity zone intervals. To simulate cycling on the roads, however, I recommend that cyclists use rollers (once they have the technique down).

Most of the drills and certainly any of the training intensity zone workouts can be done on these devices. However, the LTR is just another way to add variety and effective training to your program. It is not so much a drill in itself as a way to do any of the above drills indoors. Simply inflate the tire pressure to about 80 psi and do your workout. The first thing you will notice is that the rolling resistance is greater. In addition, the pedal stroke presses forward and downward (downstroke) more strongly, as in riding uphill. In general, the entire workout will be more intense using this technique.

CYCLING INTENSITY PACE CHARTS

These charts are used the same way as the swimming intensity pace charts and calculate training times based on the information in chapter 1. For a quick review, let me go over those once again. The training intensity zones (except O_2—aerobic conditioning) are: LVT cycling, VO_2 cycling, and LAC cycling. Cycling training intensity zone times are based on goal times for 40 kilometers. In other words, the best multisport competition time you can cycle 40 kilometers is the benchmark for calculating LVT training intervals.

Important Note: Rest intervals for each training intensity zone are as follows:

1. O_2 (aerobic conditioning) = Long and slow aerobic continuous training.

2. LVT (anaerobic conditioning) = Short send-off (rest) intervals (5 to 60 seconds). Sets (up to two, depending on training volume) last between 15 and 25 minutes.

3. VO_2 (aerobic capacity) = The rest time is equal to or double the interval time. Sets are 15 to 21 minutes long, with each interval lasting 2 to 8 minutes.

4. LAC (anaerobic conditioning) = Rest is double the interval time if less than 1 minute and three times the interval time if more than 1 minute. Sets last from 4 to 10 minutes, with cycling times from 10 seconds up to 2 minutes.

Training Note: Each training intensity zone has minimum amounts of exercise time. These durations are essential to achieving the right physiological training effect. Sometimes VO_2 and LAC training intensity zone durations may fall below those minimums, usually during early base preparatory phases when training time and distance are lowest. If this is the case, it is appropriate to complete less than the minimum VO_2 or LAC.

How to Use the Cycling IPCs

Locate your cycling time in the column headed "Time/40K." This is your LVT pace, and the miles per hour are displayed to the right (third column). The LVT is the pace you maintain for 40 kilometers (multisport) during a time trial or competition.

For interval training, let's say an LVT workout is 15,000 meters and your 40-kilometer trial time is 01:00:00. Read across the chart rows from left to right for goal times for the LVT cycling distance. In this case, the goal time for 5,000 meters is 07:30. When the distance chosen is not displayed, you may have to add two or more distances together. In this case, you'll need to multiply $3 \times 7{:}30$ to get the 15,000-meter goal time of 22:30.

Cycling times will vary according to terrain (unless, of course, you are riding on an indoor trainer). However, you may have one or several routine courses that can be used. A good plan is to have several LVT, VO_2, and LAC interval courses measured and usable.

In the above example, a VO_2 workout of $5 \times 2{,}000$ meters has a time goal of 2:51 and a rest interval of 02:51±. For LAC training, a set of 12×250 meters has a time goal of 20 seconds and a rest interval of 40 seconds, or leaving each 1 minute.

Making the interval time is very important. If you are unable to do so, the pace is likely too fast. Keep in mind that cycling outdoors on diverse terrain and in changing conditions can make a time goal more difficult to achieve.

Some athletes choose to go for time instead of distance, which makes a lot of sense. However, be sure to keep track of how far you've ridden on that section of your course so you have a yardstick for measuring how well you do the next time.

To go at a faster LVT pace, choose a cycling goal time from the pace chart that is within reach but challenging. You should work on faster interval times when you can hold send-off intervals. In other words, if you cannot complete the new interval on the old send-off time, the pace is probably a bit too fast.

The IPC Method and Group Workouts

How does IPC training work with groups? There are no easy solutions, but I'll offer a few thoughts on how my clients deal with this issue. First, after designing your program, you'll know exactly how much training intensity zone work you need each week. That's an advantage, and likely one that most of your training friends don't have.

If you offer the workout, I'd be surprised if you'd be turned down—especially when you tell them you're going to do $5 \times 5{,}000$ meters at a 40-kilometer race pace with 1 minute of rest between repeats. Or $3(1 \times 1{,}000 + 4 \times 500)$ at 5 percent faster than a 40-kilometer pace with equal rest time after each repeat and 5 minutes between sets. In the first example, you know it's an LVT, and the second is a . . . VO_2. That's right! You're getting it now!

What do you do when the ride is to be an O_2? The same thing, except this time you do some technical drills and exercises, some high-revolution spinning in the small chain ring, or some isolated-leg spinning drills. There are numerous suggestions for getting in the training you need. Of course, your friends may have plans similar to yours. In this event, it's easy to compromise to get the best training for everyone. Last, I think it's a good idea to ride with faster riders during your harder workouts. You'll probably work a bit harder, learn from their skills, and simply have someone to mark.

TABLE 4.3 Intensity Pace Chart - LVT Cycling

Kph	Time/ 40K	Mph	10-mile trial	180K	1,000	2,000	3,000	5,000	10,000
45	0:53:20	27	22:13	04:00:00	01:20	02:40	04:00	06:40	13:20
44.5	0:53:56	26.7	22:28	04:02:42	01:21	02:42	04:03	06:44	13:29
44	0:54:33	26.4	22:44	04:05:27	01:22	02:44	04:05	06:49	13:38
43.5	0:55:10	26.1	22:59	04:08:17	01:23	02:46	04:08	06:54	13:48
43	0:55:49	25.8	23:15	04:11:10	01:24	02:47	04:11	06:59	13:57
42.5	0:56:28	25.5	23:32	04:14:07	01:25	02:49	04:14	07:04	14:07
42	0:57:09	25.2	23:49	04:17:09	01:26	02:51	04:17	07:09	14:17
41.5	0:57:50	24.9	24:06	04:20:14	01:27	02:53	04:20	07:14	14:28
41	0:58:32	24.6	24:23	04:23:25	01:28	02:56	04:23	07:19	14:38
40.5	0:59:16	24.3	24:41	04:26:40	01:29	02:58	04:27	07:24	14:49
40	1:00:00	24	25:00	04:30:00	01:30	03:00	04:30	07:30	15:00
39.5	1:00:46	23.7	25:19	04:33:25	01:31	03:02	04:33	07:36	15:12
39	1:01:32	23.4	25:38	04:36:55	01:32	03:05	04:37	07:42	15:23
38.5	1:02:20	23.1	25:58	04:40:31	01:34	03:07	04:41	07:48	15:35
38	1:03:09	22.8	26:19	04:44:13	01:35	03:09	04:44	07:54	15:47
37.5	1:04:00	22.5	26:40	04:48:00	01:36	03:12	04:48	08:00	16:00
37	1:04:52	22.2	27:02	04:51:54	01:37	03:15	04:52	08:06	16:13
36.5	1:05:45	21.9	27:24	04:55:53	01:39	03:17	04:56	08:13	16:26
36	1:06:40	21.6	27:47	05:00:00	01:40	03:20	05:00	08:20	16:40
35.5	1:07:36	21.3	28:10	05:04:14	01:41	03:23	05:04	08:27	16:54
35	1:08:34	21	28:34	05:08:34	01:43	03:26	05:09	08:34	17:08
34.5	1:09:34	20.7	28:59	05:13:03	01:44	03:29	05:13	08:42	17:23
34	1:10:35	20.4	29:25	05:17:39	01:46	03:32	05:18	08:49	17:39
33.5	1:11:39	20.1	29:51	05:22:23	01:47	03:35	05:22	08:57	17:55
33	1:12:44	19.8	30:18	05:27:16	01:49	03:38	05:27	09:05	18:11
32.5	1:13:51	19.5	30:46	05:32:18	01:51	03:42	05:32	09:14	18:28
32	1:15:00	19.2	31:15	05:37:30	01:53	03:45	05:38	09:22	18:45
31.5	1:16:11	18.9	31:45	05:42:51	01:54	03:49	05:43	09:31	19:03
31	1:17:25	18.6	32:15	05:48:23	01:56	03:52	05:48	09:41	19:21
30.5	1:18:41	18.3	32:47	05:54:06	01:58	03:56	05:54	09:50	19:40
30	1:20:00	18	33:20	06:00:00	02:00	04:00	06:00	10:00	20:00
29.5	1:21:21	17.7	33:54	06:06:06	02:02	04:04	06:06	10:10	20:20
29	1:22:46	17.4	34:29	06:12:25	02:04	04:08	06:12	10:21	20:42

(continued)

TABLE 4.3 *(continued)*

Kph	Time/ 40K	Mph	10-mile trial	180K	1,000	2,000	3,000	5,000	10,000
28.5	1:24:13	17.1	35:05	06:18:57	02:06	04:13	06:19	10:32	21:03
28	1:25:43	16.8	35:43	06:25:43	02:09	04:17	06:26	10:43	21:26
27.5	1:27:16	16.5	36:22	06:32:44	02:11	04:22	06:33	10:55	21:49
27	1:28:53	16.2	37:02	06:40:00	02:13	04:27	06:40	11:07	22:13
26.5	1:30:34	15.9	37:44	06:47:33	02:16	04:32	06:48	11:19	22:39
26	1:32:18	15.6	38:28	06:55:23	02:18	04:37	06:55	11:32	23:04
25.5	1:34:07	15.3	39:13	07:03:32	02:21	04:42	07:04	11:46	23:32
25	1:36:00	15	40:00	07:12:00	02:24	04:48	07:12	12:00	24:00
24.5	1:37:58	14.7	40:49	07:20:49	02:27	04:54	07:21	12:15	24:30
24	1:40:00	14.4	41:40	07:30:00	02:30	05:00	07:30	12:30	25:00
23.5	1:42:08	14.1	42:33	07:39:34	02:33	05:06	07:40	12:46	
23	1:44:21	13.8	43:29	07:49:34	02:37	05:13	07:50	13:03	
22.5	1:46:40	13.5	44:27	08:00:00	02:40	05:20	08:00	13:20	
22	1:49:05	13.2	45:27	08:10:55	02:44	05:27	08:11	13:38	
21.5	1:51:38	12.9	46:31	08:22:20	02:47	05:35	08:22	13:57	

MODEL CYCLING TRAINING SETS

These cycling workouts are designed to provide several models for training. The models are organized within the training intensity zones described in chapter 1. There are four examples: an LVT, a VO_2, an LAC, and a mixed model set (combining several training intensity zones). O_2 training is included within each workout model. Also, each workout includes TF drills and exercises.

LVT Model Set

Anaerobic conditioning (LVT—lactate ventilatory threshold) sets are workouts done at or near 40-kilometer race pace. The send-off times are short rests of 5 to 60 seconds. LVT training increases race pace endurance using the perceived exertion of somewhat hard to energetically hard. Finally, these are great exercises for the windload indoor trainer and my recommended roller workouts.

I. Warm-up:

A. 30 minutes O_2 of HRPM spinning in small chain ring at 105 rpm

B. TF drills: 2(4 × 2 minutes), two sets of the following:

1. S for 15-second intervals each stroke (2 minutes)

2. DISO for 2 minutes

3. ISO for 15-second intervals each leg (2 minutes)

4. S for 2 minutes (working the back-stroke and upstroke sectors)

II. LVT main set:

A. 6 × 4,000 meters in 6 minutes plus 1 minute of HRPM spinning
or

B. 8(2,000 in 3 minutes plus 30 seconds, then go 1,000 in 1:30 plus 15 seconds)

TABLE 4.4   Intensity Pace Chart - VO2 Cycling

Kph	Time/ 40K	1,000	1,500	2,000	2,500	3,000	3,500	4,000	5,000
45	0:53:20			02:32	03:10	03:48	04:26	05:04	06:20
44.5	0:53:56			02:34	03:12	03:51	04:29	05:07	06:24
44	0:54:33			02:35	03:14	03:53	04:32	05:11	06:29
43.5	0:55:10			02:37	03:17	03:56	04:35	05:14	06:33
43	0:55:49			02:39	03:19	03:59	04:38	05:18	06:38
42.5	0:56:28		02:01	02:41	03:21	04:01	04:42	05:22	06:42
42	0:57:09		02:02	02:43	03:24	04:04	04:45	05:26	06:47
41.5	0:57:50		02:04	02:45	03:26	04:07	04:48	05:30	06:52
41	0:58:32		02:05	02:47	03:29	04:10	04:52	05:34	06:57
40.5	0:59:16		02:07	02:49	03:31	04:13	04:56	05:38	07:02
40	1:00:00		02:08	02:51	03:34	04:16	04:59	05:42	07:07
39.5	1:00:46		02:10	02:53	03:36	04:20	05:03	05:46	07:13
39	1:01:32		02:12	02:55	03:39	04:23	05:07	05:51	07:18
38.5	1:02:20		02:13	02:58	03:42	04:26	05:11	05:55	07:24
38	1:03:09		02:15	03:00	03:45	04:30	05:15	06:00	07:30
37.5	1:04:00		02:17	03:02	03:48	04:34	05:19	06:05	07:36
37	1:04:52		02:19	03:05	03:51	04:37	05:24	06:10	07:42
36.5	1:05:45		02:21	03:07	03:54	04:41	05:28	06:15	07:48
36	1:06:40		02:23	03:10	03:58	04:45	05:32	06:20	07:55
35.5	1:07:36		02:25	03:13	04:01	04:49	05:37	06:25	
35	1:08:34		02:27	03:15	04:04	04:53	05:42	06:31	
34.5	1:09:34		02:29	03:18	04:08	04:57	05:47	06:37	
34	1:10:35		02:31	03:21	04:11	05:02	05:52	06:42	
33.5	1:11:39		02:33	03:24	04:15	05:06	05:57	06:48	
33	1:12:44		02:35	03:27	04:19	05:11	06:03	06:55	
32.5	1:13:51		02:38	03:30	04:23	05:16	06:08	07:01	
32	1:15:00		02:40	03:34	04:27	05:21	06:14	07:08	
31.5	1:16:11		02:43	03:37	04:31	05:26	06:20	07:14	
31	1:17:25		02:45	03:41	04:36	05:31	06:26	07:21	
30.5	1:18:41		02:48	03:44	04:40	05:36	06:32	07:29	
30	1:20:00		02:51	03:48	04:45	05:42	06:39	07:36	
29.5	1:21:21		02:54	03:52	04:50	05:48	06:46	07:44	
29	1:22:46		02:57	03:56	04:55	05:54	06:53	07:52	

(continued)

TABLE 4.4 *(continued)*

Kph	Time/40K	1,000	1,500	2,000	2,500	3,000	3,500	4,000	5,000
28.5	1:24:13	02:00	03:00	04:00	05:00	06:00	07:00	08:00	
28	1:25:43	02:02	03:03	04:04	05:05	06:06	07:08		
27.5	1:27:16	02:04	03:07	04:09	05:11	06:13	07:15		
27	1:28:53	02:07	03:10	04:13	05:17	06:20	07:23		
26.5	1:30:34	02:09	03:14	04:18	05:23	06:27	07:32		
26	1:32:18	02:12	03:17	04:23	05:29	06:35	07:40		
25.5	1:34:07	02:14	03:21	04:28	05:35	06:42	07:49		
25	1:36:00	02:17	03:25	04:34	05:42	06:50	07:59		
24.5	1:37:58	02:20	03:29	04:39	05:49	06:59			
24	1:40:00	02:23	03:34	04:45	05:56	07:08			
23.5	1:42:08	02:26	03:38	04:51	06:04	07:17			
23	1:44:21	02:29	03:43	04:57	06:12	07:26			
22.5	1:46:40	02:32	03:48	05:04	06:20	07:36			
22	1:49:05	02:35	03:53	05:11	06:29	07:46			
21.5	1:51:38	02:39	03:59	05:18	06:38	07:57			

Goal LVT 40-kilometer pace: 1:00:00 or 40 kilometers per hour

C. HRPM: 3 × 3 minutes at 100, 105, 110 rpm in small chain ring

III. Warm-down (TF drills): ISO for 5 minutes, alternating every 30 seconds

Refer to table 4.3 for LVT goal times and pace. The above times are for illustration only.

VO$_2$ Model Set

VO$_2$ (aerobic capacity) sets are workout intensities above race pace by approximately 5 percent. Refer to the swimming model set for further review of this training energy system. VO$_2$max training increases the aerobic capacity or maximum oxygen capacity (aerobic power). The efforts are slightly faster than race pace, but not all out. The workouts have a perceived exertion of energetically hard to very hard.

I. Warm-up:

A. 20 minutes O$_2$ HRPM spinning in small chain ring at 100 rpm

B. 10 minutes high end of O$_2$ working the downstroke TF

II. VO$_2$ main set:

A. 10 × 1,500 meters in 2:08 plus 2:08 rest interval

or

B. 4 × 4,000 meters in 5:42 plus 5:42 rest interval

Goal LVT 40-kilometer pace: 1:00:00 or 40 kilometers per hour

III. Warm-down (TF drills): 20 minutes (4 × 5 minutes) of the following:

1. S (each sector for 15 seconds)
2. DISO
3. FE
4. HRPM at 110±

Refer to table 4.4 for VO$_2$ goal times and pace. The above times are for illustration only.

TABLE 4.5   Intensity Pace Chart - LAC Cycling

Kph	Time/ 40K	200	300	400	500	1,000
45	0:53:20	00:14	00:22	00:29	00:36	01:12
44.5	0:53:56	00:15	00:22	00:29	00:36	01:13
44	0:54:33	00:15	00:22	00:29	00:37	01:14
43.5	0:55:10	00:15	00:22	00:30	00:37	01:14
43	0:55:49	00:15	00:23	00:30	00:38	01:15
42.5	0:56:28	00:15	00:23	00:30	00:38	01:16
42	0:57:09	00:15	00:23	00:31	00:39	01:17
41.5	0:57:50	00:16	00:23	00:31	00:39	01:18
41	0:58:32	00:16	00:24	00:32	00:40	01:19
40.5	0:59:16	00:16	00:24	00:32	00:40	01:20
40	1:00:00	00:16	00:24	00:32	00:41	01:21
39.5	1:00:46	00:16	00:25	00:33	00:41	01:22
39	1:01:32	00:17	00:25	00:33	00:42	01:23
38.5	1:02:20	00:17	00:25	00:34	00:42	01:24
38	1:03:09	00:17	00:26	00:34	00:43	01:25
37.5	1:04:00	00:17	00:26	00:35	00:43	01:26
37	1:04:52	00:18	00:26	00:35	00:44	01:28
36.5	1:05:45	00:18	00:27	00:36	00:44	01:29
36	1:06:40	00:18	00:27	00:36	00:45	01:30
35.5	1:07:36	00:18	00:27	00:37	00:46	01:31
35	1:08:34	00:19	00:28	00:37	00:46	01:33
34.5	1:09:34	00:19	00:28	00:38	00:47	01:34
34	1:10:35	00:19	00:29	00:38	00:48	01:35
33.5	1:11:39	00:19	00:29	00:39	00:48	01:37
33	1:12:44	00:20	00:29	00:39	00:49	01:38
32.5	1:13:51	00:20	00:30	00:40	00:50	01:40
32	1:15:00	00:20	00:30	00:41	00:51	01:41
31.5	1:16:11	00:21	00:31	00:41	00:51	01:43
31	1:17:25	00:21	00:31	00:42	00:52	01:45
30.5	1:18:41	00:21	00:32	00:42	00:53	01:46
30	1:20:00	00:22	00:32	00:43	00:54	01:48
29.5	1:21:21	00:22	00:33	00:44	00:55	01:50
29	1:22:46	00:22	00:34	00:45	00:56	01:52

(continued)

TABLE 4.5 *(continued)*

Kph	Time/ 40K	200	300	400	500	1,000
28.5	1:24:13	00:23	00:34	00:45	00:57	01:54
28	1:25:43	00:23	00:35	00:46	00:58	01:56
27.5	1:27:16	00:24	00:35	00:47	00:59	01:58
27	1:28:53	00:24	00:36	00:48	01:00	02:00
26.5	1:30:34	00:24	00:37	00:49	01:01	
26	1:32:18	00:25	00:37	00:50	01:02	
25.5	1:34:07	00:25	00:38	00:51	01:04	
25	1:36:00	00:26	00:39	00:52	01:05	
24.5	1:37:58	00:26	00:40	00:53	01:06	
24	1:40:00	00:27	00:41	00:54	01:07	
23.5	1:42:08	00:28	00:41	00:55	01:09	
23	1:44:21	00:28	00:42	00:56	01:10	
22.5	1:46:40	00:29	00:43	00:58	01:12	
22	1:49:05	00:29	00:44	00:59	01:14	
21.5	1:51:38	00:30	00:45	01:00	01:15	

LAC Model Set

LAC (anaerobic capacity) training is the highest-intensity training you will do. The perceived exertion is very hard to very, very hard. Once again, if you need a brief refresher, reread the model LAC set in the swimming chapter.

I. Warm-up:

A. 12 minutes HRPM at 90 rpm, small chain ring

B. 8 minutes HRPM at 95 rpm, small chain ring

C. 4 minutes HRPM at 100 rpm, small chain ring

D. 30 minutes at low end of LVT on varied terrain, fast but not quite race pace for 40 kilometers

E. TF drills: 10 minutes DISO spins beginning with 10 spins right/left; when at zero, do 30 seconds of normal HRPM spins

II. LAC main set:

A. 10 × 500 meters in 41 seconds plus an 82-second rest interval

or

B. 10 × 200 meters in 16 seconds plus a 32-second rest interval (evens go LPDs)

Goal LVT 40-kilometer pace: 1:00:00 or 40 kilometers per hour

III. Warm-down: 20 minutes HRPM spin-down by 5-minute intervals; start at 105, 100, 95, and 90 rpm in small chain ring

Refer to table 4.5 for LAC goal times and pace. The above times are for illustration only.

Mixed Training Intensity Zone Model Set

Most workouts are a combination of all training intensity zones, planned or not. Terrain alone makes up for any lack of preplanning in terms of working harder and easier during a ride. Remember to keep the workouts interesting and include the right mix of intensity. I mentioned this in the swim chapter's model set section, but it bears repeating here. I never repeat the same swim, bike, or run workouts. If you use the guidelines of the training intensity zone, you won't have to either. Of course, there are individual sets that are worth repeating, but some part of the workout will be different. There are limitless ways to achieve the same training by adjusting the distancé, intensity, and rest interval of a training session.

Mixing the training intensity zones is appropriate, but two general rules apply. First, the highest-intensity training in any workout should come toward the end. Second, allow for enough rest between repeats and make every effort to get the right goal pace.

I. Warm-up: 1 hour of HRPM spinning at O_2 (low to high end)

A. LVT set (hill climb); 25 minutes of LVT (40-kilometer race pace) hill climb

B. O_2 10 minutes of HRPM spinning

C. TF drills: 5 minutes of sectors, 10 seconds each

II. VO_2 set:

A. 1 × 2,000 in 2:07 plus 2:07 rest interval

B. 1 × 2,500 in 3:34 plus 3:34 rest interval

C. 1 × 5,000 in 7:07 plus 7:07 rest interval

III. O_2 set:

A. 12 minutes of HRPM spinning in small chain ring at 90 rpm

B. Rehydrate—carbohydrates

IV. Warm-down (TF drills):
±10 minutes of ISO spinning

Goal LVT 40-kilometer pace: 1:00:00 or 40 kilometers per hour

Refer to tables 4.3 through 4.5 for goal times and pace. The above times are for illustration only.

5

RUNNING

Running isn't as simple as it may seem. Efficient running takes practice, motivation, conviction, and contemplation about how a runner runs. As coaches, we are expected to have all the answers for a runner to run faster. The truth is, everyone cannot run the same way, and the mixed bag of kinetic, psychological, and physical energy each individual possesses attests to this.

Further, some athletes succeed with what are obviously poor running styles. Runners like six-time Hawaii Ironman champion Dave Scott agree that you don't need good form to run fast. Dave once told me: "I look like a wounded water buffalo. Yet I've proven time and again I am one of the fastest runners in Kona." I sometimes wonder how changes in his biomechanics would affect his already world-class performance? It's an interesting thought, but I wouldn't modify much, if any, of Dave's running style. Athletes need to work within and believe in their own ability and capacity. This is the key to discovering the competitive edge.

Everyone knows what good running form looks like—relaxed, effortless, and efficient. But how does a runner get to this point? Is it through self-optimization over seasons of training, exercising mind over matter, or just plain old genetics? Perhaps it's a combination of these things and a bit more. Learning to run faster and more efficiently begins with understanding basic mechanical concepts and applying them to the runner's unique style. In addition, making the right choice in running shoes is important.

This chapter begins with a discussion on assessment of foot biomechanics and selection of the right running shoe. Following this, we'll look at the characteristics of good running technique as well as the kinds of running styles frequently associated with poor running mechanics. Then I'll describe exercises and drills for elevating your running to a level you may never have thought possible. Next, I'll explain how the running intensity pace charts will help you target the right training pace, and finally, I'll present several workout models based on the intensity training zones and techniques.

FOOT BIOMECHANICS AND SHOE TYPE

First off, I think every endurance athlete should see a podiatrist. The expertise of doctors like podiatrist Richard Blake, DPM, of the Center for Sports Medicine (St. Francis Memorial Hospital) in San Francisco, is invaluable in treating endurance athletes. In the 10 years I've been referring athletes to Dr. Blake for conditions such as low back pain, knee ailments, hip length disproportion, ankle, shin, and foot pain, and related biomechanical abnormalities, I can think of few instances where his treatment has not been successful. In particular, a qualified sport podiatrist may help increase efficiency of energy use by correcting running mechanics that may be causing overuse injury. Such problems can be alleviated with custom-made in-shoe orthotics or by making corrections to the shoe itself. Additionally, rehabilitative exercises are often prescribed to strengthen muscles weakened as a result of injury. Finally, a podiatrist knowledgeable in the biomechanics of running and up-to-date shoe technology is the best resource for help in selecting the right shoe for your particular needs.

When choosing a running shoe, perhaps the most important consideration is your foot biomechanics. You'll need to choose the type of shoe construction that is best suited to your footstrike characteristics. Running shoes are designed with lasts that differ in both construction (cardboard, combination, and slip lasted) and shape (straight, semicurved, and curved) to fit various types of foot profiles.

Typically, athletes have primarily pronator, supinator, or neutral (normal) footstrike mechanics (see fig. 5.1a-c), but every runner pronates (rolls inward) or supinates (rolls outward) to some degree. However, neither overpronation or oversupination are desirable characteristics. When either of these characteristics are present, the excessive motion can result in any number of injuries to the foot, shin, knee, hip, and back. Thus quality shoes with the correct motion control features, last construction, and in some cases, orthotics, are a sensible choice for these runners. Also, a properly selected shoe will allow for the natural supination and pronation of the neutral footstrike.

Running shoes are made on three types of lasts or forms: curved, semicurved, or straight. If you have a flat foot, you are an overpronator. Your foot will collapse more toward the inside (fig. 5.1a) during the footstrike, so you'll need a motion-control straight-lasted shoe. Athletes with high arches are oversupinators. Their feet roll toward the outside (fig. 5.1b) during the footstrike. These athletes should buy shoes with a curved last that permits a flexible range of foot motion. Athletes with a neutral (normal) foot position land primarily in the middle of the heel (fig. 5.1c) at footstrike. These runners will do well with shoes that have a semicurved last and moderate direction- and foot-control features.

After consulting with a podiatrist about your running biomechanics, your next stop should

FIGURE 5.1a Pronation at footstrike.

FIGURE 5.1b Supination at footstrike.

FIGURE 5.1c Normal running footstrike.

be a specialty running shoe store with knowledgeable salespeople who can help you get the right fit. Beyond the profile and type of last, fit is also very important. First, you should have ample room in the toe box (about 1/4 inch) to avoid toe blisters and black toenails due to chafing. Second, the heel of the shoe should fit snugly yet comfortably. It should not rub or slip when you walk or jog. If the shoe doesn't fit in either of these areas, it will be less stable and the potential for injury will be greater.

In addition, your feet swell when running, which can make for an extremely uncomfortable fit if not taken into account when selecting shoes. Your feet are more swollen in the afternoon, so this is the best time to try on running shoes. It's also a good idea to run, jog, or at least walk in the shoes for several minutes (most better stores allow this). If they don't feel good at once, don't buy them—period! They are not likely to feel any better once you get them home.

To summarize, as an endurance runner, you should select shoes of a design, quality, and fit that work best for you. Ads and athlete endorsements don't mean a thing if the shoes don't meet your own biomechanical needs. Thus it is important to understand your foot biomechanics and the type of training you plan to do before buying running shoes.

TECHNIQUES OF GOOD RUNNING

It's easy to spot differences in runners' techniques. Such differences are apparent in every aspect of a runner's style: agility, flexibility, power, stride length, biomechanical profiles, the movements of each part of the body, and so on. However, what's not so apparent is how to coach a runner on improving technique.

The human body is remarkable in its ability to make physiological and, indeed, psychological modifications to improve its exercise potential. Thus it is possible for anyone to learn to become a faster and more efficient runner. The body will adapt to the physical intensity and stress of training by facilitating greater degrees of efficiency and ability. Yet it won't just let go

of old habits without the mind first being receptive to change and motivated to succeed. This is where mental determination combined with technical drill training come in to ensure that those changes occur.

The following section reviews the basic running characteristics I have found to be important in efficient running. Less skilled runners can learn to improve technique by understanding and implementing these elements when running. More skilled runners, on the other hand, may not know why they run well. For them, this information will be useful in fine-tuning and maintaining economical running form.

Body Alignment Techniques

Improving body alignment requires keeping the center of body mass (CBM) over the leg making contact with the ground (footstrike). This ideal alignment can be achieved by keeping the iliac crest of your pelvis (hips) rotated slightly forward so that your foot lands more directly under your body and your leg pushes backward, propelling you forward.

Forward Hips (Iliac Crest)—An effective technique for learning to rotate the hips forward can be done on the track using a bicycle, a belt, and a 20- to 30-foot length of stretch band (surgical tubing or bungee cord). One end of the cord is attached around the belt at navel height and the other end to the bicycle. A partner or coach then rides the bicycle, leading the runner around the track at a pace that forces the hips to come forward. Besides feeling slightly goofy, the runner will feel his CBM being pulled forward so the stance phase (touchdown to pushoff) is well under the body with the legs pushing off in a backward manner (fig. 5.2). The importance of this is discussed in the section on reducing braking force.

Although tipping the pelvis slightly forward is desirable, leaning forward is not (fig. 5.3). This common running error wastes a tremendous amount of energy. In running, the hamstrings (rear thigh muscle group—semimembranosus, biceps femoris, semitendinosus) and the quadriceps (front thigh muscle group—vastus medialis, vastus lateralis, rectus femo-

BUNGEE RUNNING

Bungee running is a technique I developed for athletes who simply cannot get the feel of running tall (hips forward) and achieving a vertical footstrike and pushoff. It's a simple technique, sort of like motor pacing, except in this case a bicycle is used instead of a car. Using 20 to 30 feet of 1/2-inch stretch band (surgical tubing), secure one end around the waist of the athlete. That's the tricky part, but it can be done with a little innovation. I started out by using a belt to hold the stretch band, but have now gotten more sophisticated by using a harness system (NZ Manufacturing in Kent, Washington, makes one for swimmers that works great in this setting too). Connect the other end of the stretch band to the bike at a level slightly above the runner's hips. Begin riding the bicycle and pulling the athlete around the track. You should feel a noticeable resistance from the runner but should keep pedaling so the athlete has no choice but to keep up by running with his hips forward and his footstrike centered under his body. It will no doubt be the fastest mile he's ever run!

FIGURE 5.2 Forward hips.

FIGURE 5.3 Leaning forward.

ris, sartorius) work together with the hips and other muscle groups to provide forward movement. Leaning forward when the hips are behind the center of mass at footstrike can cause the runner to "sit in" and unnecessarily overactivate the quadriceps. Try it! Rotate your hips backward and take a short run. You'll quickly notice that with your hips lower, your foot strikes the ground with the heel braking, and your back forms a C-shaped curve as your shoulders round forward—none of which are very efficient. Sitting in causes a runner to drop the buttocks and flex too deeply at the knee. Increased knee flexion at foot contact accompanied by forward lean is oxygen depleting. Consequently, the runner must lift the body farther upward after each footstrike to maintain forward momentum. Forward trunk lean often occurs as compensation for lack of hip mobility. By contrast, an increase in hip flexibility can lead to a more vertical, energy-efficient running style.

Braking Force—To reduce the amount of braking force—or the amount of slowdown as the foot strikes the ground—a runner should lean only slightly forward from the hips. Braking force is demonstrated by extending the lower leg past the vertical angle of the knee. This vertical angle is indicated by an imaginary line drawn from the ankle through the center of the knee at footstrike (fig. 5.4). When the foot strikes the ground in front of the knee, a braking action results, increasing resistance and slowing forward momentum. A certain amount of braking force occurs naturally. The idea is to reduce this force as much as possible.

Further, if the stride length is too long, the foot makes contact with the ground too far forward of the CBM, increasing the braking force. To demonstrate how differences in stride length affect braking force, stand upright, feet together, with your hands on your hips. Take a long step forward (much longer than normal) with your right foot. When your right foot makes contact with the ground, you will notice a sudden forceful impact, similar to the braking forces that occur while running. Your rear (left) foot will feel stuck, and the quadriceps of your right leg will bear most of the weight. Now start from the same upright position and take a shorter step forward. At im-

FIGURE 5.4 Braking force.

pact, the forces on the quadriceps will be minor as your rear foot begins to move forward freely into the swing phase.

If your lower leg is at an angle such that foot contact is beyond being centered under your knee, your stride is probably too long. This not only causes you to expend more energy, it also slows you down. This angle increases the braking force because the heel makes contact first, stopping your forward momentum. The most efficient stride is one in which the lower leg lands directly under the knee at footstrike.

Head Position—When running, the head should be aligned with the spinal column and above the shoulders. Where the head goes, the spine will follow. If you look down, your back will arch forward, causing you to lean over at the hips. Needless to say, running this way requires more energy per footstrike. Leaning your head back or to the side causes still other complications. Although some great runners are successful with this running style, for the most part, I encourage my runners to keep their head in a neutral, relaxed position with the eyes looking forward.

Incorrect head and trunk posture surface frequently when an athlete becomes fatigued. Fatigue causes many problems, but poor technique only adds to them. Although your shoulders, hands, arms, and facial muscles should be relaxed yet controlled, don't let your head drop under any circumstances. It is best to keep your head aligned vertically with your spine. For some, this may mean moving the neck slightly backward to a more neutral position. Remember that many running traits are habitual, and it will take time to learn new anatomical positions.

Rigidness—To improve your athletic performance, you must learn to relax your body. This will occur over time as you gain confidence in your physical abilities and technique. Whenever a new sport is being learned, there is a period of tenseness while the motor skills are being learned. With practice, it requires less and less effort to recall and perform the motions of the skill. The best tips for improving relaxation in the short term are to:

1. keep the facial muscles, particularly the jawbone, loose (let it drop freely);
2. relax the leg muscles and ankle during the forward swing phase—after the pushoff;
3. avoid raising or tightening the shoulders; and
4. keep the arms, wrists, hands, and fingers relaxed and unrestrained (tapping lightly).

Upper Body Form: Relaxed but Controlled

The key elements of upper body running form are a proper arm and trunk position and a relaxed but controlled motion. In this section, I'll review arm carriage techniques and describe a few wasteful upper body movements and ways to correct them.

Arm Action—Keeping the arms relaxed but controlled is most effective for running. Many athletes think the arms help you drive forward, but this is not so. They do, however, provide lateral balance and keep you moving forward instead of wasting energy with too much side-to-side motion. Your arms should be loosely flexed with the elbows at ±90 degrees. Your elbows should be close to the sides of your body (but not touching) as they move downward past the hip. Bring your hand and forearm up parallel with the middle of your chest (but do not move your arm across your body), then lead with your elbow down and back toward and past your hip.

Arm Carriage—It really bothers me to see runners "holding" their arms too low. Not only does this awkward position use a lot of energy, it tenses the muscles. It's better to bring the arms up into a relaxed position with the elbow at about a 90-degree angle (forearms just above parallel with the ground). You'll know when you've found the right position because it feels relatively comfortable to hold the arms this way. Conversely, runners often hold their arms too high when fatigued or sprinting. In the first case, fatigue will cause tenseness in the shoulders and facial muscles in an unwary runner. This results in the runner tightening the arms and bringing them up too high. Stay relaxed in the shoulders, hands, and arms, keeping the elbow at the 90-degree position.

Thumb and Index Finger—How the hands are held while running is a small point but nonetheless important. I like my runners to cup the middle, ring, and small fingers loosely against the palm of the hand. The tip of the thumb should be placed under the index finger at the middle joint. This helps maintain proper arm position, balance, and relaxation.

Thumb to Chest—I see too many runners flapping their arms, often to compensate for other improper techniques. With your thumb and index finger in the correct position, bring the top side of your thumb to the middle of your chest during the forward arm swing (fig. 5.5). You don't necessarily have to touch your chest, but the motion of each arm should be directed toward the middle of the pectoral area on that side. Many runners don't seem to know what to do with their arms, and this technique provides a target for where to direct the arms during the upswing.

FIGURE 5.5   Thumb to chest.

Loose Wrists—With the hands gently cupped and the proper thumb and index finger positioning, the wrist should be loose but controlled. Former Humboldt State University track coach Jim Hunt referred to this motion as "tapping." He described the runner holding a little tapping (tack) hammer in each hand. The hammer is held ever so gently between the thumb and index finger and flexes upward and downward toward and away from the chest. His analogy makes a lot of sense and works well with any of the hand and arm positions.

Arms Cross Over Vertical—In running, if the arms swing across the imaginary vertical line that bisects the body, it causes excessive rotation and twisting of the upper body. This results in an opposite reaction in the hips and lower legs, and the net effect is squandered energy. Athletes should focus on maintaining forward momentum, with all parts of the body in line with the direction of travel. If they cannot do this easily, there may be biomechanical imperfections that a sports podiatrist could help correct.

Footstrike, Stride Length, and Vertical Lift

Foot Placement—Although there are conflicting opinions on this aspect of the running gait, I prefer my athletes to make contact with the ground slightly to the outside at midfoot. From this point, the foot rotates inward toward the ball, continuing diagonally until pressing off the big toe (fig. 5.6). In my view, this is the most efficient footstrike.

The opposite view is for the foot to strike the ground in a heel-to-toe fashion. However, this type of running gait increases the braking forces known to exist at footstrike, causing the runner to slow down. For the heel to strike first, the runner's foot must land so that the lower leg is ahead of the center of body mass. This puts the body's weight behind the footstrike and increases the force of impact. Thus forward momentum may be inhibited by the braking contact of this type of foot placement. In contrast, a midfoot landing does not impede forward momentum in this manner, but permits the

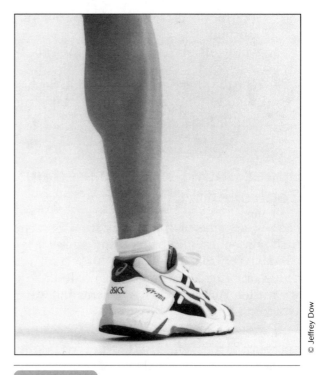

FIGURE 5.6   Foot placement.

runner to engage the ground with the least amount of braking force.

Stride Length—The most important thing to remember about stride length is that you should not make a conscious attempt to change it. In my view, stride length is intrinsic to each runner—an unconscious choice that is affected by running speed, muscle fiber composition, flexibility, terrain (uphill, rolling, downhill, level), and other related biomechanical and physical elements. Runners should not attempt to shorten or lengthen their stride length.

However, there are instances where a runner has learned overstriding as a result of poor coaching. I coached one young triathlete who seemed to overreach in every discipline. When running mile repeats on the track with professionals, it was amazing how he managed to keep in contact with such an unwieldy gait. He had a great deal of talent but was somewhat lacking in technique. Eventually he learned to take a more natural stride by keeping his body mass centered and improved his running considerably. Years after working with this young man, I remember seeing him running away from the field in a triathlon in northern California. It was incredible how much his stride had changed for the better. In fact, he went on to win the triathlon world championships for his age group.

Stride length is essentially the distance covered in sequential contacts with the ground by the same foot. Overstriding, or making contact with the ground ahead of the center of body mass, will cause an increase in the braking forces mentioned earlier in this chapter. The result is that the runner will slow down and use more energy for a given speed. Understriding, on the other hand, is when the footstrike is behind the CBM. This, again, is an unnatural stride and a poor choice of running style. Understriding unnecessarily increases stride rate while reducing stride length. The result is loss of speed and a decrease in forward propulsion and leverage at pushoff. My advice is to run in such a manner that the center of body mass is neither ahead of nor behind the footstrike at first contact with the ground. This should result in a footstrike that is on the outside edge at midfoot, producing the most efficient stride for you.

Stride Frequency—In elite distance runners, footstrike contact time is brief. This means the stride rate, or the number of stride cycles per minute, is particularly high. (A stride cycle begins when the right foot makes contact with the ground and ends the next time the right foot makes contact.) In training, the length of the stride increases more than stride frequency, but drills to improve the kinetic feel are important. Try the following: On a track, run four 200-meter repeats, one at each of the four training intensity zones. Run the first interval at O_2 pace, followed by one at LVT, VO_2, and LAC pace, respectively. At each of these perceived intensities, count the number of stride cycles over the distance (how many times the right foot makes contact with the track). You will notice that as you increase the intensity and speed of your running, the number of strides will increase also.

To optimize this motion, the center of body mass, footstrike, and body alignment must all be correct. To achieve the highest number of stride cycles and be able to propel forward at pushoff, the runner's body needs to be in the most effective position. This means pushing the body forward rather than upward.

Reducing Vertical Oscillation—Vertical oscillation refers to the up-and-down movement of your body while running. Although I see fewer triathletes and duathletes doing this, some still expend too much energy running upward. "Run forward, not upward" is an often-used training adage that reminds the runner to run horizontally, not vertically. Correct body alignment is one technique that helps keep you running forward, but many multisport athletes and marathoners have also adopted a shuffling stride that reduces the amount of knee lift during the forward leg swing prior to footstrike. Elite runners also slow or decelerate less during each footstrike compared to non-elite runners. This is achieved in part by generating a powerful pushoff and the foot striking the ground with the center of the body in alignment. On the other hand, running upward (springing up) at foot pushoff produces excessive loads when the foot makes contact with the ground again, forcing the knee to flex considerably to withstand the greater forces at footstrike. A high vertical displacement (oscillation)

PREVENTING COMMON INJURIES

Injury to the Knee: Patellofemoral Syndrome

The knee is the most frequently reported site of injury or pain in the endurance athlete. Interestingly, though, very few athletes actually seek medical attention. Of knee injuries, patellofemoral syndrome is consistently the number one running injury. Common symptoms include pain, swelling, and crepitus (grating sounds). The problem may be related to certain biomechanical patterns that predispose an athlete to this syndrome. Rest, inflammation control through icing, anti-inflammatory medications, and orthotics have been used therapeutically, but I recommend consulting with a sports podiatrist if you have the symptoms of this injury.

Injury to the Foot: Achilles Tendinitis

Achilles tendinitis is the most common injury to the foot and ankle in runners. The source of this problem is thought to be excessive pronation of the hindfoot. Pronation is an inward (medial) movement and places strain on the Achilles tendon. Rest, anti-inflammatory agents, and orthotics have proven to be effective treatments for this injury.

Low Back Pain and Running

Low back pain in runners is a common overuse injury. Running can tighten the lower back muscles and fascia, causing several back conditions that can become aggravated through further training. Stretching the lower back and hamstrings and strengthening the abdominal muscles are excellent training supplements for preventing this condition. An examination by a qualified sport podiatrist may be warranted, as hip displacement and leg length discrepancies can be associated with the pain. In-shoe orthotics such as lifts, wedges, or castings may help relieve the condition.

Iliotibial Band (ITB) Friction Syndrome

Pain and tenderness on the lateral side of the knee is a characteristic symptom of ITB syndrome. Other symptoms include radiating pain and pain descending onto the ITB. The iliotibial tract is a fibrous tissue extending from the gluteal muscles (buttocks), along the outer thigh, connecting to the lateral aspect of the patella (kneecap) and onto the tibia (lower leg). ITB problems are associated with overuse caused by excessive friction along the lateral side of the knee, resulting in bursitis and inflammatory conditions.

The most common causes of ITB friction syndrome are related to running surface, increased distance, type of running, and alterations in an athlete's training program. Certain mechanical (structural) conditions such as pronation and leg length differences also predispose athletes to this condition. If you experience pain, stop the exercise and consult with a professional to determine the cause of the discomfort.

This condition is best treated by rest, correcting the causes (possibly through use of an orthotic), eliminating training errors, stretching the ITB (chapter 6), anti-inflammatory agents, ice, heat, ultrasound, and for more severe cases, electrical stimulation.

Shin Splints

Anterior (front) and posterior (back) shin splints are commonly caused by a combination of the following: biomechanical abnormalities, poor fitness, and incorrect training. Anterior shin splints cause pain and tenderness near the front and side of the shin. Heel striking, causing excessive force at impact with the ground, may be a significant cause of this problem. Pain due to posterior shin splints presents on the back of the calf (most likely the lower third). Overpronation (inward roll of the foot at footstrike), poor footwear, training oversights, and tightness in the Achilles tendon may cause this condition.

The following are treatments for shin splints:

- Rest for from one day to several weeks, depending on severity
- Ice massage
- Nonsteroidal anti-inflammatory drugs (ibuprofen, naproxen, etc.)
- Non-weight-bearing aerobic training
- Consulting a physician or podiatrist for biomechanical correction and treatment
- Stretching
- Increase in strengthening exercises
- Heat application
- Light progression of running
- Ice after exercise

Plantar Fasciitis

Plantar fasciitis, a particularly uncomfortable overuse injury, occurs in the sole of the foot. The plantar fascia is a tissue that connects the heel bone to the arch of the foot, supplying support. Tight Achilles tendons can cause this problem through repetitious irritation in running. Stretching the fascia, massaging the foot and ankle, stretching the Achilles area, wearing well-cushioned shoes, and progressing in training slowly are some preventives.

Ice

Ice has been used for many years in the treatment of soft tissue and other sport injuries: tendinitis, sprains, strains, swelling, synovitis (bursa) inflammation, and other acute conditions requiring rehabilitation. Ice packs, ice cups, and ice immersion are the more common methods of applying this treatment modality. The effects of ice on the body include

1. a decrease in metabolism,
2. a decrease in blood flow (vasoconstriction),
3. a slowing of the inflammation process, and
4. a reduction in pain and tissue temperature.

continued

PREVENTING COMMON INJURIES (cont.)

Tendinitis: Injury Due to Overuse

Tendinitis is a degenerative condition of muscle tendons. More common injuries include Achilles tendinitis, rotator cuff tendinitis, tennis elbow, and shoulder tendinitis. Rehabilitation of these conditions can be especially difficult for the endurance athlete who tends to return to training too soon, exposing the injury to ongoing stress far beyond the range of single-sport athletes. This can lead to chronic problems. Return to sport should occur only after a sound rehabilitation schedule has been followed. Consult with a physician and rehabilitate using rest, ice, massage, anti-inflammatory agents, practice range-of-motion exercises, do only low-intensity exercises, and incorporate strength work at the appropriate time.

increases the loading, because more forces are generated by the higher liftoff. Keeping the horizon level helps keep excessive vertical displacement in check.

To show just how ineffective vertical oscillation can be, I've used the following technique to demonstrate why runners shouldn't run upward. On a moderate hill, I instruct the athlete to run uphill in what feels like a normal style. Next, I have the runner exaggerate the upward liftoff after footstrike by using the legs and arms to propel upward and forward. They quickly tire and notice how exhausting and ineffective a method this is for running. The best way to run uphill is to use the arms in coordination with the legs, take short strides, and keep the body mass as low to the grade as possible. Any unnecessary upward movement increases oxygen debt and subsequently slows the runner. To a certain extent, this is also true when running on level terrain. Move forward by keeping the body upright and working efficiently in the intended direction of travel.

EXERCISE AND DRILL TRAINING

Working on technique is fundamental to improving economy, efficiency, and thus running speed. For the endurance athlete, biomechanics are highly meaningful for optimum performance. As with every sport in this book, running exercises and drill training are the bedrock of running progress. Why do these work? As I recommended in the swimming and cycling chapters, technical form training should be incorporated into all intensities of running workouts. These drills isolate running mechanics to improve overall technique. By learning to perform these skills, your running will ultimately become more coordinated, comfortable, and efficient.

Concentrating on technique becomes even more important during moments of fatigue due to dehydration, glycogen shortages, and ground force impact. The most efficient runners hold an advantage, as they are able to use energy more effectively. On the other hand, runners with less skill and technique development often fall into even poorer running postures, and the energy needed to maintain pace increases. The following exercises and drills are intended to give you the basics for training technique. Once again, they need to be practiced frequently for you to benefit. I've used these techniques for many years with great success. At first, they may seem difficult or cumbersome, even frustrating. But practicing them will make a difference—you'll become a much better runner.

I prefer to do these drills on a track, as the organization of the workouts is more easily managed, the chances of injury are decreased due to the conducive surface, and the impact on the legs is reduced. However, a slightly sloped (3 to 5 degrees) road, trail, park, or woodland area are also excellent places to do your TF training drills. While lecturing in Europe, I met a running coach who used cones for drill training. Together, in the park, we designed a sequence of intensities and drills for each cone section for the group. It was interesting for both runners and coaches and provided an opportunity to look at and critique the technique of each runner.

Sand Tracks ST

This is an excellent exercise for developing form, as running in sand (loose dirt, tall grass, snow, or lightly pebbled scree) or on any other soft surface automatically forces the runner to keep the hips forward, push off with powerful strides, lift the knees, and work the arms vigorously (fig. 5.7). Additionally, as fitness exercises go, few are more challenging. The runner should consider these LAC workouts, which are less than 2 minutes. These can be relatively

FIGURE 5.7 Sand tracks.

© Jeffrey Dow

high in intensity, so take the right amount of rest between repetitions.

As an example of STs, select a suitable surface and run eight repetitions of 20-second to 2-minute intervals. As this is an LAC drill, rest for two to three times the interval run. For those fortunate to have a nearby beach or sandy surface to run on, this drill is particularly rigorous.

Pushoffs PO

When the foot pushes off the ground, the body is airborne for a brief time. To maximize this floating time, the pushoff becomes particularly important. Actually, the ankle is a sneaky little power generator. It generates up to three times the power of the hip and knee. Therefore, ankle pushoff training should help get the most from this overlooked aspect of running.

For this exercise, exaggerate the force and ankle flexion after footstrike until pushoff. I like to have athletes use this drill during a warm-up by emphasizing this pushoff from a flexion of the ankle. When the drill is done correctly, there should be a momentary sensation of floating or gliding, sort of like bounding. Typically, the drill is performed for about 20 to 50 meters, followed by normal running for about the same distance. Do this between 5 and 15 times during the warm-up.

Footstrike FS

As discussed earlier, the way the foot makes contact with the ground is especially important in running efficiently. In this footstrike exercise, the runner should make a conscious effort to strike at the midfoot, then roll onto the forefoot.

Here's how to do this drill. Once you have sufficiently warmed up and stretched, begin by increasing the knee lift during the forward swing phase of the stride after pushoff. The running pace should be moderate, relaxed, and comfortable. As your foot initiates the footstrike, be sure to contact the ground at midfoot (not at the heel or the ball of your foot). This drill works well for a distance of 50 to 200 meters, followed by an equal distance of normal running. Or you can try an exercise Mike

Pigg once showed me at a training camp we did together. Placing his hands on his hips, he marched in place, flexing only slightly at the knee and concentrating on correct footstrike. He then began to run in place, maintaining a midfoot strike the entire time.

Hold-Ups   HU

This is an excellent exercise for checking body alignment. Place your hands behind your neck, holding this position while running for several strides, then move your arms down to their normal position. This will help you recognize when your running form is correct—chest high, hips forward, head in alignment with spine, and back straight (fig. 5.8). I like athletes to do this exercise whenever they feel their form deteriorating. It is not uncommon for runners to do this exercise during a competition, as this is often when they are most fatigued. It's a great prompt for how your form should feel and is better than sitting in or letting the hips slide back behind the center of mass.

High Knees   HK

Although you're not going to run this way in competition, it makes sense to exaggerate the high knee lift, particularly for coordination, speed, flexibility, and hip flexor conditioning. Begin by running in place. Gradually bring your knees higher (above horizontal with the ground) and quicken the pace (fig. 5.9). An option to this drill is to extend the lower leg after the knee has reached the horizontal position. The arms should work in coordination with the leg movements, with the hands open and brushing the sides of the hips (directed forward, not across the body). You can vary the forward speed from running in place to moderate, then add faster accelerations. I often prescribe a workout for this drill, such as a pyramid of various distances (50 to 200 meters) and intensities of the knee lift; for example, a set of 4 × 200, 4 × 100, and 4 × 50 meters, with the longer interval distances being faster accelera-

FIGURE 5.8   Hold-ups.

FIGURE 5.9   High knees.

tions for the high knees. The rest periods are normally one-half or less than the interval distance.

High-Knee Bounding HKB

There are many variations for this exercise, depending on whether you're running on the track, on stairs, on hills, jumping, or skipping from boulder to boulder. The best way to describe the action of this exercise is to compare it to the long jump. As the jumper approaches the takeoff, the foot strikes the marker and the arms gather down and backward. Then the knee flexes, preparing for pushoff as the arms swing forward.

Begin the drill on the flat surface of a running track or grassy area by marching for a few steps, exaggerating the downward flexion of the knee (1 to 3 inches lower than normal; fig. 5.10). After several strides, begin to run. Do each interval for no more than 20 seconds, followed by 40 seconds of jogging. Remember, this is not a beginner exercise, so take your time working up to the more complicated and stressful drills. The skilled bounder can use single- or double-leg takeoffs and landings. Additionally, when running on cross-country wooded trails, try bounding occasionally for several strides to help develop essential specific muscular strength for running.

Kick-Ups KU

This drill stretches the quadriceps and assists in training the recovery portion of the running gait cycle. Begin this exercise by running in place, kicking your buttocks with your heel during the recovery. Keep your arms working forward (not across the chest) with hands open, brushing the sides of your hips on the downward swing (fig. 5.11). Most runners will be unable to touch the buttocks with the heel. The distance for this drill ranges from 50 to 400 meters, followed by a recovery time equal to the interval time.

© Jeffrey Dow

FIGURE 5.10 High-knee bounding.

© Jeffrey Dow

FIGURE 5.11 Kick-ups.

Hands to Pockets `HP`

Have you ever seen Olympic gold medalist Carl Lewis run the 100 meters or complete the long jump? His hands are open, his knees are high, and his motion is forward. Also, his hands seem to brush the sides of his hips. His momentum is absolutely forward; no energy is wasted moving up and down or side to side-as he coordinates his arm and leg movements for maximum efficiency. I am not suggesting running all-out 100s, but I want you to imitate Lewis's motion for intervals of 50 to 400 meters. Do 4 to 10 of these drills. Open your hands, bring them high and forward, then drop them toward your sides. Put them into imaginary pockets and take them out (fig. 5.12).

Downhill Turnovers `DT`

I'm not talking about baked goods here, but rather leg speed and coordination drills using a downhill 3 to 5 percent grade, 100 to 500

FIGURE 5.12 Hand to pockets.

© Jeffrey Dow

meters long. This exercise works on several things at once. The downhill permits less footstrike opposition, making the exercise more effective and easier to do. During this drill, count the number of strides taken over a course (place cones or use natural markers) or a period of time. For each repetition (maximum of 10), try to reduce the number of strides. You should notice that braking force is reduced by keeping your hips forward and making the footstrike at mid- to forefoot. This is a superb exercise for learning how to maintain a tall posture and feel swift. Be sure not to overstride. Keep the center of body mass in line with the footstrike and work for a powerful pushoff.

Uphill Bounders `UB`

This exercise is a bounding drill done on an uphill trail. The running motion is exaggerated as you run uphill. With each footstrike, flex the knee about an inch beyond your normal stride, then bound upward forcefully. This exercise is particularly fun to do on moderate hills with large boulders or rock slabs, but it is tiring, so follow the training intensity zone guidelines for VO_2 and LAC training for perceived exertion and rest intervals. The number of repetitions and rest will depend on which training intensity zone you're using.

Light Feet `LF`

Getting off your feet quickly and without excessive noise can be accomplished by landing at midfoot and rotating onto the ball and forefoot. I stressed the importance of this footstrike technique earlier, but some runners nevertheless hit the ground too harshly. Think of this contact as a momentary instant in the running cycle, and try to make moving quickly and quietly off each foot a normal part of your running stride. For a drill, you will want to accentuate this motion by moving more forward on the footstrike, perhaps onto the forefoot or ball of the foot. This technique will teach you to land lightly and push off quickly. Variations of this drill are determined by the pace and distance of the interval. If running slowly, you can do the drill up to 400 meters. For faster speeds, I recommend 50 to 200 meters, as this drill places

UPHILL RUNNING

Relaxation, practice, short strides, and pacing (training intensity zone management) are key elements of successful uphill running. Actually, to be efficient, any type of running must be done with the body relaxed and smooth. This is especially true for uphill running, as you must work against the incline of the hill. To be a better hill runner, you must practice running hills. This will ultimately train muscle groups and motor neurons (nerves that transmit impulses to muscle), along with cardiovascular considerations.

Engaging a hill and running it well requires more than practice and relaxation, however. Management of intensity starts at the bottom of any hill. Beginning too fast will result in an oxygen debt impossible to correct unless you slow down or even begin walking. The few meters before the start of a climb are important, because as soon as you begin climbing, your oxygen consumption will increase. If you are already at your lactate threshold, it will not be long before you reach $\dot{V}O_2max$, and in just a few minutes, perhaps seconds, your pace will decline.

A good rule is to slow down slightly before beginning the climb. Once on the hill, as you gather the measure of the pace, you can increase the intensity if necessary. A good way to unnerve a competitor is to slow down intentionally as you approach a hill (letting them pass), then as the hill is collected and the pace is increased, or at least maintained, you will often pass. Be sure to work over the top of the hill to the best of your ability. Knowing the course is particularly important when pushing the pace in such a manner, but it works.

If it will take you between two and eight minutes to climb the hill, you may be able to gut out the effort and begin the charge at the bottom, as long as there is some recovery time after the top. If not, you will have too much oxygen debt, your muscles will tighten, and your pace will slow. This is another good reason to know the course and the time it may take to cover the more challenging portions. On the other hand, if it takes less than two minutes to climb the hill, you can be confident of recovering after making a strong effort. Of course, this strategy is dependent on the length of the event, but in certain instances it can be a very good one.

---

a fair amount of stress on the Achilles tendon and soleus.

In the late seventies, I watched Bill Rodgers, the famous marathoner, run by on a quiet and isolated stretch of desert in Las Vegas, Nevada. There was no sound, just this incredibly efficient running machine gliding by. It was spectacular to see. In contrast, I remember the first time I saw former world-class New Zealand triathlete Greg Wells. He was a tremendous force in swimming and cycling, but his early years of running were excruciating to watch. Even though there were other runners all around him, I could distinctly hear the thud of his heavy footstrike. Each step sounded like a youngster making a cannonball splash from the high dive. Running lightly is relaxed running. Every muscle in the body must be fluid and balanced to achieve the most efficient and effective result.

Hip Tips HT

This drill closely approximates the way a runner should run. As discussed earlier, the number one technique a runner should have is correct center of body mass position. As a drill, I have the runner slightly overexaggerate tipping the hips forward. This permits the footstrike to land well under the CBM, sort of like running in a squirrel's cage or on a treadmill. A footstrike that is too far forward (hips back) will result in overstriding and stumbling, whereas with the hips forward and the vertical angle in line, the runner will maintain an optimum stride.

Do this drill 5 to 20 times for 50 to 100 meters, followed by an equal-distance jogging recovery. The top of the pelvis should be rotated forward and pushed ahead, as if you're being pulled from the waist with a cord. The point of this drill is to emphasize the importance of keeping the center of body mass in line at footstrike. If it is not, the CBM is likely behind the footstrike, which can increase both braking force and oxygen consumption. Under normal running conditions, of course, you should maintain the in-line posture, not the slightly overexaggerated one described. This drill isolates the technique of keeping the hips forward when running.

Arm Swings AS

Sit on the ground with your legs together out front, arms at your sides (elbows at 90 degrees),

hands open. Begin pulling your right elbow back and upward until your open hand brushes the side of your body. Now bring your right arm forward as your left elbow pulls back and up until the hand brushes your body (fig. 5.13). Continue this correct arm motion for one minute, increasing the pace of the elbow swing every 15 seconds. By the last 15 seconds, your arms should be moving quite quickly. After one minute, slow down to the starting rate for another 15 seconds. During this drill, keep the facial, shoulder, and hand muscles tension free. In fact, every time the pace increases, try to relax even more. The reason for sitting is to isolate the arm motion so the athlete can move the arms without having to coordinate the increased speed with the legs.

A variation of this drill can be done while running too. It follows the same intervals and arm-swing rates, but because the arms work in coordination with the legs, you are not likely to reach the same rates as when sitting. Nevertheless, running is obviously a good way to work the technique. Begin by marching slowly while moving the arms quickly, then run for 50 meters. For example, run 8 × 50 meters with

FIGURE 5.13   Arm swings.

50 meters of recovery jogging. Every two intervals, increase the rate of the arm movement while maintaining the relaxation elements described.

OTHER TRAINING METHODS

LAC-Downs LD

This exercise is more of a training intensity zone application. These high-intensity repetitions are to be performed on a downhill slope. Refer to the intensity pace chart for the duration and rest periods of this training intensity zone. The incline should be about 10 to 20 degrees on a soft surface such as grass. Run down the slope fast, keeping your arms relaxed but controlled. Not only does this exercise train the anaerobic capacity, it also works on leg speed and coordination. It is a great exercise for tapering, as it gets the legs moving fast (feeling the speed), but be careful, as downhill running will make the muscles sore due to eccentric movement.

LAC-Ups LU

These are the same as LDs, but are done on an uphill slope with the same degree of incline. Use your arms, shorten your stride, and keep your hips ahead of the center of body mass.

VO₂-Ups VU

These are the same as the LUs, except the duration is longer and the rest interval time is equal to the interval time. The length is from two to eight minutes, so the runner will need a longer hill.

Fartlek Accelerations FA

Fartlek workouts, Swedish for "speed play," typically involve placing periodic surges into a run or activity. I recommend doing this type of workout on a varied course with uphills and downhills. During a steady state run, accelerate your pace for a designated period of time (one to three minutes) or distance (300-800 meters). During this interval, accelerate your pace while focusing on good technique. Following each interval, drop back down to your steady state run to allow for complete recovery.

DOWNHILL RUNNING

The biggest mistake I see in runners going downhill is breaking momentum with footstrikes that hit heel first. This restricts forward movement, much like putting on the brakes in your car. Some braking is necessary for very steep terrain, but you might try holding your arms farther out in this situation, rather than hitting heel first.

To run downhill most efficiently, make sure the footstrike is at mid- to forefoot. Also, land with your hips leaning slightly forward, and do not allow the ankle (at footstrike) to be in front of the knee. The ankle should be vertically aligned directly under the knee. Hold your arms out just slightly at the elbow (more on steeper terrain). Allow the ground to move under your body as quickly as possible, as if running down an upward-moving conveyor. Keep yourself as limber as possible. The object is to run down the hill with as little slowing down (braking) as possible. To do this, you must remain relaxed (shoulders, face, and hands), have a fast turnover, and land when each foot is under your body, not ahead of it.

RUNNING INTENSITY PACE CHARTS

The running intensity pace charts (IPCs), like those in the swimming and cycling chapters, work in relation to the training intensity zones discussed in chapter 1. Everything is linked in accordance with the periodization, the training zones, and finally, the program design. The charts serve as an easy reference for determining the interval time for each training intensity zone.

Although I reference heart rate zone as an indicator of exertion and performance, it can be less effective than using the perceived

TRAINING OVERSIGHTS AND ERRORS IN RUNNING

In an article in the *Journal of Athletic Training*, authors and sport physical therapists John Sallade and Steve Koch (1992) present 10 of the most common training errors and treatment strategies for long-distance runners. Here's a brief overview of the tips they suggest:

1. Distance runners commonly run on crowned roads, which place the left leg downhill (when running facing traffic). This causes the right foot to overpronate (move inward at footstrike) and puts increased stress on the ITB. To remedy this, simply run equal distances on both sides of the road and, whenever possible (safe, low traffic, country roads), run in the center on top of the crown.

2. Excessive hill running may put abnormal stress on the Achilles tendon, leading to tendinitis and possible strain. To cure this problem, gradually stretch the heel cord by running on the balls of your feet when going uphill. Also, increase the duration of your hill running gradually.

3. Track running in only one direction also causes excessive pronation of the inside foot and supination of the outside foot. This ongoing stress can cause injury to the shin and knee. The simple solution is to change the direction of training during workouts or run in opposite directions on different days.

4. Running on hard surfaces is particularly damaging to runners with high arches and those who cannot effectively absorb the shock of foot impact. Properly cushioned shoes (not too worn) may help, along with running on somewhat softer surfaces. Shoes should be replaced regularly, not necessarily according to the number of miles but depending on how the shoes feel. Hold one shoe with both hands (toe and heel) and flex and twist it gently. A worn shoe will feel soft and spongy, whereas a good shoe will rebound somewhat. The endurance athlete is wise to own several pairs of shoes too. Rotating the shoes you wear for training on alternate days will increase the life of the shoe and ensure better support. Replace worn-out shoes immediately. Don't risk injury by using ill-cushioned, flat, or unstable shoes.

5. Running on unstable terrain such as grassy fields, sand, or dirt may exaggerate overpronation or -supination in athletes who are prone to such problems. Instability as opposed to shock (impact from footstrike) plays a greater role in such injuries. Choose appropriate shock-absorbing shoes with proper motion control for your particular needs. A running specialty store and/or sport podiatrist can help you determine the best shoe for you.

6. Changing shoes can cause musculoskeletal problems too. When you find a good pair of shoes, it might be wise to buy another pair or two, as manufacturers seem determined to replace shoe models sooner rather than later. When breaking in new shoes, don't make any changes (especially drastic ones) in your training program for a while.

7. In the spring, as the weather improves and race season approaches, there is a natural tendency to increase training volume too rapidly. Use the 10 percent rule for managing this potential problem. Increase training volume no more than 10 percent each week, and don't continue increasing volume unnecessarily beyond what seems appropriate for your competitive needs.

8. Increasing training speed and intensity is much the same as increasing volume, as there is an ever-increasing chance of injury with intense exercise. To run fast, you must train fast, but you need adequate time to adjust to increases in training load. Periodization in training ensures that this will occur through gradual increases in the volume and intensity of training.

9. Not listening to your body's signal to back off is a problem when following a structured program or training with a group or friends. The pressure is on to complete the distance regardless of how you are feeling. Many athletes train because the program or group says so. Listen to your body; periodic restorations and days off are as important to the training process as hard training sessions.

10. Lack of variety in training is typically not a problem for the multiple-sport endurance athlete; however, the weekly training flow should be designed to include variability in intensity, volumes achieved, group training, and rest periods. Failure to do so can lead to overuse injury, undertraining, and inability to adapt to ongoing training load due to inadequate rest periods between workouts.

exertion methods. Use heart rate in combination with the perceived exertion applications for best results. To cite an instance, as fitness improves, cardiac output increases and heart rate goes down for a given pace. In this case, the athlete may be undertraining if using heart rate as the only measure of pace. The more I see how variable heart rate training and monitors can be, the more I believe in using them only in conjunction with perceived exertion principles. Monitors are neat little devices, but they aren't always a precise indicator of intensity. Use monitors for overtraining and estimation of recovery, as opposed to training intensity (chapter 1). You'd be wise to invest in more appropriate running shoes or orthotics (if needed) than in a heart rate monitor.

The intensity pace charts and the training intensity zones manage pace and physiological training. How? They provide parameters for the length of training time, intensity of training time, and rest intervals.

LVT, VO_2, and LAC running are shown in the following charts. Running intensity training zones are based on anticipated, actual, or goal times for 10K (multisport).

1. O_2 (aerobic conditioning) = Long and gradual continuous aerobic training.

2. LVT (anaerobic conditioning) = Short rest intervals of 5 to 60 seconds.

Note: Sets last for 15 to 25 minutes, and occasionally two sets are called for.

3. VO_2 (aerobic capacity) = The rest time is equal to the interval time, or "double interval time."

Note: Sets last for 15 to 21 minutes, with the intervals lasting from 2 to 8 minutes.

4. LAC (anaerobic conditioning) = Rest is two times the interval if less than 1 minute of interval time and three times the interval if more than 1 minute.

Note: Sets are 4 to 10 minutes with intervals between 15 and 120 seconds.

> *Training Note:* Each training intensity zone has required durations of exercise time. These durations are necessary to achieve the correct physiological training effect. In the VO_2 and LAC intensity training zones, the minimum requirements of training volume sometimes are not met when an athlete's weekly volume is particularly low. This usually occurs during base preparatory phases. If this is the case, it is appropriate to complete less than the minimum VO_2 or LAC within a training session.

In table 5.1, locate the appropriate 10K (10,000-meter) goal time in the left-most column. The columns and rows to the right display the interval time for each training intensity zone. For example, if the LVT portion of a workout is 4 miles and your 10K goal time is 40:00, simply go to the correct row under the "10K time" column. Four miles is approximately 6,400 meters (4 3 1.609 = 6,436 meters). To convert miles to meters, multiply the number of miles by 1.609. In the above example, a set of 4 3 1,600-meter repeats would be run with an average time of 6:24 and a send-off interval of ±7:30. The 6,400 meters could be broken up into numerous different sets or even done in a continuous 4-mile or 6,400-meter race pace time trial. If you want to move up the pace, simply go to the charts and select the split times for any distance you choose.

> *Training Note:* Move up the chart only when you can make the full distance on a faster or at least the prior send-off interval.

MODEL RUNNING TRAINING SETS

LVT Model Set

LVT (anaerobic conditioning) sets and interval training are workouts done at or near 10K race pace. The send-off interval times are the same as for swimming and cycling, 5 to 60 seconds. That's how much rest should be taken between intervals. LVT training raises race pace stamina using the perceived exertion of somewhat hard to energetically hard.

I. **Warm-up: 1 to 1.5 miles O_2 pace (light jogging, break a sweat)**

II. **TF training: 16 minutes: 4(4 × 30 seconds + 30 seconds O_2 running)**
   1. PO
   2. HU
   3. HKB
   4. LF

III. **Main set: 6,000 meters**
   A. 3 × 2,000 meters in 8 minutes plus 1 minute walking/jogging

   or

   B. 1 × 3,000 meters in 12 minutes plus 1 minute walking/jogging, then 3 × 1,000 meters in 4 minutes plus 30 seconds between sets

IV. **Warm-down: 9 minutes TF: 6 × 1 minute plus 30 seconds**
   1-3. HT
   4-6. LF

Goal LVT 10,000-meter pace: 40:00 or 6:27 per mile, 4:00 per 1,000 meters

Note: Refer to table 5.1 for LVT goal times and pace. The above times are for illustration only.

TABLE 5.1   Intensity Pace Chart - LVT Running

10K time	1K LVT split	Mile LVT split	Marathon	400	1,000	1,600	5,000
0:30:00	03:00	04:50	2:06:28	01:12	03:00	04:48	15:00
0:30:30	03:03	04:55	2:08:35	01:13	03:03	04:53	15:15
0:31:00	03:06	05:00	2:10:41	01:14	03:06	04:58	15:30
0:31:30	03:09	05:05	2:12:47	01:16	03:09	05:02	15:45
0:32:00	03:12	05:10	2:14:54	01:17	03:12	05:07	16:00
0:32:30	03:15	05:15	2:17:00	01:18	03:15	05:12	16:15
0:33:00	03:18	05:19	2:19:07	01:19	03:18	05:17	16:30
0:33:30	03:21	05:24	2:21:13	01:20	03:21	05:22	16:45
0:34:00	03:24	05:29	2:23:20	01:22	03:24	05:26	17:00
0:34:30	03:27	05:24	2:25:26	01:23	03:27	05:31	17:15
0:35:00	03:30	05:39	2:27:33	01:24	03:30	05:36	17:30
0:35:30	03:33	05:44	2:29:39	01:25	03:33	05:41	17:45
0:36:00	03:36	05:48	2:31:46	01:26	03:36	05:46	18:00
0:36:30	03:39	05:53	2:33:52	01:28	03:39	05:50	18:15
0:37:00	03:42	05:58	2:35:59	01:29	03:42	05:55	18:30
0:37:30	03:45	06:03	2:38:05	01:30	03:45	06:00	18:45
0:38:00	03:48	06:08	2:40:12	01:31	03:48	06:05	19:00
0:38:30	03:51	06:13	2:42:18	01:32	03:51	06:10	19:15
0:39:00	03:54	06:17	2:44:24	01:34	03:54	06:14	19:30
0:39:30	03:57	06:22	2:46:31	01:35	03:57	06:19	19:45
0:40:00	04:00	06:27	2:48:37	01:36	04:00	06:24	20:00
0:40:30	04:03	06:32	2:50:44	01:37	04:03	06:29	20:15
0:41:00	04:06	06:37	2:52:50	01:38	04:06	06:34	20:30
0:41:30	04:09	06:42	2:54:57	01:40	04:09	06:38	20:45
0:42:00	04:12	06:46	2:57:03	01:41	04:12	06:43	21:00
0:42:30	04:15	06:51	2:59:10	01:42	04:15	06:48	21:15
0:43:00	04:18	06:56	3:01:16	01:43	04:18	06:53	21:30
0:43:30	04:21	07:01	3:03:23	01:44	04:21	06:58	21:45
0:44:00	04:24	07:06	3:05:29	01:46	04:24	07:02	22:00
0:44:30	04:27	07:11	3:07:36	01:47	04:27	07:07	22:15
0:45:00	04:30	07:15	3:09:42	01:48	04:30	07:12	22:30
0:45:30	04:33	07:20	3:11:49	01:49	04:33	07:17	22:45
0:46:00	04:36	07:25	3:13:55	01:50	04:36	07:22	23:00

(continued)

TABLE 5.1   *(continued)*

10K time	1K LVT split	Mile LVT split	Marathon	400	1,000	1,600	5,000
0:46:30	04:39	07:30	3:16:01	01:52	04:39	07:26	23:15
0:47:00	04:42	07:35	3:18:08	01:53	04:42	07:31	23:30
0:47:30	04:45	07:40	3:20:14	01:54	04:45	07:36	23:45
0:48:00	04:48	07:45	3:22:21	01:55	04:48	07:41	24:00
0:48:30	04:51	07:49	3:24:27	01:56	04:51	07:46	24:15
0:49:00	04:54	07:54	3:26:34	01:58	04:54	07:50	24:30
0:49:30	04:57	07:59	3:28:40	01:59	04:57	07:55	24:45
0:50:00	05:00	08:04	3:30:47	02:00	05:00	08:00	25:00
0:50:30	05:03	08:09	3:32:53	02:01	05:03	08:05	
0:51:00	05:06	08:14	3:35:00	02:02	05:06	08:10	
0:51:30	05:09	08:18	3:37:06	02:04	05:09	08:14	
0:52:00	05:12	08:23	3:39:13	02:05	05:12	08:19	
0:52:30	05:15	08:28	3:41:19	02:06	05:15	08:24	
0:53:00	05:18	08:33	3:43:26	02:07	05:18	08:29	
0:53:30	05:21	08:38	3:45:32	02:08	05:21	08:34	
0:54:00	05:24	08:43	3:47:38	02:10	05:24	08:38	
0:54:30	05:27	08:47	3:49:45	02:11	05:27	08:43	
0:55:00	05:30	08:52	3:51:51	02:12	05:30	08:48	
0:55:30	05:33	08:57	3:53:58	02:13	05:33	08:53	
0:56:00	05:36	09:02	3:56:04	02:14	05:36	08:58	
0:56:30	05:39	09:07	3:58:11	02:16	05:39	09:02	
0:57:00	05:42	09:12	4:00:17	02:17	05:42	09:07	
0:57:30	05:45	09:16	4:02:24	02:18	05:45	09:12	
0:58:00	05:48	09:21	4:04:30	02:19	05:48	09:17	
0:58:30	05:51	09:26	4:06:37	02:20	05:51	09:22	
0:59:00	05:54	09:31	4:08:43	02:22	05:54	09:26	
0:59:30	05:57	09:36	4:10:50	02:23	05:57	09:31	
1:00:00	06:00	09:41	4:12:56	02:24	06:00	09:36	
1:01:00	06:06	09:50	4:17:09	02:26	06:06	09:46	
1:02:00	06:12	10:00	4:21:22	02:29	06:12	09:55	
1:03:00	06:18	10:10	4:25:35	02:31	06:18	10:05	
1:04:00	06:24	10:19	4:29:48	02:34	06:24	10:14	
1:05:00	06:30	10:29	4:34:01	02:36	06:30	10:24	

*Distances are in meters

VO$_2$ Model Set

VO$_2$ (aerobic capacity) sets are workout intensities above LVT by approximately 5 percent. $\dot{V}O_2$max training increases the aerobic capacity or maximum oxygen capacity (aerobic power). The efforts are slightly faster than race pace but not all out, and intervals are 2 to 8 minutes in duration. The total training of any one set is 21 minutes. VO$_2$ workouts have a perceived exertion of energetically hard to very hard.

I. **Warm-up:**
   A. 2 miles at O$_2$ pace
   B. TF every 4 minutes for 4 minutes
      1. PO
      2. KU
      3. DT
      4. AS
   C. Stretch 6 minutes or more, then jog 3 minutes

II. **Main set: 4,000 meters**
   A. 5 × 800 meters in 3:03 plus 3:03 resting/walking/jogging

or

   B. 4 × 1,000 meters in 3:49 plus 3:49 resting/walking/jogging

III. **Warm-down:**
   A. 1 to 1.5 miles of O$_2$ running
   B. TF: 6 minutes of the following:
      1. HP 3 × 1 minute
      2. FS 6 × 30 seconds

Goal LVT 10,000-meter pace: 40:00 or 6:27 per mile, 4:00 per 1,000 meters

Refer to table 5.2 for VO$_2$ goal times and pace. The above times are for illustration only.

LAC Model Set

LAC (anaerobic capacity) training is the highest-intensity (fastest speeds) training you will do. The perceived exertion is very hard to very, very hard. Once again, LACs are intervals from 10 to 120 seconds and are continued for a combined time of 4 to 10 minutes. The rest periods are twice the interval time for intervals of less than 1 minute of exercise time and three times the interval time for intervals of more than 1 minute. For example, 100 meters in 20 seconds will have an additional rest time of 40 seconds; however, 800 meters in 2 minutes will have an additional rest time of 4 minutes. An important point to remember is that the final repetition of any LAC set should be equal to or faster than earlier repetitions. Also, refer to the IPC for the "right" training pace for these intervals. When you've completed the training program in chapter 2, you'll know just how much of each training intensity zone work you need to do each week.

I. **Warm-up: 24 minutes of the following:**
   A. 8 minutes of O$_2$ jogging
   B. 6 minutes of FA (15 seconds on, then 45 seconds O$_2$)
   C. 4 minutes of stretching, more if needed
   D. 4 minutes of TF drill: HK
   E. 2 minutes of stretching

II. **Main set: 1,200 meters**
   A. 6 × 200 meters in 43 seconds plus 2 × interval time or leave on 1:30

or

   B. 12 × 100 in 22 seconds plus 2 × interval time or leave on 1:10 (LD)

III. **Warm-down: 1 to 1.5 miles soft-surface jogging, working relaxed, tall posture, and light feet**

Goal LVT 10,000-meter pace: 40:00 or 6:27 per mile, 4:00 per 1,000 meters

Refer to table 5.3 for LAC goal times and pace. The above times are for illustration only.

Mixed Training Intensity Zone Model Set

The following workout is representative of most training sessions. Typically, workouts are composed of this type of training, whether the athlete knows it or not. For example, running or cycling over moderately hilly terrain will

TABLE 5.2   Intensity Pace Chart - VO$_2$ Running

10K time	1K LVT split	Mile LVT split	600	800	1,000	1,600	2,400
0:30:00	03:00	04:50		02:17	02:51	04:34	06:50
0:30:30	03:03	04:55		02:19	02:54	04:38	06:57
0:31:00	03:06	05:00		02:21	02:57	04:43	07:04
0:31:30	03:09	05:05		02:24	03:00	04:47	07:11
0:32:00	03:12	05:10		02:26	03:02	04:52	07:18
0:32:30	03:15	05:15		02:28	03:05	04:56	07:25
0:33:00	03:18	05:19		02:30	03:08	05:01	07:31
0:33:30	03:21	05:24		02:33	03:11	05:06	07:38
0:34:00	03:24	05:29		02:35	03:14	05:10	07:45
0:34:30	03:27	05:34		02:37	03:17	05:15	07:52
0:35:00	03:30	05:39	02:00	02:40	03:19	05:19	07:59
0:35:30	03:33	05:44	02:01	02:42	03:22	05:24	
0:36:00	03:36	05:48	02:03	02:44	03:25	05:28	
0:36:30	03:39	05:53	02:05	02:46	03:28	05:33	
0:37:00	03:42	05:58	02:07	02:49	03:31	05:37	
0:37:30	03:45	06:03	02:08	02:51	03:34	05:42	
0:38:00	03:48	06:08	02:10	02:53	03:37	05:47	
0:38:30	03:51	06:13	02:12	02:56	03:39	05:51	
0:39:00	03:54	06:17	02:13	02:58	03:42	05:56	
0:39:30	03:57	06:22	02:15	03:00	03:45	06:00	
0:40:00	04:00	06:27	02:17	03:02	03:48	06:05	
0:40:30	04:03	06:32	02:19	03:05	03:51	06:09	
0:41:00	04:06	06:37	02:20	03:07	03:54	06:14	
0:41:30	04:09	06:42	02:22	03:09	03:57	06:18	
0:42:00	04:12	06:46	02:24	03:12	03:59	06:23	
0:42:30	04:15	06:51	02:25	03:14	04:02	06:28	
0:43:00	04:18	06:56	02:27	03:16	04:05	06:32	
0:43:30	04:21	07:01	02:29	03:18	04:08	06:37	
0:44:00	04:24	07:06	02:30	03:21	04:11	06:41	
0:44:30	04:27	07:11	02:32	03:23	04:14	06:46	
0:45:00	04:30	07:15	02:34	03:25	04:16	06:50	
0:45:30	04:33	07:20	02:36	03:27	04:19	06:55	
0:46:00	04:36	07:25	02:37	03:30	04:22	07:00	

(continued)

TABLE 5.2 *(continued)*

10K time	1K LVT split	Mile LVT split	600	800	1,000	1,600	2,400
0:46:30	04:39	07:30	02:39	03:32	04:25	07:04	
0:47:00	04:42	07:35	02:41	03:34	04:28	07:09	
0:47:30	04:45	07:40	02:42	03:37	04:31	07:13	
0:48:00	04:48	07:45	02:44	03:39	04:34	07:18	
0:48:30	04:51	07:49	02:46	03:41	04:36	07:22	
0:49:00	04:54	07:54	02:48	03:43	04:39	07:27	
0:49:30	04:57	07:59	02:49	03:46	04:42	07:31	
0:50:00	05:00	08:04	02:51	03:48	04:45	07:36	
0:50:30	05:03	08:09	02:53	03:50	04:48	07:41	
0:51:00	05:06	08:14	02:54	03:53	04:51	07:45	
0:51:30	05:09	08:18	02:56	03:55	04:54	07:50	
0:52:00	05:12	08:23	02:58	03:57	04:56	07:54	
0:52:30	05:15	08:28	03:00	03:59	04:59	07:59	
0:53:00	05:18	08:33	03:01	04:02	05:02		
0:53:30	05:21	08:38	03:03	04:04	05:05		
0:54:00	05:24	08:43	03:05	04:06	05:08		
0:54:30	05:27	08:47	03:06	04:09	05:11		
0:55:00	05:30	08:52	03:08	04:11	05:13		
0:55:30	05:33	08:57	03:10	04:13	05:16		
0:56:00	05:36	09:02	03:12	04:15	05:19		
0:56:30	05:39	09:07	03:13	04:18	05:22		
0:57:00	05:42	09:12	03:15	04:20	05:25		
0:57:30	05:45	09:16	03:17	04:22	05:28		
0:58:00	05:48	09:21	03:18	04:24	05:31		
0:58:30	05:51	09:26	03:20	04:27	05:33		
0:59:00	05:54	09:31	03:22	04:29	05:36		
0:59:30	05:57	09:36	03:23	04:31	05:39		
1:00:00	06:00	09:41	03:25	04:34	05:42		
1:01:00	06:06	09:50	03:29	04:38	05:48		
1:02:00	06:12	10:00	03:32	04:43	05:53		
1:03:00	06:18	10:10	03:35	04:47	05:59		
1:04:00	06:24	10:19	03:39	04:52	06:05		
1:05:00	06:30	10:29	03:42	04:56	06:11		

*Distances are in meters

TABLE 5.3   Intensity Pace Chart - LAC Running

10K time	1K LVT split	Mile LVT split	100	200	400	600
0:30:00	03:00	04:50	00:16	00:32	01:05	01:37
0:30:30	03:03	04:55	00:16	00:33	01:06	01:39
0:31:00	03:06	05:00	00:17	00:33	01:07	01:40
0:31:30	03:09	05:05	00:17	00:34	01:08	01:42
0:32:00	03:12	05:10	00:17	00:35	01:09	01:44
0:32:30	03:15	05:15	00:18	00:35	01:10	01:45
0:33:00	03:18	05:19	00:18	00:36	01:11	01:47
0:33:30	03:21	05:24	00:18	00:36	01:12	01:49
0:34:00	03:24	05:29	00:18	00:37	01:13	01:50
0:34:30	03:27	05:34	00:19	00:37	01:15	01:52
0:35:00	03:30	05:39	00:19	00:38	01:16	01:53
0:35:30	03:33	05:44	00:19	00:38	01:17	01:55
0:36:00	03:36	05:48	00:19	00:39	01:18	01:57
0:36:30	03:39	05:53	00:20	00:39	01:19	01:58
0:37:00	03:42	05:58	00:20	00:40	01:20	02:00
0:37:30	03:45	06:03	00:20	00:40	01:21	
0:38:00	03:48	06:08	00:21	00:41	01:22	
0:38:30	03:51	06:13	00:21	00:42	01:23	
0:39:00	03:54	06:17	00:21	00:42	01:24	
0:39:30	03:57	06:22	00:21	00:43	01:25	
0:40:00	04:00	06:27	00:22	00:43	01:26	
0:40:30	04:03	06:32	00:22	00:44	01:27	
0:41:00	04:06	06:37	00:22	00:44	01:29	
0:41:30	04:09	06:42	00:22	00:45	01:30	
0:42:00	04:12	06:46	00:23	00:45	01:31	
0:42:30	04:15	06:51	00:23	00:46	01:32	
0:43:00	04:18	06:56	00:23	00:46	01:33	
0:43:30	04:21	07:01	00:23	00:47	01:34	
0:44:00	04:24	07:06	00:24	00:48	01:35	
0:44:30	04:27	07:11	00:24	00:48	01:36	
0:45:00	04:30	07:15	00:24	00:49	01:37	
0:45:30	04:33	07:20	00:25	00:49	01:38	
0:46:00	04:36	07:25	00:25	00:50	01:39	

(continued)

TABLE 5.3 *(continued)*

10K time	1K LVT split	Mile LVT split	100	200	400	600
0:46:30	04:39	07:30	00:25	00:50	01:40	
0:47:00	04:42	07:35	00:25	00:51	01:42	
0:47:30	04:45	07:40	00:26	00:51	01:43	
0:48:00	04:48	07:45	00:26	00:52	01:44	
0:48:30	04:51	07:49	00:26	00:52	01:45	
0:49:00	04:54	07:54	00:26	00:53	01:46	
0:49:30	04:57	07:59	00:27	00:53	01:47	
0:50:00	05:00	08:04	00:27	00:54	01:48	
0:50:30	05:03	08:09	00:27	00:55	01:49	
0:51:00	05:06	08:14	00:28	00:55	01:50	
0:51:30	05:09	08:18	00:28	00:56	01:51	
0:52:00	05:12	08:23	00:28	00:56	01:52	
0:52:30	05:15	08:28	00:28	00:57	01:53	
0:53:00	05:18	08:33	00:29	00:57	01:54	
0:53:30	05:21	08:38	00:29	00:58	01:56	
0:54:00	05:24	08:43	00:29	00:58	01:57	
0:54:30	05:27	08:47	00:29	00:59	01:58	
0:55:00	05:30	08:52	00:30	00:59	01:59	
0:55:30	05:33	08:57	00:30	01:00	02:00	
0:56:00	05:36	09:02	00:30	01:00		
0:56:30	05:39	09:07	00:31	01:01		
0:57:00	05:42	09:12	00:31	01:02		
0:57:30	05:45	09:16	00:31	01:02		
0:58:00	05:48	09:21	00:31	01:03		
0:58:30	05:51	09:26	00:32	01:03		
0:59:00	05:54	09:31	00:32	01:04		
0:59:30	05:57	09:36	00:32	01:04		
1:00:00	06:00	09:41	00:32	01:05		
1:01:00	06:06	09:50	00:33	01:06		
1:02:00	06:12	10:00	00:33	01:07		
1:03:00	06:18	10:10	00:34	01:08		
1:04:00	06:24	10:19	00:35	01:09		
1:05:00	06:30	10:29	00:35	01:10		

*Distances are in meters

automatically include several training intensity zones. The athlete will attain several training intensity zone continuum benefits during any one workout. These workouts are best when doing longer-duration sessions.

Once again, as mentioned in the swimming and cycling chapters, mixing the intensity training zones is appropriate, but two general rules apply. First, the highest-intensity portions should come toward the end of the workout. Second, allow for enough rest between repeats and make every effort to get the right goal pace.

I. **Warm-up: 2 to 2.5 miles O_2 technical form/ TF (4 × 5 minutes)**
   1. ST
   2. HU 10 seconds on and 50 seconds off for the 5 minutes
   3. KU
   4. PO

II. **LVT set: 5,000 meters: 1 × 5,000 meters in 20 minutes**

III. **O_2 set: 5 minutes of O_2 jogging**

IV. **VO_2 set: 4,000 meters: 2 × 2,000 in 7:38 plus 7:38 rest interval**

V. **O_2 set: 6 minutes of O_2 jogging TF at LF**

VI. **Warm-down (TF drills): 10 minutes (5 × 2:00)**
   1. AS
   2. FS
   3. HT
   4. KU
   5. HU

Goal LVT 10,000-meter pace: 40:00 or 6:27 per mile, 4:00 per 1,000 meters

6

SUPPLEMENTAL TRAINING

Undeniably, every sport requires a measure of endurance, strength, and power, but the differentiating characteristics of sport performance determine how a supplemental training program is developed. Athletes who run marathons, swim long distances, cycle centuries, or race in triathlons or duathlons have muscular needs other athletes don't have. For example, an endurance athlete does not need all of the explosive power of a 350-pound NFL lineman. Rather, endurance athletes' strength requirements are proportionate to long-duration athletic competitions. This type of strength requires high-intensity repetitive contractions at or near the anaerobic threshold, sometimes for hours on end. Athletes do supplemental training to enhance sport performance, prevent injury, promote flexibility, and increase endurance, strength, and power.

Supplemental training is exactly that—*supplemental.* Although I stress the necessity for this type of training, it must not interfere with your sport-specific improvement. For this reason, supplemental training (except flexibility training) always follows an athlete's swimming, cycling, or running workouts. Supplemental strength gains through nonspecific training are important up to a point. Essential supportive musculoskeletal groups are strengthened and will help support improved performance through injury reduction and improved postural endurance.

However, sport training is notably specific to the muscles being used. Each of the respective swimming, cycling, and running chapters

clearly shows the need for specificity in training. Strength gains from supplemental training are also specific to the exact muscles being trained. Therefore, a fast swimmer will not become faster by gaining strength using a supplemental program. However, athletes who need more strength for a sport will gain from a supplemental program. On the other hand, competitive and elite-level athletes' gains from supplemental training are again for supportive and postural training. Both are important to the overall program, but an athlete needs to understand that, for the most part, improvements come from training in the actual sport. There is little crossover from the weight room to swimming, biking, or running. Yet, when done appropriately, a supplemental training program can significantly improve performance, in particular, by increasing the intrinsic strength of the athlete, reducing the occurrence of injury due to overuse, and aiding in strengthening the postural/core muscles of the trunk, spine, and shoulders (see figs. 6.1 and 6.2).

The importance of supplemental exercise for the endurance athlete is aptly supported by David Martin and Peter Coe (1997) in *Better Training for Distance Runners, Second Edition:* "Such training can contribute to making the difference between winning and simply performing well, and between being injury-prone and injury-resistant"(281). This observation characterizes my feelings about supplemental training. However, athletes and coaches should

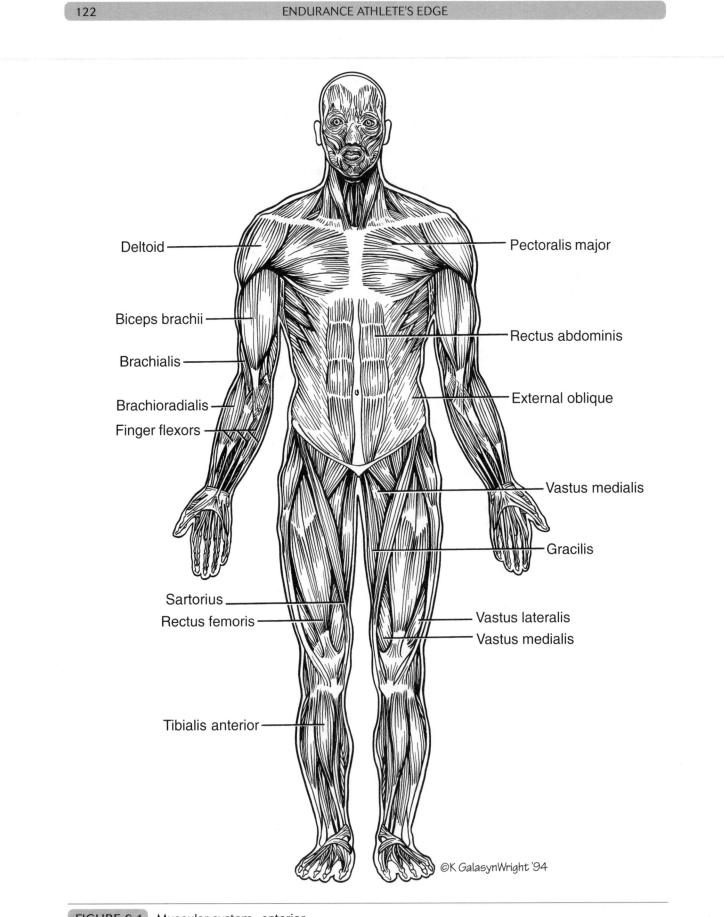

Deltoid

Biceps brachii

Brachialis

Brachioradialis

Finger flexors

Pectoralis major

Rectus abdominis

External oblique

Vastus medialis

Gracilis

Sartorius

Rectus femoris

Tibialis anterior

Vastus lateralis

Vastus medialis

©K GalasynWright '94

FIGURE 6.1 Muscular system—anterior.

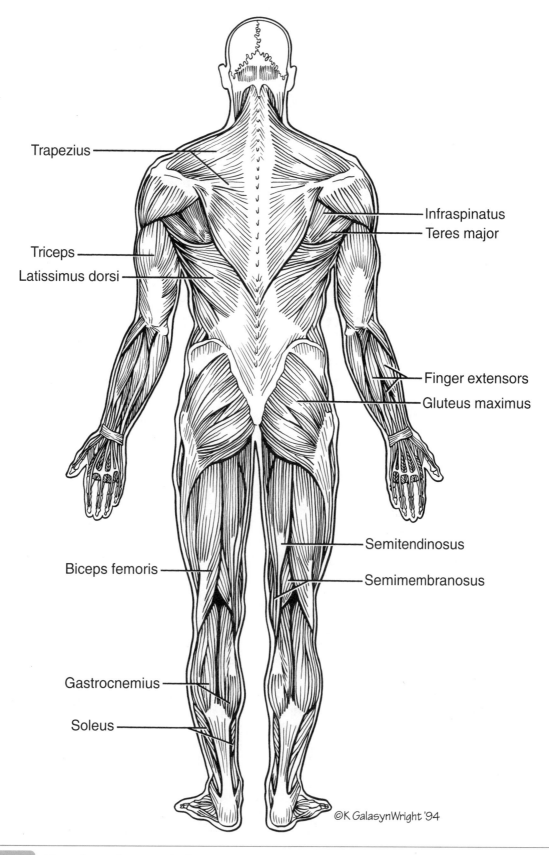

Trapezius

Infraspinatus
Teres major

Triceps
Latissimus dorsi

Finger extensors
Gluteus maximus

Semitendinosus

Semimembranosus

Biceps femoris

Gastrocnemius

Soleus

©K GalasynWright '94

FIGURE 6.2 Muscular system—posterior.

know about certain limitations before blindly beginning a supplemental program.

The supplemental training program outlined in this chapter includes flexibility training (stretching), isotonic (weight) training, calisthenics, plyometrics, and functional isokinetic training. Isometric training in which you use muscle tension against fixed objects is another effective supplemental training method, but it is not included here. This type of training is excellent for rehabilitation of specific areas of the body when full range of motion is not possible. Physical therapists often have helped injured athletes perform this type of strength work when it is not possible to train the entire muscle group.

IMPROVING YOUR STRENGTH, POWER, AND ENDURANCE

Strength is an athlete's capacity to use or resist force. The ability to lift, press, or curl a heavy weight is one example. Power is the consequence of both strength and muscle contraction (speed). In other words, how much weight can an athlete lift and how fast a contraction is an athlete capable of? Finally, muscular endurance is defined as an athlete's ability to perform successive contractions against resistance. Although the endurance athlete needs each of these capabilities, it remains important for supplemental training to be guided by the rules of right practice, specificity of practice, and intensity of practice outlined in chapter 1.

Briefly, flexibility training (stretching) helps increase range of motion and reduce muscle tension. Additionally, strength is improved through the proprioceptive neuromuscular facilitation (PNF) methods described later. Isotonic (weight) training reduces the occurrence of injury by strengthening musculoskeletal interdependence and increasing muscular endurance, power, and strength. Calisthenics increase muscular endurance and postural muscle strength. Plyometrics improve power, or the speed of muscle contractions. Finally, functional isokinetic training develops muscular endurance in a highly sport-specific manner.

The goal of these exercises is to develop whole-body training. As with all of the training systems in this book, the supplemental program integrates the training intensity zones described in chapter 1. Again, the purpose is to use the concept of effective periodization, or the muscular and cardiovascular overloading of stress and recovery, to develop optimum strength, power, endurance, and flexibility.

Each program described below is designed for a three-week rotation (periodization). Each week, there are changes in the total training time and the rest interval for each exercise, similar to what a typical swim, bike, or run training program advises. In other words, three weeks of buildup in volume and intensity are followed by a restoration period (recovery week).

Training Muscle Fibers

Muscles have four important characteristics:

1. *Elasticity,* or the ability to change length and stretch
2. *Extensibility,* or the ability to shorten and return to normal length
3. *Excitability,* or the capacity to respond to stimulation from the nervous system
4. *Contractility,* or the capability to contract in response to neural commands

Within each muscle are fast- and slow-twitch muscle fibers (plus additional subtypes). These fibers respond to commands for movement in opposite ways. Fast-twitch fibers respond by generating highly powerful forces or muscular contractions and have a low oxidative capacity (better for sprinters). Slow-twitch fibers respond most effectively to endurance activities and are highly oxidative. Genetics, not training, determines the ratios of these fibers in a person; that is, you cannot convert slow-twitch fibers to fast-twitch fibers or vice versa. However, you can enlarge each type of fiber through training, and you can train each type of fiber differently, depending on how you work the muscle.

For example, deliberate movements using heavy resistance and low repetitions result in training more fast-twitch fibers. These fibers are made up of metabolic and contractile qualities that respond to explosive, powerful movement. On the other hand, slow-twitch fibers are developed most effectively through high-repetition, low-resistance exercise such as swimming, cycling, or running. Slow-twitch fibers are slower to fatigue compared to fast-twitch fibers. In effect, fast-twitch fibers are more responsive to anaerobic activities (without oxygen), whereas slow-twitch fibers work best aerobically (in the presence of oxygen).

To get the greatest neuromuscular benefit from a supplemental training program, an athlete should be aware of the speed of the movements (contractions) for each exercise. Whenever possible, an athlete should try to exceed or match the limb and joint speeds for each sport. Similarly, an athlete should vary the velocities of exercise contractions to train greater numbers of muscle fibers and enhance nervous system adaptability.

Crossover Training

The rules of right practice, specificity of practice, and intensity of practice tell us training needs to be specific to competition to have the greatest benefit. Again, no amount of supplemental training will improve your swimming, cycling, or running better than actually doing those sports. Strength, power, and endurance can be advanced in sport-specific training, because VO_2 and LAC training are specific power and strength builders within your swimming, cycling, or running program. Swimming 16×50 meters at 95 to 100 percent effort with 1 to 3 minutes of rest trains fast-twitch muscle fibers, which translates to increased strength. The same can be said for cycling and running workouts of short duration, high intensity, and relatively high work-to-rest ratios.

Although supplemental exercises cannot be absolutely sport-specific, the more similarity to those used in competition, the greater the crossover effects of such training. In my opinion, any contribution to improving primary, synergist, stabilizer, and neutralizer muscle functions (roles different muscle have in various joint actions) along with strength, power, and flexibility will significantly affect endurance sport performance. That is exactly what this supplemental program does.

Again, although supplemental training is important, it does not replace specific training in each sport. Athletes who are relatively new to multisport endurance events should spend more time working on the actual sport. For the experienced endurance athlete, supplemental training can provide the competitive edge you are looking for.

FLEXIBILITY TRAINING

Every sport requires physical ranges of movement to be performed properly. There are obvious style and technical differences, but an athlete with superior range of movement for a particular sport will often outperform an athlete who lacks flexibility. These same athletes may have reversed roles in another sport. Often when we watch elite athletes in action, they make their event look effortless. Certainly, many seasons of training influence the fluidity and economy of movement of these athletes, but consistent flexibility training is also a factor.

Incorporate flexibility training into your schedule the same way regular workouts are performed. Set aside a prescribed time for it. Casually stretching before, during, and after workouts has some benefit, but it isn't going to improve performance significantly. Certainly, warming the muscles and tendons gently before stretching or working out lessens the likelihood of injury, and any stretching, when done correctly, is beneficial. However, I like my athletes to make flexibility exercise an actual "workout." This is an excellent example of a workout that can be done with a partner or in a group.

Benefits of Stretching

Proper stretching can reduce tension within the muscles, joints, ligaments, and tendons, warm muscles, reduce soreness, improve flexibility and range of motion, develop coordination skills, and help prevent injury by increasing muscle and connective tissue motion. Why should an endurance athlete stretch to improve flexibility? Tight muscles and tendons can limit effective range of motion and reduce performance. An inflexible endurance athlete, and there

THE REHABILITATION PROCESS

The five essential components to building a base preparatory phase or for rehabilitating an injury are as follows:

Flexibility—There is typically a loss in range of motion following injury. Flexibility is the first goal of rehabilitation and includes active, active-assisted, and passive joint range-of-motion techniques. Injured athletes tend to "guard" an injury for protection from further harm. In this regard, physical therapy and the qualified assistance of a therapist in the proper reintroduction of movement to the injured area are beneficial. Briefly stretching the injured area under the direction of a physician and physical therapist will hasten the recovery process.

Strength—The second goal of a rehabilitation program is to strengthen the injured area. This can be accomplished in several ways, depending on the history of the patient. The rehabilitation of an endurance athlete, for example, will likely be much different from that of a sedentary individual. The injured area needs to be taken through a progressive resistance program, avoiding reinjury through the use of isokinetic, isotonic, and isometric methods.

Endurance—The third goal of rehabilitation is increased muscular and cardiovascular aerobic endurance. This is accomplished by slowly progressing training load through swimming, cycling, resistance exercise, use of stair climbers or cross-country ski machines, and walking or running. The eventual goal is to return athletes to their competitive sport by training in supplemental sports during rehabilitation.

Proprioception—The fourth goal of rehabilitation is regaining proprioception or the application of balance of the muscular system. This is done using devices such as balance boards for training and testing the muscles' ability to regain balance capacity.

Agility and skill—The fifth rehabilitation goal is agility and skill training. Such training fine-tunes the athlete for the eventual return to competition.

are thousands, is susceptible to muscle injury and has less power due to decreased range of movement (eccentric and concentric contractility).

Stretching before and after training and competition is one method of flexibility training. However, although stretching may help warm the muscles beforehand and reduce posttraining soreness, over the long run it will not improve flexibility the way a more deliberate stretching program will. A planned stretching workout improves the body's response to a training load (range of motion). This translates to improvement in range of motion of the specific muscles to be used in competition.

As a general rule, for swimming, stretch the shoulder, triceps, deltoid, latissimus dorsi, neck, and finger muscles a few minutes before entering the water. Then, after a warm-up, stretch those muscles again. Before a running workout, always warm up gently and then stretch the major running muscles (gastrocnemius/soleus, hamstring, hip flexors, etc.). For cycling, stretch the entire body lightly for a few minutes beforehand.

For the more structured stretching program detailed later in this chapter, the athlete should stretch after the day's workouts have been completed. In this case, it is not necessary to warm up. The athlete's muscles, tendons, and ligaments will already be warm from the preceding workouts. Stretching is an important part of your training program, so allow ample time. Flexibility and proprioceptive neuromuscular facilitation exercises for weeks 1, 2, and 3 require 9, 10, and 12.5 minutes separately. Stretch five to seven days a week throughout your training season. Isotonic (weight) training exercises in weeks 1, 2, and 3 require approximately 45, 56, and 70 minutes to complete the program. Calisthenics, with 17 exercises, requires 25, 31, and 37 minutes for weeks 1, 2, and 3, respectively. Plyometrics, with only three exercises, requires just 3, 4.5, and 5 minutes for weeks 1, 2, and 3. Last, functional isokinetics, with nine exercises, requires about 12, 15, and 17.5 minutes in weeks 1, 2, and 3.

In table 6.1, I have outlined the durations for each stretch on a three-week cycle. This will correspond to the periodization in the program and the step-up from weeks 1 through 3. In the fourth week, a restoration week, stretching is done, but without the structure shown in the table. Again, this fourth week is for physiological and psychological restoration. Therefore, this week is not structured, except that stretching is done five to seven times.

TABLE 6.1   Flexibility and PNF Method Exercises

	Exercise	Week 1 time	Week 1 sets	Week 2 time	Week 2 sets	Week 3 time	Week 3 sets
1.	Side stretch	00:10	2	00:15	2	00:20	2
2.	Hip flexors I, kneeling	00:15	3	00:20	2	00:25	2
3.	Hip flexors II, lunge	00:20	1	00:25	1	00:30	1
4.	Quadriceps I, under	00:20	1	00:25	1	00:30	1
5.	Quadriceps II, kneeling	00:20	1	00:25	1	00:30	1
6.	Hamstrings I, sitting	00:15	3	00:20	2	00:25	2
7.	Iliotibial band (ITB) I, standing	00:20	1	00:25	1	00:30	1
8.	Iliotibial band (ITB) II, floor	00:20	1	00:25	1	00:30	1
9.	Gluteals/hips, sitting	00:15	3	00:20	2	00:25	2
10.	Hip external rotation	00:15	3	00:20	2	00:25	2
11.	Achilles tendon and soleus	00:20	1	00:25	1	00:30	1
12.	Shoulder flexors PNF	00:10	2	00:15	2	00:20	2
13.	Shoulder extensors PNF	00:10	2	00:15	2	00:20	2
14.	Triceps PNF	00:15	3	00:20	2	00:25	2
15.	Shoulders PNF	00:15	3	00:20	2	00:25	2
16.	Hamstrings II, lying PNF	00:20	1	00:25	1	00:30	1
17.	Ankle flexors PNF	00:10	2	00:15	2	00:20	2
18.	Ankle extensors PNF	00:10	2	00:15	2	00:20	2
19.	Quadriceps III, wall PNF	00:20	1	00:25	1	00:30	1

Frequency and Duration of Stretching

The athlete will spend 9, 10, and 12.5 minutes stretching in any one session, depending on the week periodization (week 1, 2, or 3).

Base preparation: Five to seven sessions per week

Base transition: Five to seven sessions per week

Race preparation: Five to seven sessions per week

Peak transition: Five to seven sessions per week

Dynamic Versus PNF Stretching

Flexibility is specific to certain muscle groups. In other words, having flexible ankles does not ensure flexibility in your shoulders. Additionally, one shoulder or ankle can be more or less flexible than the other. The type of flexibility endurance athletes use in sport-specific training and competitions is dynamic flexibility; that is, they move their joints through a variety of motions and speeds.

Dynamic flexibility is important, as it relates to the range of motion an athlete is capable of during athletic movements. Once a muscle has contracted, if restrictive limitations to this specific range of motion exist, poor performances are likely. For example, having the massive physique of a competitive bodybuilder would limit the optimal ranges of motion necessary for swimming, cycling, and running. This is evident when watching bodybuilders perform just about any routine motion, but is particularly noticeable during endurance activities that require repetitive muscle contractions.

Dynamic stretches are those that increase the ranges of motion needed to improve specific athletic performance. In swimming, poor ankle and shoulder flexibility hinder performance by decreasing technique and increasing energy expenditure due to increased drag. For cycling, strong, flexible postural muscles help stabilize the endurance athlete for extended training and competitions. Running is improved significantly with increases in hip flexor range of motion.

Proprioceptive neuromuscular facilitation is a rehabilitation and stretching technique developed in the 1950s. PNF stretching increases muscle length and range of movement through isometrically assisted (against an immovable object) stretching. Not only does PNF increase flexibility and help in injury rehabilitation, it also improves muscular strength. There are several PNF stretching techniques, but for simplicity and effectiveness, I will describe only one.

The PNF method I use is the contract-relax technique and is done as follows:

1. The athlete should be warmed up.
2. A partner, towel, or stretch band is needed to perform each stretch.
3. The athlete relaxes the muscle to be stretched.
4. The partner applies pressure to slowly lengthen (stretch) the muscle.
5. When limitation of stretch is felt, the athlete contracts (pushes) the muscle against the force (isometric hold) of the partner for 5 seconds.
6. The athlete relaxes and then the partner restretches the muscle until limitation is felt again.
7. These steps are repeated until progression of the stretch appears to be minimal.

Dynamic and PNF Flexibility Exercises

The following flexibility exercises are organized with the dynamic stretches first followed by the PNF stretches. Once again, working through the exercises with a training group or partner is helpful and can provide valuable and much-needed socialization for the endurance athlete. The first time or two through the exercises may seem difficult, but you'll quickly achieve the skill and dexterity to do each of them correctly.

Side Stretch

This prestretch/exercise and warm-up is particularly useful before competition swim starts (stretches the latissimus dorsi, shoulders, triceps, ITB, lower back, and hip flexors). Standing with your left arm down at your side, bend to your left from the waist while raising your right hand above your head to a full extension. Do three to four stretches on each side with your hand open, then lightly closed. A variation for this exercise would be to place your hands on your hips.

FIGURE 6.3   Side stretch.

Hip Flexors I, Kneeling (Stomach and Ankle Extensors)

Kneeling, put both hands on your lower back and lean slowly backward while pushing your hips forward (tightening your buttocks). Lay your head back and exhale while sliding your hands onto your heels. Then return to the starting position by lowering your chin back toward your chest. Use a cushion for your knees, and have a partner stabilize you, if necessary.

Hip Flexors II, Lunge

Standing with both hands on your buttocks, lunge forward with your right leg. Keeping your left heel down, gently push the buttocks forward. Repeat with the other leg.

FIGURE 6.4   Hip flexors.

Quadriceps I, Under

Lie on the floor on your back and move your right leg under your flexed left leg (sole of foot on floor). Grasp your right foot and slowly stretch (pull) your heel toward your buttocks. A PNF stretch is easily done as your hand applies pressure in the direction opposite the stretch for 5 seconds. Then relax and stretch the muscle fully. Repeat on the other side.

Quadriceps II, Kneeling

Starting in a lunge position with your weight on your right knee, brace yourself with your right hand on the floor. Grasp your right foot with your left hand and pull your heel into your buttocks, moving in small increments to a point of stretch. Next, press your foot against your hand (PNF) for 5 seconds, then pull your heel into your buttocks again. Repeat with your other leg.

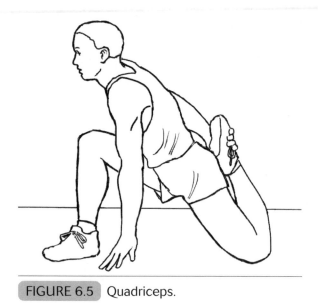

FIGURE 6.5 Quadriceps.

Hamstrings II, Sitting

Sit on the floor with your left leg straight and your right leg flexed, with your right heel resting against the inside of your left leg. Gently grasp your left thigh with both hands and slowly slide your hands down your leg, arching your head downward toward your thigh while exhaling. Flex and extend your ankle as you do this stretch. Don't bounce. Repeat on the other side.

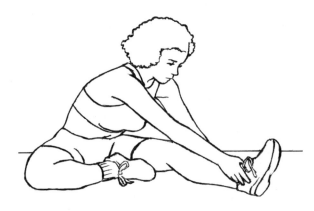

FIGURE 6.6 Hamstrings.

Iliotibial Band (ITB) I, Standing

Stand with your left hand on your left hip and your right hand over your head. Cross your left foot over your right foot. With your left hand, push your hip sideways as your right hand and arm stretch overhead. Repeat on the other side. A second way to do this exercise, which may be more effective for those who have ITB syndrome, is to bring your left foot 12 to 24 inches behind your right leg. You'll need to hold onto a table or counter. Then roll into your left hip and stretch the length of your ITB.

Iliotibial Band (ITB) II, Floor

In a supine position on the floor, place your flexed left leg over your straight right leg. Your right hand should be atop your left knee and gently pressing downward. Your left arm should be outstretched from the shoulder.

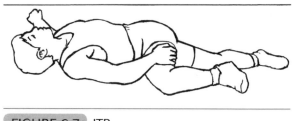

FIGURE 6.7 ITB.

Repeat on the other side. Straightening the cross-over leg for some may add to this stretch.

Gluteals/Hips, Sitting

Sit upright on the floor with your left leg crossed under your right leg (knee touching the floor). Steady yourself with your left hand on the floor. Place your right hand on or toward your right ankle. Exhale slowly, bending down toward your left knee. Relax and repeat on the other side.

Hip External Rotation

Lie on your back with your knees bent (feet flat on the floor). Lift your right ankle onto the front of your left upper thigh. Hold your right ankle with your left hand and push against your right knee. A PNF stretch can also be used here by pressing your knee against the resistance of your hand. Repeat on the other side.

FIGURE 6.8 Gluteal and hips.

Achilles Tendon and Soleus

Stand with your feet together, 2 to 4 feet from a wall (hands on wall at shoulder height). Step backward with your right leg (heel down). Move your hips forward and downward to achieve the stretch.

FIGURE 6.9 Achilles and soleus.

Shoulder Flexors PNF (A and B)

This works better as a partner stretch but can be done alone using a wall, stretch band, or simply as a slow, active stretch. Place both hands behind and away from your back with palms facing upward. The direction of the stretch is upward in stretch *a* and downward in stretch

b. Follow the directions for PNF application below:

1. Standing or sitting, place both hands behind your back.
2. Relax the muscle to be stretched.
3. Apply pressure against your partner's hands in the *opposite* direction of the stretch. Your partner should maintain resistance during the 5-second contraction.
4. After 5 seconds, relax the muscle as your partner moves the muscle in the stretch direction.
5. Continue repetitions until the range-of-movement limit in the stretch direction seems to have been reached or you feel discomfort.

Shoulder Extensors PNF (A and B)

This also is an effective partner stretch. Sit on the floor or in a chair and raise both hands and arms together straight overhead. Your partner will apply the PNF resistance in the opposite direction of the stretch. The direction of the

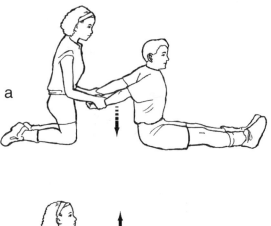
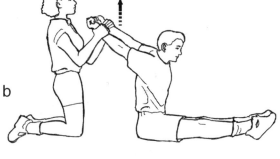

FIGURE 6.10 Shoulders (*a* and *b*).

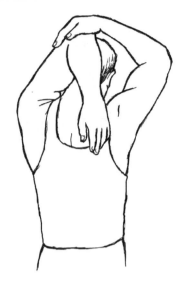

FIGURE 6.11   Triceps.

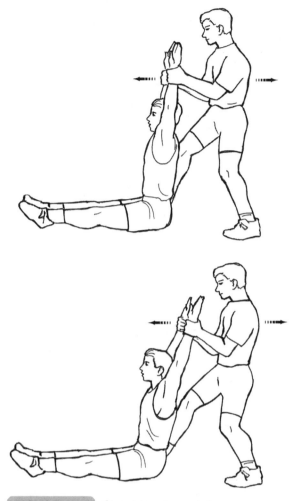

FIGURE 6.10   Shoulders (c and d).

stretch is backward in stretch *a* and forward in stretch *b*. Follow the directions for PNF application as in the shoulder flexors.

Note: Stretch *a* can be done easily using a stretch band connected to a wall or doorknob to apply the PNF.

Shoulders PNF

Starting with your arms held straight in front of your body, hold your right elbow by locking it in your left forearm. Pull your right shoulder away from your left hand for 5 seconds (PNF). Relax and then stretch the muscle in the opposite direction, pulling across your chest. Repeat with your other arm.

Triceps PNF

Sit or stand with your arms straight overhead. Bend your left arm at the elbow and, with your right hand, grasp your elbow behind your neck. Press your elbow against your hand for 5 seconds (PNF), then relax and stretch the muscle in the opposite direction by pulling downward. Repeat with your other arm.

Hamstrings I, Lying PNF

Connect a stretch band to the bottom of your right foot and lie on your back. Keeping both legs straight, pull your right leg up toward your chest until you feel a moderate stretch reflex. Resist the band with your foot (PNF) for 5 seconds and relax. Once again, pull the extended leg toward your chest to full range. Repeat with your left leg.

Ankle Flexors PNF

From a sitting position with legs extended together in front, place a towel or stretch band (or have your partner apply pressure) around the ball of your feet. Press (PNF) your feet away from your body for 5 seconds. Relax and stretch your ankles in the opposite direction (dorsiflexion). Repeat.

a

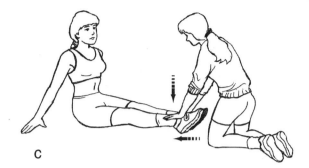

c

b

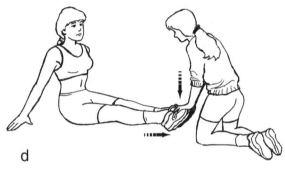

d

FIGURE 6.12   Ankle flexors (*a* and *b*); extensors (*c* and *d*).

Ankle Extensors PNF

From a sitting position with your legs extended together in front, have your partner apply downward pressure by pushing on the tops of your feet. Pull up (PNF) against your partner's hands for 5 seconds. Relax and then have your partner stretch the ankle in the opposite direction (toes pointed—plantar flexion). Repeat.

Quadriceps III, Wall PNF

Stand facing the wall, approximately 1 foot away, with your right hand on the wall for balance. Reach behind your body and hold your right foot with your left hand. Press your foot into your hand for 5 seconds, applying PNF. Relax, then restretch the quadriceps by pulling upward toward your buttocks. Repeat with your other leg.

ISOTONIC TRAINING

Isotonic contractions are those in which the muscle generates force as a result of resistance. This resistance causes the muscle to change length in two ways. The first is concentric contraction, where the muscle contracts (shortens) as in lifting or curling. The second is eccentric contraction, in which the muscle lengthens as a result of lowering or extending an object (weight, body, etc.). Isotonics can include more than lifting weight, and as a later section on plyometrics shows, the body also can be used isotonically. In fact, swimming, cycling, and running are other forms of isotonic contraction. For example, a runner uses concentric muscle contraction at the footstrike and eccentric contraction during the pushoff.

Benefits of Isotonic Training

Isotonic training is used foremost by endurance athletes I coach for injury prevention by strengthening tendons and muscles. But isotonic training is also beneficial for strengthening the postural muscles of the spine, shoulders, and trunk or for maintaining strength. Again, never allow this or any of the supplemental training disciplines to interfere with sport-specific training. Fatigue resulting from supplemental training can extend into sport-specific training. In this case, movements, technique, and skills can diminish. Strength gains provide limited benefit to the endurance athlete. Beyond this point, attempts to improve strength may only compromise sport performance. Muscle hypertrophy (increase in muscle size) may be detrimental to the endurance athlete when those gains are beyond what is necessary to the sport. To work optimally, large muscles require corresponding and proportional oxidative capacities. Therefore, the endurance athlete's weight training should be developed with the goal of bringing about the strength needed for competition, no more.

Establishing the proper level of strength for any discipline is difficult for endurance athletes. However, the athlete must first focus on performance in each respective sport. For example, poor swimmers with large muscles don't need more strength. I recently watched two triathletes swimming in the lane next to mine. Both were heavily muscled in the upper body and needed significant rest after each interval before the next repeat. As noted in previous chapters, high-intensity and long rest intervals such as the VO_2 and LAC training intensity zones train more anaerobic pathways. In effect, these poor swimmers were increasing strength, whereas more concentration on short rest intervals and technique, in particular, propelling efficiency (S-shaped curvilinear strokes), would be more beneficial.

Although each of the following exercises uses slightly different techniques and movements, they all share several lifting technique characteristics. Most of the following tips are related to preventing back injury while lifting weights. I encourage you to follow them closely and to wear a back support belt, use moderate weight (weight you can control), and take extra care with each exercise.

- Lift the weight mostly with your legs, keeping your back straight.
- Keep the weight close to your body.
- Stand with your feet at least shoulder-width apart.
- Keep your back in alignment (straight) with your head and your chin up.
- Lift the weight smoothly; don't jerk it into position.
- Breathe in during the lifting phase.

YEAR-ROUND WEIGHT TRAINING

Should you weight train all year? There is no simple answer to this question, but I will try to be brief. First, I have my athletes do supplemental training all year round and especially during the base preparation phase. Three to four weeks before major competitions, discontinue isotonic training. I have most athletes do one weight training (isotonic) session per week at any time of the year. Sometimes, when an athlete needs to gain strength, I will recommend two sessions. The rest of the supplemental training program consists of calisthenics, plyometrics, isokinetics, and stretching. Strength can be maintained by decreasing the frequency of training sessions during the race preparatory phase. In other words, weight training every two weeks or so will keep your strength up and not detract from performance.

Frequency and Duration of Isotonic Training

The athlete will spend 45, 56, and 70 minutes in any one session, depending on the week periodization (week 1, 2, or 3).

Base preparation: One to two sessions per week

Base transition: One to two sessions per week (small reduction in volume)

Race preparation: One to two sessions per week, but none three to four weeks prior to important competitions

Peak transition: None

Endurance athletes need one or two isotonic training sessions each week. Any more than that will likely detract from specificity in training. One session each week will maintain all the strength and connective tissue benefits an endurance athlete needs. For the most part, weight training is continued throughout the season but is discontinued during restoration, three or four weeks before important event and peak transitions. Isotonic training should always follow the sport-specific training. To do otherwise only diminishes specific training effects, as fatigue from isotonic training will bring about changes in technique in the primary sports.

Isotonic Weight Training Exercises

Refer to table 6.2 for the repetitions, sets, and rest intervals for the following exercises. Remember to apply proper techniques as described earlier and use moderate weights at first.

TABLE 6.2 Isotonic: Weight Training Exercises

	Exercise	Training zone	Wk1 reps & % RM	Weight	Wk1 rest	Wk1 sets	Wk2 reps & % RM	Weight	Wk2 rest	Wk2 sets
1.	Side bends	LVT	20+35		00:10	3	25+40		00:15	3-4
2.	Wrist curls	LVT	20+35		00:10	3	25+40		00:15	3-4
3.	Clean and press	LVT	20+35		00:10	3	25+40		00:15	3-4
4.	Upright row	VO$_2$	15+60		00:20	3	12+65		00:25	3
5.	Triceps kickbacks	LAC	8+80		00:30	3	6+85		00:45	3
6.	Triceps extensions	LAC	8+80		00:30	3	6+85		00:45	3
7.	Two-arm curl	VO$_2$	15+60		00:20	3	12+65		00:25	3
8.	Bench press	VO$_2$	15+60		00:20	3	12+65		00:25	3
9.	Lat pull-downs	VO$_2$	15+60		00:20	3	12+65		00:25	3
10.	Lateral arm raises	VO$_2$	15+60		00:20	3	12+65		00:25	3
11.	Calf raises	LVT	15+60		00:10	3	25+40		00:15	3-4
12.	Lunges	LVT	20+35		00:10	3	25+40		00:15	3-4
13.	Half squats	VO$_2$	15+60		00:20	3	12+65		00:25	3
14.	Hamstring curls	LAC	8+80		00:30	3	6+85		00:45	3

DETERMINING THE AMOUNT OF WEIGHT TO LIFT

You can determine how much weight to lift by using an estimator called the repetition maximum (RM). In the isotonic program detailed in this chapter, the exercises are executed using weights determined by a percentage of your RM. Your RM is determined after warming up in the exercise you'll be testing. For example, the bench press is performed for two sets of 12 to 15 repetitions with 2 minutes of rest between sets. The weight should be easily manageable for the purpose of loosening up the muscles. Once you have warmed up thoroughly, estimate and place on the bar or machine the amount of weight you believe you can bench press one time only. If you're not sure, estimate the amount based on the warm-up weight you used. Make sure to have someone spot the weight when attempting the one RM. Then make your best effort to lift the weight. If you don't make the lift, that's okay. You can attempt to lift a slightly lower weight or, more practically, choose a more conservative weight and use it as your RM.

Side Bends

Stand tall with your feet 6 inches apart. Holding a dumbbell in one hand with your other hand on your hip, bend to the weight side.

Option: Use a barbell on your shoulders and bend to each side.

Major muscles exercised: Lateral trunk flexors.

Wrist Curls (Extension and Flexion)

Kneel on the floor in front of a bench, holding a dumbbell in one hand. Lay your forearm on the bench so your wrist and hand are over the edge. First, with the palm down, flex your wrist downward and then extend it upward. Second, with the palm up, extend your wrist downward and flex it upward. You can also try these wrist curls while seated on a bench by placing your forearms on your legs, weight in hands. Stretch bands can also be used for this exercise.

Major muscles exercised: Flexor carpi radialis, flexor carpi ulnaris, and forearm extensors and flexors.

Clean and Press

Grasping the bar with your hands shoulder-width apart (knees inside of arms), lift the bar bell off the floor. Slowly stand upright using your legs to lift the weight until it is just below your hips (arms straight). Now clean (lift) the weight to your chest and pause for one count, then press overhead for another count. Keep the shoulder-width stance during the entire movement. If you need to move your feet or adjust your stance, the weight is too great. Return the weight to your chest, then your hips, and then lower it to the floor. It is important to keep your back straight while lifting.

Major muscles exercised: Quadriceps, gluteus maximus, erector spinae (back), abdominals and hip flexors, deltoids, trapezius, biceps, and radial flexors.

Upright Row

Begin by gripping the bar with an overhand grip. Your hands should be close together and your arms extended. Your back should be straight. Clean the weight to your hips, then lift the bar to your chin, keeping your elbows high and the bar near your body. Slowly lower the bar to your hips; pause and repeat according to the sequence described in table 6.2.

Major muscles exercised: Trapezius (upper back), deltoids, biceps, brachialis (lateral biceps), and brachioradialis (forearm).

Triceps Kickbacks

While standing, bend at the waist to 90 degrees. With a dumbbell in one hand and supporting your body with the other, let the weight hang straight down. Now curl the weight to your biceps. Kick the weight down and back, extending your triceps fully (your arm will be parallel with the floor). After completing the indicated repetitions, repeat with your other arm.

Major muscles exercised: Triceps (brachii long and lateral head) and radial flexors.

Triceps Extensions

Using an overhand grip, with 10 inches between your hands, place the bar across your neck and shoulders. Your elbows should be close to your head and pointing forward. Press (extend) your arms overhead to a full extension, then lower them back to your shoulders for the duration of the set.

Major muscles exercised: Extensors of the arms (triceps, brachii long, and lateral head).

Two-Arm Curl

Standing upright, sitting, or from an inclined position (incline bench), use either a curling bar or a pair of dumbbells. With an underhand grip, lift the weight to your hips. Keeping your elbows still and close to your body, curl your arms to chest and shoulder height.

Major muscles exercised: Biceps, radial flexors, and brachioradialis.

Bench Press

From a supine position on the bench, with hands gripped shoulder-width apart, press the bar overhead. Inhale and then lower the bar to your chest, touching lightly, pause for a moment, and then press again.

Major muscles exercised: Pectoralis major, deltoid, and triceps brachii.

Lat Pull-Downs (Using Lat Machine or Overhead Stretch Band Connection)

Using a wide overhand grip (seated or kneeling), pull the bar down behind your neck. Extend your arms to the starting position. Do not pull a weight that lifts you off the bench or floor.

Major muscles exercised: Latissimus dorsi, biceps, trapezius, and brachioradialis.

Lateral Arm Raises

With a dumbbell in each hand, stand with your feet shoulder-width apart and your arms extended at your sides, palms inward. Keeping your arms extended, raise them sideways until the weights are even with your head. Lower to the starting position and repeat. Your arms should be straight throughout the movement.

Major muscles exercised: Deltoids (shoulders) and supraspinatus.

Calf Raises

Perform this exercise with a barbell across your shoulders or dumbbells in each hand at your sides and your feet 8 inches apart. Raise up onto your toes to a maximum extension, holding for a count of three. Slowly lower to the starting position.

Major muscles exercised: Gastrocnemius and soleus.

Lunges

Holding a barbell on your shoulders or dumbbells in each hand, stand upright in a ready position with your hands at your sides. Lunge forward with one leg, bending until the quadriceps are nearly parallel with the floor. Return to the starting position (spring back gently) and repeat with your other leg. Keep your back straight, and use a weight that allows you to maintain control.

Major muscles exercised: quadriceps, gluteus maximus, and hamstrings.

Half Squats

Place a barbell on your shoulders, gripping it with your hands at shoulder width. Your feet should be a little more than shoulder-width apart, and your heels should be raised 1 or 2 inches (use a piece of wood or two 5-pound weights under each heel to maintain stability). Squat halfway down, keeping your back straight and your knees aligned with your big toes. Do not lean too far forward. Beginners may want to use a bench between the legs and a waist belt for added protection.

Major muscles exercised: Extensors of the thigh, quadriceps, gluteus maximus, hamstrings, and erector spinae (back).

Hamstring Curls

Perform this exercise on the hamstring or leg curl machine in the prone position. Flex your knee, bringing your foot toward your buttocks, then return slowly to the starting position.

Major muscles exercised: Hamstrings and gluteus maximus.

CALISTHENIC TRAINING

The athletes I coach say the calisthenic program is the hardest workout they do but also the most fun. Some may remember calisthenics as those simple exercises we used to do in grade school. Calisthenics are meant to provide a vigorous and comprehensive body-conditioning workout.

Benefits of Calisthenics

Group training in calisthenics is a change of pace many endurance athletes could use. These exercises are tough, and the conditioning benefits are numerous. Working through these exercises with a group of friends is good for morale. They provide injury protection as well as increases in tensile strength, flexion, extension, and shock absorption capacities of the muscles.

Calisthenics condition intrinsic muscles such as those used in stabilization. Finally, calisthenics develop the muscular coordination, timing, and rhythm so sorely needed by many endurance athletes. Involving many energy and muscular systems, calisthenics strengthen the muscles of the spine, shoulders, and trunk. The program that follows is an energetic and substantial cardiovascular workout as well.

Frequency and Duration of Calisthenics

The athlete will spend 25, 31, and 37 minutes in any one calisthenic session, depending on the week periodization (week 1, 2, or 3).

Base preparation: Two to three sessions per week

Base transition: One to two sessions per week

Race preparation: One session per week (none three weeks before competitions)

Peak transition: None

As with each supplemental discipline, calisthenic training is adjusted with the season periodization. The purpose of these adjustments, described earlier, is to allow adequate rest from sport-specific training. The athlete should follow the program outlined in table 6.3 for a three-week periodization. The durations of exercise and rest and number of sets are indicated. There is no calisthenic training during restoration weeks.

TABLE 6.3   Calisthenic Exercises

	Exercise	Training zone	Wk1 time	Wk1 rest	Wk1 sets	Wk2 time	Wk2 rest	Wk2 sets	Wk3 time	Wk3 rest
1.	Abdominal crunches	LVT	00:25	00:10	3	00:30	00:10	3	00:40	00:10
2.	Abdominal twists	LVT	00:25	00:10	3	00:30	00:10	3	00:40	00:10
3.	Abdominal V-ups	LVT	00:25	00:10	3	00:30	00:10	3	00:40	00:10
4.	Abdominal R and L	LVT	00:25	00:10	3	00:30	00:10	3	00:40	00:10
5.	Two-leg laterals	VO_2	00:15	00:15	2	00:20	00:20	2	00:25	00:20
6.	Back raises	VO_2	00:15	00:15	2	00:20	00:20	2	00:25	00:20
7.	Push-ups	VO_2	00:15	00:15	2	00:20	00:20	2	00:25	00:20
8.	Push-ups inclines	LAC	00:10	00:20	2	00:30	00:15	2	00:20	00:30

	Exercise	Training zone	Wk 1 time	Wk 1 rest	Wk1 sets	Wk 2 time	Wk 2 rest	Wk2 sets	Wk 3 time	Wk 3 rest
9.	Mountain climbers	LVT	00:25	00:10	3	00:30	00:10	3	00:40	00:10
10.	Squat scissors	LVT	00:25	00:10	3	00:30	00:10	3	00:40	00:10
11.	Tele arc squats	LVT	00:25	00:10	3	00:30	00:10	3	00:40	00:10
12.	Toe/calf raises	LVT	00:25	00:10	3	00:30	00:10	3	00:40	00:10
13.	Walking lunges	LVT	00:25	00:10	3	00:30	00:10	3	00:40	00:10
14.	Dips (seated push-ups)	LVT	00:25	00:10	3	00:30	00:10	3	00:40	00:10
15.	Bench step-ups	LVT	00:25	00:10	3	00:30	00:10	3	00:40	00:10
16.	Tri squats	VO_2	00:15	00:15	2	00:20	00:20	2	00:25	00:20
17.	Chin-ups	LAC	00:10	00:20	2	00:15	00:30	2	00:20	00:30

Calisthenic Exercises

I recommend you go through these exercises one at a time. This rehearsal will familiarize you with the movements for a better workout routine. Again, these are great exercises to do with a partner. Play some good music and have someone responsible for keeping time and leading each exercise.

Abdominal Crunches

From a supine position, raise your feet 6 inches off the floor (legs can be straight or knees bent) with ankles crossed. Place your hands with fingertips lightly touching behind your head, keeping your elbows parallel with the floor. Keep the lower part of your back flat on the floor. Movement is begun from the lower abdomen and lower back. Raise up 6 to 8 inches off the floor and lower yourself back down (not quite all the way to the floor). Do slow, controlled repetitions, focusing on contracting and relaxing the abdominal muscles.

Major muscles exercised: Rectus abdominis, internal and external obliques, and lumbodorsal fascia of lower back.

Abdominal Twists

Use the same starting position and movement as for the abdominal crunch, with the addition of touching your right elbow to your left knee and then your left elbow to your right knee.

Major muscles exercised: Rectus abdominis, internal and external obliques, and lumbodorsal fascia of the lower back.

Abdominal V-Ups

From a supine position (lying on your back), with your hands/elbows on the floor overhead

FIGURE 6.13 Abdominal V-ups.

© Jeffrey Dow

and your feet 12 inches apart, raise your legs and arms simultaneously (keeping them straight) until your hands touch your knees. Next, lower your legs toward the floor (not quite all the way) and hold for 2 seconds, then return your feet to the floor.

Major muscles exercised: Rectus abdominis, internal and external obliques, and lumbodorsal fascia of the lower back, as well as the tensor facial latae (hip flexors).

Abdominal R and L (Right Arm, Left Leg Up)

Lying on your back with both arms stretched overhead, raise your left leg and right arm and touch your right knee with your left hand. Repeat on the other side (right leg, left arm). The back should have a gentle C shape.

Major muscles exercised: Rectus abdominis, internal and external obliques, and lumbodorsal fascia of the lower back, as well as the tensor facial latae (hip flexors).

Two-Leg Laterals (Raises)

Lie on your side with your head resting on your outstretched arm and shoulder. Place your feet on top of one another. Raise both legs together laterally 4 to 8 inches off the floor. Hold for a count of three and lower your legs to the floor. After a set of repetitions on the one side, repeat for the other side.

Major muscles exercised: External abdominis (obliques), hip abductors and adductors, lateral trunk muscles, hip flexors, gluteus maximus, iliotibial band, and lower back muscles.

Back Raises

Lying on your stomach with your hands locked behind your head, arch your back upward, raising your shoulders and chest 4 to 6 inches off the floor. Hold this position for 2 to 3 seconds.

Major muscles exercised: Erector spinae, gluteus maximus, hamstrings, and abdominal muscles.

FIGURE 6.15   Back raises.

Push-Ups

Lie prone, supporting your weight on your hands and toes (or knees). Your back should be straight and your head facing forward diagonally. Your hands should be slightly more than shoulder-width apart. Lower your chest to the floor and then raise it.

Major muscles exercised: Arm extensors and shoulder flexors.

Push-Up Inclines

Use the same position and movements as above, except place your feet on a bench. Start

FIGURE 6.14   Two-leg laterals.

with a low bench height, then move on to more challenging levels.

Major muscles exercised: Arm extensors and shoulder flexors.

FIGURE 6.16   Push-up inclines.

Mountain Climbers

Start in a squatting position with your right leg extended and your left leg under your chest. Now switch leg positions (right leg under chest, left leg extended). The cadence of this exercise should be fast as your left and right legs move forward and backward.

Major muscles exercised: Extensors and flexors of the knee and hip.

FIGURE 6.17   Mountain climbers.

Squat Scissors

Place your hands on your hips (hips forward) and keep your eyes looking forward. Put your left foot 12 inches ahead of your right foot, then hop (scissors fashion) back and forth, hopping only high enough to get your feet off the ground. Keep your knees slightly flexed.

Major muscles exercised: Anterior thigh muscles (rectus femoris, vastus medialis and lateralis), gluteus, hamstring extensors, and hip extensors.

FIGURE 6.18   Squat scissors.

Tele Arc Squats

Standing with your hands on your hips, step forward with your right leg until the heel of your left foot is 2 to 3 inches off the floor. It is important that your weight be equally distributed on your right and left feet. Your right foot should be flat, and you should be up on the ball and toes of your left foot (weight balanced equally). From this position, squat down slowly until the front of your left tibia is parallel with the floor. Keep your knee aligned with your big toe as you squat (head and back erect), then raise upward to nearly full extension. Remember to keep the middle of your knee in line with your big toe both going down and coming up, and make sure your weight is always equally distributed on both feet. Switch to the other side and repeat.

Major muscles exercised: The patellar tendons, anterior thigh muscles, and gluteal and hip extensors.

© Jeffrey Dow

FIGURE 6.19 Tele arc squats.

© Jeffrey Dow

FIGURE 6.20 Walking lunges.

© Jeffrey Dow

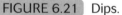

FIGURE 6.21 Dips.

Toe/Calf Raises

Stand with your hands on your hips and your feet 3 inches apart. Raise upward, fully flexing up onto your toes, then lower slowly. Add weight or use stretch bands connected to the floor for more resistance as needed.

  Major muscles exercised: Gastrocnemius and soleus.

Walking Lunges

Stand with your hands on your hips. Take an extended step forward on one leg, keeping the opposite leg extended backward. Walk forward with the opposite leg, squatting slightly, and reverse the motion to return to the starting position.

  Major muscles exercised: Quadriceps, gluteus maximus, and hamstrings.

Dips (Seated Push-Ups)

Use a dipping bar or two facing chairs. With chairs, use a supine position with your heels

on one chair and your hands supported on the other. Dip down and press up.

  Major muscles exercised: Triceps, anterior shoulder and chest muscles, and upper back muscles.

Bench Step-Ups

Stand facing a sturdy bench or chair with your hands on your hips. Step onto the bench one foot at a time, then step off one foot at a time. Repeat on the other side. Variations include using one leg in sets of 5 to 10+ or standing sideways to the bench and using stretch band or weights (dumbbells) for added resistance.

© Jeffrey Dow

FIGURE 6.22   Bench step-ups.

Major muscles exercised: Anterior thigh extensors (quadriceps) and gluteus maximus extensors.

Tri Squats

Start by standing with your feet together, then squat down into a ball and place your hands on the floor. Next, kick both feet straight backward (you are now in the push-up position). Then spread (kick) your feet outward (spread eagle) and then inward. Next, hop forward to the ball position, then return to the starting position.

Major muscles exercised: Extensors of the spine, hips, knees, and ankle; abdominal adductors and abductors.

Chin-Ups

Grasp a chinning bar with an overhand grip, shoulder-width apart. Pull up in a slow, controlled manner. If you are unable to do this exercise, attach a stretch band above your head (to ceiling, door, or rafter) and pull the stretch band downward to shoulder height.

Major muscles exercised: Biceps, triceps, posterior shoulder muscles, latissimus dorsi, and muscles of the chest and abdomen.

Plyometrics

Plyometrics are a method of generating greater muscle force during eccentric contractions (muscle is extending). Muscles exert more force during this lengthening than when contracting concentrically (flexing and shortening). An example of this is the stance phase during running. When the foot strikes the ground, the body lowers slightly as the eccentric forces attempt to resist the impact of body weight on the muscle. In effect, sprint training is plyometric, as the exaggerated muscle contractions lead to a more powerful concentric motion and lengthening of the muscle. I have included three modified plyometric (plyo) exercises in this portion of supplemental training. However, caution must be given to athletes who are in the early stages of fitness, who are new to sports training, or who have or are susceptible to knee and lower back injury. Plyometrics are powerfully explosive exercises and may cause injury.

Benefits of Plyometrics

Plyometric exercises are generally used to improve power. Power is the amount of force and the time in which a contraction or movement can be performed. Strength, on the other hand, is related to the amount of force the muscle can generate, and endurance is a measure of strength and power over an extended period. So where does power come in for the endurance athlete? In cycling and running, the forward and downward press and the stance to push-off, respectively, are the power-generation points. The more power (faster movement) generated, the greater the speed. The following modified plyometric exercises are intended to provide the competitive edge in these two important areas.

TABLE 6.4   Plyometric Exercises

Exercise	Training zone	Wk1 time	Wk1 rest	Wk1 sets	Wk2 time	Wk2 rest	Wk2 sets	Wk3 time	Wk3 rest	Wk3 sets
1. Squat plyo jump	LAC	00:10	00:20	2	00:15	00:30	2	00:20	00:30	2
2. Split plyo jump	LAC	00:10	00:20	2	00:15	00:30	2	00:20	00:30	2
3. Incline plyo jump	LAC	00:10	00:20	2	00:15	00:30	2	00:20	00:30	2

Frequency and Duration of Plyometrics

The athlete will spend 3, 4.5, and 5 minutes in any one session, depending on the week periodization (week 1, 2, or 3).

Base preparation: One to two sessions per week

Base transition: One session per week

Race preparation: None

Peak transition: None

Again, with periodization changes, the number of weekly plyometric training sessions changes. Table 6.4 details the duration, rest period, and number of sets of each exercise for the three-week periodization. The athlete should do these training exercises during the base training phases only. Once into the race preparation phase, there is no need to continue to train at this intensity. Be sure to warm up fully, stretch, and do these exercises only after completing the sport-specific workouts for the day.

Plyometric Exercises

Squat Plyo Jump

Stand with your back straight and your arms at your sides or your hands clasped behind your head. With your feet shoulder-width apart, squat a third of the way down, then spring upward to maximal height. This exercise can also be done on stadium stairs as part of a running technical form workout.

Major muscles exercised: Extensors and flexors of the hips, knees, and ankles.

Split Plyo Jump

Begin in a one-quarter lunge position with your right leg forward (a moderately long step). Spring upward forcefully as high as possible and, while in the air, switch your left leg to the front. The cadence here should be jump-2-3-jump.

Major muscles exercised: Extensors and flexors of the hips, knees, and ankles.

Incline Plyo Jump

Stand facing a 5-degree incline (such as a grassy slope, stairs, or a steep driveway) with your hands clasped behind your head. Jump forward up the grade at a rate of one jump every 3 to 5 seconds.

Major muscles exercised: Extensors and flexors of the hips, knees, and ankles.

FIGURE 6.23   Squat plyo jump.

Adapted, by permission, from D.A. Chu, 1992, *Jumping Into Plyometrics* (Champaign, IL: Human Kinetics), 31.

FIGURE 6.24 Split plyo jump.

Adapted, by permission, from D. A. Chu, 1992, *Jumping Into Plyometrics* (Champaign, IL: Human Kinetics), 28.

FIGURE 6.25 Incline plyo jump.

Adapted, by permission, from D. A. Chu, 1992, *Jumping Into Plyometrics* (Champaign, IL: Human Kinetics), 40.

FUNCTIONAL ISOKINETIC TRAINING

Now, before the exercise scientists disagree too quickly, first let me define what I mean by functional isokinetics. *Functional* means *practical*, and isokinetic exercises relate to constant speeds and variable forces. I believe this relates well to stretch-band training, in addition to the high degree of specificity attainable (see table 6.5).

I like this type of training very much because the resistance is variable, thus the maximum capability is always being trained. I believe it provides a certain amount of automatic overload and underload, meaning that when an athlete is feeling strong or weak, the resistance adapts to the athlete's current capacity. So, in contrast to using a 100-pound barbell, the resistance is only as great as that applied by the athlete.

Convenience is another factor that makes this training effective and efficient. With stretch bands, there are few, if any, obstacles such as cumbrous equipment. But perhaps most important, movements can be made that are very similar to the sport, such as a swimming pull and curvilinear patterns. Isokinetic training offers the athlete an effective training tool that permits adaptation and overload almost automatically. As an athlete's strength improves, greater tension will be applied to each contraction.

Benefits of Isokinetics

Functional isokinetic stretch band training is popular because it requires little equipment and many exercise movements can be performed with it. In fact, there are few, if any, machine or free-weight exercises that cannot be done with a stretch band. Also, the resistance adjusts to the amount of pulling or extending force used, making this type of training similar to the movements of swimming, cycling, and running.

Your swim coach can probably help you find stretch bands, or check with a medical supply store. Ask for a 10-foot length of quarter- to half-inch-diameter stretch band. Take an old pair of swimming paddles and attach them to the cord through the existing paddle holes. Alternatively, you can simply wrap the cord once around your hand or connect it to a cylinder or round piece of wood to use as a handle. That's all you need to do all the exercises shown. One company, NZ Manufacturing in Kent, Washington, has developed a well-designed and affordable variable-resistance stretch band system called StretchCordz.

TABLE 6.5 Functional Isokinetic Exercises

Exercise	Training zone	Wk 1 time	Wk 1 rest	Wk 1 sets	Wk 2 time	Wk 2 rest	Wk 2 sets	Wk 3 time	Wk 3 rest	Wk 3 sets
1. Two-arm pull	LVT	00:25	00:10	3	00:30	00:10	3	00:40	00:10	3
2. Triceps extensions	LVT	00:25	00:10	3	00:30	00:10	3	00:40	00:10	3
3. Two-arm press	VO_2	00:15	00:15	2	00:20	00:20	2	00:25	00:20	2
4. Two-arm curl	VO_2	00:15	00:15	2	00:20	00:20	2	00:25	00:20	2
5. Medial rotator	VO_2	00:15	00:15	2	00:20	00:20	2	00:25	00:20	2
6. Hip flexors	LVT	00:25	00:10	3	00:30	00:10	3	00:40	00:10	3
7. Leg extension	VO_2	00:15	00:15	2	00:20	00:20	2	00:25	00:20	2
8. Hamstrings curls	VO_2	00:15	00:15	2	00:20	00:20	2	00:25	00:20	2
9. Concentric squats	LVT	00:25	00:10	3	00:30	00:10	3	00:40	00:10	3

Frequency and Duration of Isokinetic Exercises

The athlete will do 12, 15, and 17.5 minutes in any one session, depending on the week periodization (week 1, 2, or 3).

Base preparation: Three to four sessions per week

Base transition: Two to three sessions per week

Race preparation: One (none two weeks prior to competition)

Peak transition: None

Isokinetic training is perhaps the most important of the supplemental disciplines. As a rule, whenever a supplemental discipline needs to be left out, save the isokinetics for last. In table 6.5, the training intensity, duration, rest intervals, and number of sets are organized for each three-week periodization. Again, do these after completing the sport-specific training. As indicated above, the periodization for isokinetic training adjusts with the phase of training. This is necessary for adaptation to sport-specific training when volume and intensity require adjustment.

Isokinetic Exercises

Remember to pack your stretch bands whenever you travel. For the times when your regular workout or supplemental training isn't possible, you can do almost all of the following exercises anywhere.

Two-Arm Pull (Freestyle Pull)

Attach the bands to a doorknob or other fixture between shoulder and waist height. Bend forward from the hips and stretch backward until your arms are fully outstretched. Keep your head up and look diagonally forward. Begin by pulling both arms in a keyhole motion similar to the underwater pull of a butterfly stroke. Keep your elbows higher than your hands and pointing upward and outward. Rotate your palms slightly toward your thighs as you reach full extension (keep your fingertips pointing toward the floor until then). The speed of this movement should be at least as fast as when swimming.

FIGURE 6.26 Two-arm pulls.

Triceps Extensions

Connect the stretch bands to a doorknob or other fixture between shoulder and waist height and stand away to full tension. Bend at the waist 75+ degrees, placing your elbows at your sides. Extend your forearms backward to full extension, keeping your elbows stationary and your fingertips pointing toward the floor. Then, at

FIGURE 6.27 Triceps extension.

nearly full extension, rotate your palm toward your thigh. Maintain a fast speed throughout the movement.

Two-Arm Press

Place stretch bands under both feet. Raise the stretch bands to chest height and press overhead, then lower them to your chest and repeat.

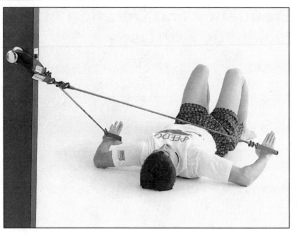

FIGURE 6.29 Medial rotator.

should be moderate tension in the stretch bands. Raise (arc) your forearms and hands (not elbows) forward off the floor until they touch the floor again near your hips.

Hip Flexors

Anchor the stretch bands at doorknob height. Using Velcro straps, connect one band to each ankle. Standing (back facing the anchor point),

FIGURE 6.28 Two-arm press.

Two-Arm Curl

Place stretch bands under both feet with arms at your sides. Curl the stretch bands upward to your chest and lower them to your hips.

Medial Rotator

Anchor the stretch bands low to the floor or at doorknob height. Lie on your back (head toward the anchor point) with your elbows at shoulder height and touching the floor. There

FIGURE 6.30 Hip flexors.

stretch the band to moderate tension, then raise your knee forward and parallel with the ground (as in running). The movement should be fast, and you should work one leg at a time without pausing during the interval. The motion is just like running, except the knee lift is exaggerated.

Leg Extension

Anchor the stretch bands at doorknob height. Using Velcro straps, fasten the stretch bands around both ankles. Stand facing away from

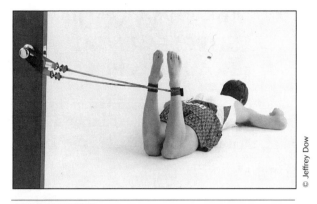

FIGURE 6.32   Hamstrings curl.

Concentric Squats

Stand on the stretch bands with both feet, holding one end in each hand, with approximately 1 foot of band showing. Squat downward while curling your arms slightly. Raise up, adjusting the tension concentrically (stretching/lengthening the muscle) with the leverage of your arms.

FIGURE 6.31   Leg extension.

the anchor point and raise and lower each leg to full extension, or sit on a chair facing away from the anchor point and extend and lower each leg.

Hamstrings Curls

Connect the stretch bands to a doorknob. Lie on the floor facing away from the connection point and secure the stretch bands over your ankles or feet. Curl the hamstrings by moving both feet toward your buttocks.

FIGURE 6.33   Concentric squats.

CREATING YOUR SUPPLEMENTAL TRAINING PLAN

Tables 6.1 through 6.5 described each of the exercises in the supplemental training program. Note that the training intensity zones are used in a different manner than for the regular sports, as described below.

1. The first column on the left of tables 6.1 through 6.5 indicates the exercise and preferred order of completion.

2. The second column of tables 6.2 through 6.5 indicates the training intensity zones. These are recommendations for intensity and rest intervals for each exercise. The supplemental exercises do not attain the volume or time requirements, but the athlete will use the same perceived exertion for those exercises. To illustrate, there are references to three training intensity zones: LVT, VO_2, and LAC (O_2 is not used for supplemental training intensity). The corresponding durations, rest intervals, and number of sets indicate the degree of intensity to be used. Any LAC-labeled exercises are of short duration with rest cycle ratios of 2:1 or more. The training intensity zone labels convey the intensity, thus telling the athlete that a higher or lower intensity should be used (more weight, greater tension, or more energy used with exercise).

3. The third and fourth columns (except for table 6.2) indicate the week number (Wk1), time, and rest period for each exercise. For flexibility, calisthenic, plyometric, and functional isokinetic exercises, the sets are performed for periods of time, not repetitions. The rest of the columns follow this same format.

4. Isotonic weight training follows the same training intensity zone format. Beginning with the third column, "Wk1 reps & % RM" refers to the week in a three-week periodization, the number of repetitions, and the amount of weight expressed as a percentage of the athlete's repetition maximum. The RM is found by estimating or completing the exercise (after a thorough warm-up) with a weight that can be lifted a single time. The percent of RM is then a multiple of the RM, such as 0.35 percent of 100 pounds, or 35 pounds. It is absolutely necessary for athletes to figure out their RM so that they can determine the intensities of their isotonic program. The progression in weeks 2 and 3 follows the uniform method as described above. The fourth column is for entering the weight actually lifted.

5. For each supplemental group, a three-week progressive overload is designed. The exercises are again organized in the order to be performed, with times or repetitions indicated for each.

6. Beneath the respective exercise descriptions are the recommended number of supplemental workouts for a given week. Typically, the periodization of weeks 1, 2, and 3 follows the stair-step buildup of the regular training program. Therefore, week 4 will normally be a restoration week (no supplemental training except flexibility).

7. It is important to remember that supplemental training is secondary to primary sport training. Less strong or injured athletes perhaps can gain the most advantage from a supplemental program, but only up to a point. Never let the supplemental training oppose gains or interfere with specific-sport fitness. Strength and power should not exceed the needs of the sport (this is true for the elite athlete as well). Therefore, for endurance athletes, strength and cardiorespiratory endurance must be counterbalanced to achieve the greatest benefit.

7

DESIGNING YOUR TRAINING PROGRAM

This chapter completes the training program begun in chapter 2. Along with the principles of training volume and periodization cycles discussed in chapter 2, the sport-specific techniques and drills presented in the swimming, cycling, running, and supplemental training chapters are used to develop the program and workouts here. This chapter will provide information to help you set up your weekly training goals, including overdistance workouts; the periodization of your individual swimming, cycling, and running workouts; recovery; and how to chart workouts and progress.

PROGRAM MANAGERS

The program overview manager (described in steps 1 through 7 in chapter 2) is important because it is an overview of the entire season. It's where the training program design begins to take shape and where the athlete can see the entire season at a glance. I won't explain each portion again, however, several specific training components are meaningful to illustrate here.

Step 8:
Specifying Weekly Training Goals

Important columns of the POM—"Swim, bike, and run week target"—indicate the training emphasis or goal in each discipline for that week. These columns provide a more general but important training management purpose. I use these chiefly for noting and managing the longest workouts of the week, generally the O_2 overdistance workouts, or for important time trials, competitions, or restorations. Thus it becomes a comprehensive picture of the entire season of training.

© Richard Etchberger

How the athlete or coach chooses to use this section is a matter of preference, but some type of ongoing overall training management should be planned. This allows you to match up your workouts more appropriately across disciplines. For example, you might schedule 50-, 65-, 75-, and 100-mile bike rides on consecutive weeks. The long runs in each of those weeks might be 20, 16, 13, and 10 miles, respectively. In other words, the longest bike ride combines with the shortest run and the shortest bike ride with the longest run. For the swim, the overdistance workouts are managed similarly, with 1,600, 1,800, and 2,000 meters on successive weeks. Forty-four weeks of swim-

ming, cycling, and running week targets are depicted in the sample POM.

It's important to keep your workouts structured such that the distances are fairly consistent. This means organizing the long swims, rides, or runs in a way that progressively overloads the athlete and permits periodic restoration phases. In my programs, I tend to follow three weeks of progressive distance and intensity increases with a recovery week. The recovery week generally consists of O_2 training and technical form work, and the overall weekly volume is reduced by 20 to 50 percent.

Follow my guidelines or develop your own weekly goals, but keep in mind the importance

OVERDISTANCE TRAINING: HOW FAR TO SWIM, BIKE, AND RUN

How much overdistance (O_2) volume is needed relative to a particular competitive distance? Further, how much of this aerobic overdistance training will be needed 20, 15, 10, or even 3 weeks before a competition of minor importance during the base preparation, base transition, race preparation, and peak transition phases? Tables 7.1 through 7.4 offer some guidelines for overdistance training.

The tables work well for almost any competitive distance. In the examples, multipliers are shown for each of the respective training cycles. The tables are used with competitive distance targets of 1,500 meters of swimming, 40 kilometers of cycling, and 10 kilometers of running. The results have been rounded up.

Use these tables as follows:

1. Note the respective distance of the competition disciplines (swim, bike, run, triathlon, or duathlon) alongside the competition distance.

2. Determine the period (bp, bt, rp, or pt) in which a competition falls. *Note:* Recovery (r) is built into the charts.

3. Decide how many weeks from this competition date each training week falls.

4. Multiply the competition distance by the multiplier. The product is the estimated volume for a single overdistance training workout for the week.

Planning Note: The multipliers and training volumes may need to be changed slightly for some athletes. When an athlete plans to compete at several different distances in any one or more periods, the amount of weekly aerobic training should be tapered accordingly. Refer to table 7.4 (peak transition) for recommended reductions. These recommendations should be followed with respect to competitive distance, training background, and goals; that is, the periodic step-up or step-down of distance along with the periodic restoration periods will vary depending on the cycle of training.

TABLE 7.1 Percentage of Competition Volume for Weekly O_2 Training: Base Preparation Phase

Week number	Swim competition distance		Bike competition distance		Run competition distance	
	Percentage of race distance	Volume	Percentage of race distance	Volume	Percentage of race distance	Volume
20	70.0	1,050	75.0	19	75.0	5
19	80.0	1,200	85.0	21	85.0	5
18	90.0	1,350	95.0	24	95.0	6
17	60.0	900	65.0	16	65.0	4
16	80.0	1,200	85.0	21	85.0	5
15	90.0	1,350	95.0	24	95.0	6
14	100.0	1,500	105.0	26	105.0	7
13	60.0	900	65.0	16	65.0	4
12	80.0	1,200	85.0	21	85.0	5
11	90.0	1,350	95.0	24	95.0	6
10	100.0	1,500	105.0	26	105.0	7
9	70.0	1,050	75.0	19	75.0	5
8	110.0	1,650	115.0	29	115.0	7
7	120.0	1,800	125.0	31	125.0	8
6	130.0	1,950	135.0	34	135.0	8
5	70.0	1,050	75.0	19	75.0	5
4	110.0	1,650	115.0	29	115.0	7
3	120.0	1,800	125.0	31	125.0	8
2	130.0	1,950	135.0	34	135.0	8
1	100.0	1,500	100.0	25	100.0	6

TABLE 7.2 Percentage of Competition Volume for Weekly O_2 Training: Base Transition Phase

Week number	Swim competition distance		Bike competition distance		Run competition distance	
	Percentage of race distance	Volume	Percentage of race distance	Volume	Percentage of race distance	Volume
6	125.0	1,875	130.0	33	130.0	8
5	65.0	975	70.0	18	70.0	4
4	105.0	1,575	110.0	28	110.0	7

(continued)

TABLE 7.2   *(continued)*

Week number	Percentage of race distance	Volume	Percentage of race distance	Volume	Percentage of race distance	Volume
3	115.0	1,725	120.0	30	120.0	7
2	125.0	1,875	130.0	33	130.0	8
1	75.0	1,125	75.0	19	75.0	5

TABLE 7.3   Percentage of Competition Volume for Weekly O_2 Training: Race Preparation Phase

	Swim competition distance		Bike competition distance		Run competition distance	
Week number	Percentage of race distance	Volume	Percentage of race distance	Volume	Percentage of race distance	Volume
8	115.0	1,725	120.0	30	120.0	7
7	125.0	1,875	130.0	33	130.0	8
6	135.0	2,025	140.0	35	140.0	9
5	75.0	1,125	80.0	20	80.0	5
4	115.0	1,725	120.0	30	120.0	7
3	110.0	1,650	150.0	38	150.0	9
2	95.0	1,425	90.0	23	90.0	6
1	50.0	750	50.0	13	50.0	3

TABLE 7.4   Percentage of Competition Volume for Weekly O_2 Training: Peak Transition Phase

	Swim competition distance		Bike competition distance		Run competition distance	
Week number	Percentage of race distance	Volume	Percentage of race distance	Volume	Percentage of race distance	Volume
3	85.0	1,275	90.0	23	90.0	6
2	70.0	1,050	75.0	19	75.0	5
1	50.0	750	50.0	13	50.0	3

of following a reasonable buildup in volume, and periodically test fitness with time trials and competitions.

Step 9: Customize the Swimming, Cycling, and Running Program Managers

The swimming, cycling, and running program managers specify the periodization of the weekly training volumes for each of the four training intensity zones: O_2 (aerobic conditioning), LVT (anaerobic conditioning), VO_2 (aerobic capacity), and LAC (anaerobic capacity). The swimming program manager is described below and details the total season and training intensity zone volumes.

Details of the Swimming Program Manager

1. *Period:* Swim periodization is determined by the table of periodization and periodization cycles. Enter the periodization here from the POM (chapter 2).

2. *Weekly target:* A training week goal is indicated here. This target has already been entered onto the POM (chapter 2). This is not necessarily the hardest workout, but a memorandum of the longest-duration workouts and time trials or tests. For swimming, you might see 3,000 meters O_2 (continuous aerobic swimming); for cycling, 60 + 10TT (60 miles including a 10-mile time trial); or for running, 10 O_2 (10 miles of aerobic running). (Using tables 7.1 through 7.4 may be helpful here.)

3. *Volume:* The total training volume for the week is the result of step 4 (following).

4. *Pct:* Percentage from the periodization cycle step-up (chapter 2, table 2.5).

5. O_2: Total week volume (meters) of aerobic conditioning training intensity zone (from the table of periodization (chapter 2, table 2.6).

6. *LVT:* Total week volume (meters) of anaerobic conditioning training intensity zone (anaerobic threshold).

7. VO_2: Total week volume (meters) of aerobic capacity training intensity zone (maximal O_2 consumption).

8. *LAC:* Total week volume (meters) of anaerobic capacity training intensity zone (lactate).

9. *Season volume:* Indicate the total volume for the entire season.

10. *PI volume:* The result of dividing the season volume by the number of weeks in the entire season.

Only use those program managers applicable to your sports. For example, duathletes (run and bike) will not use the swimming manager, and single-sport endurance athletes may use any one of the program managers but not the other two.

Step 10: Determining Supplemental Exercise Periodization

The supplemental exercise periodization is summarized at the far right of the POM (the exercises were described in chapter 6). This column serves as a guide for which supplemental discipline to do each week. For the most part, I prescribe some type of supplemental training for all periodization cycles of the season. I generally do not have athletes do much, if any, supplemental exercise during restoration weeks, except for daily stretching. Before top-ranked competitions, I discontinue supplemental training (except stretching) during the race preparation and peak transition phases. Supplemental training periodization follows the same weekly step-up as the specific sport training weeks.

In the rp phase, all supplemental training except stretching is at a minimum. However, if an athlete's schedule has several weeks without competitions, I include a Wk1 or Wk2 program. Athletes and coaches must think of the rp phase as a time for peaking for competitions. Too much supplemental resistance training will overtax you physically and take away from the competitive edge. There is no supplemental training (except stretching) during any of the pt training phases.

THE WORKOUT TRAINING MANAGER

Up to this point, the central aim has been to design workouts based on calculated periodization. Through those computations, a weekly volume has been defined for each training intensity zone for each sport. All that remains is to develop the actual workouts.

The workout training manager (WTM) combines the data from the separate program managers for the purpose of writing specific daily workouts. Athletes manage their training volume for each week by periodizing volume and training intensity.

The WTM displays the actual workouts in a given week's training. The information from each sport's program manager is entered in the far right column of this worksheet. The results are calculations and periodization being applied as you decide using the table of periodization.

The sample workout training managers offer specific workouts and time intervals for each training session. Each is based on the intensity pace charts (chapters 3, 4, 5, and 6) and is especially useful for choosing the right intensity for each training session. These workouts are the result of putting the respective program manager information into practical training sessions. The swimming, cycling, and running chapters also provide sample workouts and technical form drills.

Training workouts can include all four of the training intensity zones. The separate program managers detail the total weekly volume and the total training intensity zone volume. The latter needs to be organized appropriately into the training week workout schedule. The WTMs in tables 7.5 through 7.8 show how this is done properly. The general rule is to separate same-sport high-intensity (LVT, VO_2, and LAC) workouts by at least one full day of rest. Workouts can contain several training intensity zone sets but should not exceed the durations recommended in chapter 1 (table 1.1).

Different sport workouts can be done on the same day. I have encountered no problems with this in terms of recovery or training effectiveness. In fact, this is perhaps the best way to train, as it puts the rule of specificity into practice for the multisport endurance athlete. Additionally, the order of workouts is important. In the bp and bt phases of training, weekly workouts (at least two) should be done in the order performed in competition. It's not important to do these workouts back-to-back, but simply in the sequence of competition, as this will enhance training specificity over time. In the rp phase, more race-specific transition (back-to-back) workouts are necessary, but the athlete can also use second-ranked events as preparatory nontaper workouts. Three to four weeks before a top-ranked competition, the athlete should include simulation training in workouts or a nontaper competition.

Step 1: Designing the Week's Training

There is no easy way around having to design everyday workouts individually—unless, of course, you do the same type of workouts week to week, in which case you would be able to adjust the training intensity zones and total volumes fairly easily. Individualizing workouts according to goals and ability has always been important in my training programs. I believe the training systems outlined in this book maintain a refreshing variety of workouts using the concepts of periodization and training intensity zones.

The first thing to do in developing your weekly schedule is to decide which days you will train for which sport. The training intensity zone and total volumes have already been calculated from the separate program managers for each sport. Write those numbers into the cell above the actual workout section on table A.6. Don't write any workouts until you've organized the week's flow of workout sessions.

There are virtually limitless ways to design a training week. As you structure the week, think carefully about how each training day correlates to overall training intensity and volume. Try to organize your weekly training flows to allow for adequate amounts of stress (overload) and recovery (rest). Take into consideration personal work schedule and family needs. Plan 1 or 2 days off every 7 to 10 days. Remember, recovery from workouts and competitions should be adequate to restore and improve fitness. One day before and after a competition, I like athletes to exercise lightly in each discipline and stretch for 15 to 30 minutes. Two days before and after a competition, I often schedule days off to permit enough prerace rest and postevent recovery. Symptoms of overtraining such as poor workout times,

© Ken Lee

TABLE 7.5   Base Preparation (bp) Training Model Week

Week of: 1/20/97   Week number: 3   Athlete: Model

Week targets	Monday	Tuesday	Wednesday	Thursday	Friday	Saturday	Sunday	Week volumes
Swim:		3,000	1,500	Off	2,700	Off	Off	Actual 7,200
1,000 trial	Full rest day	Warm-up S 600 O₂ at DPS; K 200 continuously O₂; TF 4(FC,SD,SC,CU) by 25 S; O₂ 200 nonfree loosen; LVT 1,000 timed-record; P 4 × 150 + 15 S LVT at BB, DPS	O₂ 3(300 + 1') loosen up mostly nonfreestyle and TF drills (FP at rest); LAC 5 × 25 + 30 S; VO₂ 250 + time rest; 225 O₂ swim down		Warm-up 4 × 75 + 10 S at O₂; TF 4 × 75 SD,CU,FC, SC; P 4 × 75 + 10 S BB; K 4 × 75 KF, KBP, KB, KBS; 1,500 O₂ continuous swim; work the length of stroke		Optional loosen up; stroke drills after run and ride (800 to 1,000)	O₂ 5,300 / LVT 1,525 / VO₂ 250 / LAC 125 / Program Manager 7,200
Results:								
Bike:		15	Off	15	Off	28	4	Actual 62
30 O₂/Brk/3mi.	Full rest day	Warm-up HRPM 15' at 105 + TF 4(1' at SU, ISO, S, T); VO₂ 1.5 miles (2.5K) in 3:34; 10' O₂ spinning TF; S; LAC .5 mile (800 MTR) in 1:13; HRPM spindowns at 105		Warm-up HRPM 4 × 5' at 90 + 5 rpm each 5'; then TF drills: 5(1' at FE, ISO, HOD, DS); O₂ warm-down		O₂ to low end of LVT for 18 miles, working HRPM and also press and backstroke, then go 4 miles (6.5K) in 9:45; followed by run	O₂ HRPM spinning after run in small ring; okay to spin on indoor trainer/rollers	O₂ 55.75 / LVT 4.25 / VO₂ 1.5 / LAC 0.5 / Program Manager 62
Results:								
Run:		Off	4	Off	3	2	7	Actual 16
7 O₂	Full rest day		Warm-up 8' forest/trail run in fartlek style, go: LVT .75, VO₂ .25 and LAC .25; take appropriate rest between each training zone		Track/drills: 6(200 meters at HU,PO,KU, and HP); TF/FA 4 × 100 + 100 O₂; stretch and warm-down	O₂ to low LVT working the bike-to-run combination; maintain form and stay relaxed	O₂ forest run working tall posture, light footstrike, and hips forward. Keep the pace low to high O₂	O₂ 15 / LVT 0.75 / VO₂ 0.25 / LAC 0.25 / Program Manager 16
Dry land:								
Wk3 CAL								
Wk3 ISK								
Wk3 IST								
Results:								Competition:
AM heart rate:								

TABLE 7.6 Base Transition (bt) Training Model Week

Week of: 7/28/97   Week number: 30   Athlete: Model

Week targets		Monday	Tuesday	Wednesday	Thursday	Friday	Saturday	Sunday	Week volumes
1,600 O₂	Swim:	1,600	Off	3,300	Off	2,800	Off	1,000	Actual 8,700
		O₂ continuous swim work the DPS, body roll, and high elbow recovery and keep intensity down	Full rest day	Warm-up 800 DS by 200's TF/DPS; K 4(25 KL,KB,KBP, KBS); LVT 3(150/ 2:07, 4 × 50/41 S) plus 10 S ± rest interval; VO₂ 2 × 250 in 3:22 + 3:30 rest; TF 2(50 PS, STS, VS)		Warm-up 3(S 125, K 50, SD 25) TF 3(25 FC, S, SD, S); LVT 3(500 + 1', 45" descend; KF 200 descend by 50 S; LAC 7 × 50 in 32 seconds on 90; P 850 BB/DPS at O₂		O₂ 300 long and loose, then go 700 nonfreestyle choice at O₂ swims; just stretch it out after running any time	O₂ 5,325
									LVT 2,525
									VO₂ 525
									LAC 350
									Program Manager 8,700
	Results:								
40 O₂	Bike:	5	Off	20	Off	10	40	Off	Actual 75
		O₂ HRPM spinning in the small ring working press and rpms of 100+	Full rest day	Warm-up 6 × 4' from O₂ to LVT/ low; VO₂ 3 × 2,600 meters in 3:34 + 4'; O₂ spin 10' TF/HRPM; LAC 4 × 500 in 41 S + 80 S; O₂ HRPM spin-down; work downstroke		Rollers/trainer Warm-up 6 × 2' > rpm each 2' by 5 from 90 rpms; TF drills 4 × 2'; each: DISO/S/B and ISOs	O₂ HRPM at 100+ for 30'; TF 5' ISOs; LVT 4 × 4,000 meters in 6' + 1' spin number 2 and 4 on hills; O₂ HRPM spin down in small ring, TF tracking		O₂ 58.25
									LVT 11
									VO₂ 4.5
									LAC 1.5
									Program Manager 75
	Results:								
9 O₂	Run:	2	Off	3	5	Off	Off	9	Actual 19
		O₂ jog/walk/ stretch TF drill: arm swings (AS) for 5 to 10 minutes	Full rest day	O₂ TF/drills, track; 4(200 HU, HK, HP, HT); stretch 10' + TF: as drill O₂ jog-down	O₂ 10' then go: low LVT "tempo" on soft surface for rest of run; work FS, HTs the whole distance			O₂ trail/forest fartlek; begin 10' O₂ then go: LVT 3,600 meters in 12:24, LAC 4 × 200 meters in 43 S + 90 S, VO₂ 2 × 800 meters in 3:02; O₂ jog-down/stretch	O₂ 15
Dry land:									LVT 2.25
Wk2 CAL									VO₂ 1
Wk2 ISK									LAC 0.5
Wk2 IST									Program Manager 19
	Results:								Competition: 0
	AM heart rate:								0

TABLE 7.7 Race Preparation (rp) Training Model Week

Week of: 8/4/97   Week number: 31   Athlete: Model

Week targets		Monday	Tuesday	Wednesday	Thursday	Friday	Saturday	Sunday	Week volumes	
	Swim:	Off	3,400	2,400	Off	2,225	1,200	Off	Actual	9,225
1,000 O₂			Warm-up S 400, KF200, P 400 TF 4/50 SD, CU) on 1:05; LVT 5/300/ 4:18 on 4:30'; 100 nonfree loosen	Warm-up 8 × 75/ 1:15 O₂/TF–DPS; K 200 KBP/KBS VO₂ 2 × 250 in 3:22 + 3:22; 200 O₂ nonfree easy P 8 × 75/1:05 BB; 400 warm-down swim/kick by 50 S		Warm-up 3 × 100/1:45 O₂/DPS; K 4 × 50/1:20 freestyle; LVT 6 × 200 in 2:50 on 3'; 100 loosen swim; LAC 7 × 50 in 32 S cn 90 S warm-down 200 TF at WAS, FF	O₂ continuous swim; work the downsweep and hand pitch/angle of attack; keep the swim intensity light		O₂	5,600
									LVT	2,700
									VO₂	560
									LAC	375
									Program Manager	9,225
	Results:									
	Bike:	Off	21	Off	19	Off	5	35	Actual	80
35 O₂			Warm-up HRPM 42 × 19-21 20'; TF 4 × 3' DS, ISO, S, T; LVT 3 × 6,000 meters in 9' + 1'; O₂ HRPM spin-down, work the backstroke at 100+		Rollers/trainer or road warm-up 4 × 3' > rpm by 5 from 95-plus TF each at S, ISO, B, S, all HRPM spinning in small chain ring		O₂ HRPM spinning after run; easy spinning; loosen up the legs	O₂ HRPM spins at 105 + 30'; TF drills 10' at 2.5' each: SU/ISOs and DISOs; VO₂ 2 × 4,000 meters in 5:42 + 6'; O₂ HRPM 10' small ring; LAC 3 × 800 meters in 1:05 + 3'	O₂	61.5
									LVT	12
									VO₂	4.75
									LAC	1.5
									Program Manager	80
	Results:									
	Run:	8	Off	3	4	Off	6	Off	Actual	21
6 O₂		Fartlek: warm-up 12' O₂ jog forest/trails/ soft surface; LVT 4 × 1,000 meters in 4' +1'; O₂ 4' light jogging; VO₂ 2 × 800 meters in 3:02 + 3'; LAC 4 × 200 meters in 43 S + 90 S		O₂ TF immediately after swim; work hips, footstrike, head alignment, and relaxation	Easy combination run following bike, keep intensity low to high O₂; work TF/HTs and footstrike (push off)		O₂ aerobic, working hips, posture, and light feet; run easy and with good form		O₂	17
Dry land:									LVT	2.5
									VO₂	1
Off CAL									LAC	0.5
Wk1 ISK									Program Manager	21
Off IST										
	Results:								Competition:	0
	AM heart rate:									0

TABLE 7.8 Peak Transition (pt) Training Model Week

Week of: 11/3/97 Week number: 44 Athlete: Model

Week targets	Monday	Tuesday	Wednesday	Thursday	Friday	Saturday	Sunday	Week volumes
Swim:	Off	2,400	Off	1,000	Off	800	1,500	Actual 5,700
Trirace 1.5K		Warm-up S 300, K 150, P 250; LVT 12 × 50/42; in 45 seconds; TF 5 × 50 SD/swims O2; on easy interval ± 15 S warm-downs 4 × 100 + 30 S at DPS		Warm-up S 200, K100; P 200; VO2 2 × 150 in 2:40 ÷ 2:40; O2 200 loosen; warm-down, work the entry and high elbow recovery	Full rest day; stretch; Optional: 5 minute swim, loosen up only	O2 loosen up 400, part of swim course; LAC 6 × 25 in 16 S + 30 S rest; O2 warm-down at DPS ** early in the morning	Triathlon #1 ranking; warm-up 5' to 10'; sight course (landmark) ** race distance not included in week volume	O2 3,125; LVT 600; VO2 300; LAC 150; Program Manager 4,175
Results:								
Bike:	15	Off	20	Off	Off	6	25	Actual 61
Trirace 40K	Warm-up O2 HRPM 30' at 100's; LVT 4 × 1,000 in 1:30 + 20 S; each at 40K pace; O2 HRPM spin-down, working down/ backstroke		Warm-up 12' HRPM at 105+; low LVT 10' "tempo"; O2/TF-DISO, ISO, T for 10'; VO2 2 × 2K in 2:51 + 3'; O2 HRPM spin-down small ring at 105 rpm		Full rest day; stretch; ** drive course early	O2 HRPM spinning 14'; LAC 4 × 400 meters in 32 S + 1+; O2 HRPM spin-down, small ring at 100 rpm ** early in the morning	Triathlon #1 ranking; review transition area entrance/exit/ race entrance ** race distance not included in week volume	O2 30; LVT 2.25; VO2 3; LAC 1; Program Manager 36
Results:								
Run:	Off	5	Off	4	Off	2	6.2	Actual 17.2
Trirace 10K	Stretch 20'	Warm-up 12' O2 light; stretch 5'; LVT 1,200 meters in 4:45; O2 5'; LAC 3 × 200 meters in 43 S + 90 S; O2 loosen down		Warm-up 12' relaxed/loose stretch 5' to 10'; VO2 2 × 800 meters in 3:00 with 3' rest between; O2 warm-down light with 2 × 20 S + 40 S FAs	Full rest day; stretch; ** drive course early	O2 loosen up jog 10'; TF/FA 2 × 100 meters in 21 S + 42 S; O2 warm/ down/ stretch ** early in the morning	Triathlon #1 ranking; review transition area entrance/exit/ race entrance ** race distance not included in week volume	O2 7; LVT 0.5; VO2 0.75; LAC 0.25; Program Manager 9
Dry land:								
Off CAL								
Off ISK								
Off IST								
Results:								Competition:
AM heart rate:								1.5, 40, 10 kilometer triathlon

lethargy, elevated resting pulse, and irritability may indicate a need to reduce training stress and include more recovery time for a few days or weeks. Tables 7.5 through 7.8 show examples of how weekly training workouts and intensity flow might be designed.

Step 2: Entering the Training Intensity Zone Volume and Weekly Targets

On the rightmost side of your WTM copied from the appendix, enter the total volume for the week, including a breakdown of volumes for each training intensity zone. These amounts are taken from the respective swimming, cycling, and running program manager's weekly volume and training intensity zone amounts for O_2, VO_2, LVT, and LAC.

In the leftmost column are the weekly targets for each sport. Enter those targets (from the POM) into the days most appropriate for your schedule. Most athletes do the longer aerobic training on the weekends, when they have more time to devote to training. Scheduling the remainder of the training week is a process of organizing each workout using the IPCs and dividing the right amount of each training intensity zone into workouts.

I focus on LVT, VO_2, and LAC volumes. Those amounts of weekly volume for each respective intensity zone provide the basis for laying out the week and writing the workouts. I organize these intensity volumes into individual (or in some cases, the same) workouts and in relation to each sport. For example, duing week 1 (swim), the total week's LVT volume is 1,350 meters. On Wednesday, the LVT portion of the workout might include 4 × 1200 meters on a 3:00 send-off time and an average swim time of 2:50 plus 11 × 50 meters on a 0:50 send-off time. The VO_2 (swim) would total 200 meters, and on the following Friday it would come near the end of the workout as "VO_2 200/2:41 recorded." This means the goal time for the 200 meters would be 2:41. Finally, the LAC (swim) would also be on Wednesday as "LAC 4 × 25 in 16 seconds + 32 seconds." This means you would swim 4 × 25 meters in

16 seconds, taking another 32 seconds of rest. Be sure to look up your own pace on each of the IPCs.

Essentially, the same process continues for each sport and workout. Keep in mind how competitions, workout volume, and intensity relate to the other sports' workouts (preceding and following) and upcoming competitions.

Step 3: General Guidelines for Recovery Between Workouts

Multisport training is more complex than training in only one discipline; the training intensity zones must be integrated across each competitive sport. For example, an LVT- or LAC-based swim workout will impact cycling or running workouts done later that day or the next day. You don't need to write anything down in this step; rather, use the information here for planning workouts and the necessary recovery between them.

To recover fully from exercise and restore carbohydrates, consider how much time you'll need between workouts. Recovery can take on different meanings for different athletes. Some athletes respond better to days of complete rest, whereas others recover from training with easy, short-duration workouts. Table 7.9 offers basic guidelines for planning how much time to allow between various types of training intensity zone sessions.

In the future, perhaps, we'll actually see athletes taking numerous rest days on a regular basis. That, of course, is not common behavior today, as athletes seem to fear taking too much time off and thus losing some of their fitness. It's just not easy for some athletes to understand that at times rest is better than training.

Rest days are important, and athletes need to take them regularly. For some, two days or more per week are right, depending again on the athlete's individual goals and athletic ability and history. In another case, a full day off from training every 6 to 10 days seems right. Some professionals I've coached schedule a different type of "days off," ones that involve light swimming, biking, and running for 20 to 30 minutes.

SCHEDULING MODERATE OVERLOAD TRAINING

Sometimes, I intentionally cluster workouts on successive days. This bunching produces a certain overload that simulates competitions of longer duration (6 hours or longer). Although this is somewhat contrary to the rules mentioned earlier, some athletes respond quite well to this type of scheduling, particularly when followed by one or more days off or very light training. Clusters consist of combination training intensity zone workouts on consecutive days. This could mean back-to-back swim, bike, and run combination workouts of high intensity and/or volume. Essentially, higher training intensity zones are bunched together to achieve a greater training overload.

Also, the athlete can include several training intensity zones in a workout. Additionally, I include TF training (drills) in most every workout. These are great technique enhancers and provide a stimulating variety for every workout. You'll need to refer to the separate chapters on swimming, cycling, and running for definitions of the drill and exercise acronyms used.

The competitive endurance athlete should schedule several periodic restoration periods in the base preparatory, base transition, and race preparatory cycles of training. These "breaks," which are generally seven days long, consist of a 25 to 40 percent reduction in weekly training volume and include only aerobic conditioning exercises (no hard interval training). These regular minibreaks will keep an athlete motivated and restored during a long competitive season. When beginning another training phase after restoration, the athlete should build slowly for the first day or so.

The workout models presented later in this chapter can be of certain value to athletes and coaches in structuring weekly training flows among the respective disciplines. The intensity and discipline relationships provide excellent templates for organizing a separate plan. By the way, whether one is a triathlete, duathlete, or single sport endurance athlete the flows of these model training weeks are sound. The athlete can

TABLE 7.9   Training Intensity Zones (Recovery After Exercise)

Intensity of exercise	Time for recovery
Low O_2 training	8 hours
High O_2 training	8 to 12 hours
Low LVT training	24 hours
High LVT training	24 to 36 hours
Low VO_2 training	36 hours
High VO_2 training	36 to 48 hours
LAC training	36 to 48 hours

simply remove the swimming component or perhaps include some of the technical form swim workouts for recovery.

Step 4:
Writing the Workouts

Finally, although the POM is designed for the season in advance, the WTMs should only be completed one or two weeks ahead of the workout weeks (table A.6). The reason is that innumerable changes can occur to cause adjustments in the training week (injury, illness, family, work, race cancellation, or change of date). Also, it takes 15 to 20 minutes to write the workouts for each week. The respective swimming, cycling, and running chapters include model sets and respective intensity pace charts to guide you through the workout design process. In addition, tables 7.5 through 7.8 show how workouts are organized and designed. However, if time is short, the total weekly volume for each respective sport is sometimes enough to get the right training done. For example, week 31 on the cycling program manager shows a total volume of 80 miles, of which 61.5 miles are O_2, 12 miles are LVT, 4.75 miles are VO_2, and 1.5 miles are LAC training (see chapter 2, page 32). For this week, instead of actually writing out every day's workout, arrange the workout week (flow of training week) according to the time and sport(s) to be done. Thus, starting on Tuesday of week 31, for example, ride 25 miles but include a 12-mile LVT section.

RECOVERY IN THE
OFF-SEASON

Even though athletes have begged me to do so, I refuse to design off-season training programs. The off-season is a time to let go of the structure, but without getting out of shape entirely. Swimming, cycling, and running activities should not be organized, and the volume and intensity should be light and stress-free. Athletes should also move into more diverse aerobic athletic activities. Off-season activities can include almost any sport, but I favor winter aerobic and mobility types of training such as cross-country,

telemark, and skate skiing. Hiking, rock climbing, in-line skating, snow shoeing, surfing, and wind surfing are also excellent off-season choices.

A prolonged off-season training break is essential for psychological and physiological balance. However, during this time, it is important to maintain cardiovascular endurance through supplemental exercises and participate in cross-training exercises as a form of active restoration. Some athletes should also take this time to focus on their weakest discipline, preferably early in the training break period.

The length of the training break depends on an athlete's competitive goals and level of fitness. Generally, four to eight weeks of nonspecific off-season training are recommended following the training season. However, supplemental cardiovascular training needs to be continued during this time. Otherwise, endurance athletes will detrain quickly, and retraining may take longer for them than for less well-trained athletes (Wilmore and Costill 1988).

The off-season is also a time for replanning and beginning the process of setting goals and designing the training program for the next season. The athlete will once again make the move into base preparatory training, which will serve as the foundation for the upcoming season. To do this, competitive season goals and the past season will need to be studied in detail.

Many athletes continue to include off-season activities during the base preparatory phase. Although the elite athlete should concentrate on sport-specific skills, I see no disadvantage in using the activities mentioned above and others during this time. In fact, adding further cross-training activities is likely beneficial for overall physical conditioning.

How Much Time Off Will Cause Loss of Endurance?

An interesting fact about endurance training is that when a highly trained athlete takes time off, the loss of fitness is swift. Such losses are apparent through reductions in maximal oxygen consumption (VO_2max), stroke volume, cardiac output, and total blood volume. In one study, a 21-day bed rest resulted in up to 27 percent reductions in several cardiovascular functions. Compared to the sedentary subjects, the losses were greater in the endurance athletes. These data strongly suggest that well-trained endurance athletes cannot afford to take too much time off from aerobic training or strength and flexibility training.

It also takes the highly trained athlete longer to regain pre-rest-period fitness levels. After just a few weeks of no training, the athlete may require several months to regain fitness. In reality, then, there is no such thing as a complete off-season for the serious endurance athlete. Rather, the training break should include activities that will keep the athlete in good physical condition and exercise that stimulates muscles similar to those used in the athlete's competitive sports.

How many consecutive days off will result in decreases or decline in muscular strength, endurance, and flexibility? There is no easy answer to the question. In my experience, you should take no more than seven consecutive days off in any one period of the year. Of course, this does not include those days when the athlete is participating in other disciplines, such as backpacking, skiing, and so on.

Overtraining: Signs and Symptoms

Overtraining can be defined simply as the point at which an athlete cannot continue with effective training. The athlete becomes stale and is fatigued. Overtraining can be recognized by both physical and psychological symptoms. The following are some common signs:

Physical signs and symptoms:
High resting, recovery, and morning heart rates (5 to 10 beats per minute)
Slower return to normal heart rate following exercise and interval training
Increased body temperature
Weight loss and increased thirst
Bowel disorders

Psychological signs and symptoms:
Changes in sleeping patterns
Lowered self-confidence
Drowsiness
Irritability
Loss of motivation
Loss of appetite
Chronic fatigue
Depression
Anxiety
Poor concentration
Confusion

Managing overtraining includes both physical and emotional treatment. Physically, the volume and intensity of training need to be reduced, and the athlete needs time for complete rest. Nutritional needs should be looked at as well. Is the athlete getting enough carbohydrates, fluids, and calories to meet training demands? Light exercise in the athlete's regular discipline is an effective way to get through an overtraining period; in addition, including other activities that are aerobic in nature can offer an effective "break" as well. Make sure you allow for adequate time for recovery. If any symptoms continue or reappear, more rest is needed.

Psychologically, it may be more difficult to identify the best treatment or prevention for overtraining. However, I have found it helpful to (1) change the training pattern more frequently, (2) include regular restoration periods (breaks), and (3) use concrete mental imagery techniques such as asking what the athlete intends to accomplish in a particular section of a workout (see chapter 9).

CHARTING YOUR PROGRESS

Recording information helps an athlete recognize patterns in training that result in good performances. Measuring progress and achievement generates positive reinforcements that assist in charting goals. The athlete can gauge training by what may have gone right or wrong.

Athletes can keep a written record of their fitness progress in several ways. One way is to use the various forms offered as part of this training plan—thus keeping the workouts and results in one handy place. Another is to develop a separate training log.

Using the Workout Training Manager

The WTM is like a training diary and is perhaps a step above most methods for charting workouts and fitness progress. The WTM includes every aspect of the planned training workouts, and the results can be entered in the space provided beneath the workouts. The results can include physical data such as pace, interval, and so on, as well as perceptions and feelings. Logging the results of training is important for establishing a permanent manifest of what an athlete has done. Keeping your program managers will also allow you to track your workouts over time. Still, some may prefer to use a diary, ledger, or one of several training logs available commercially.

Using the Heart Rate Training Manager

The heart rate training manager (see chapter 1) is another excellent companion to the training diary. It reflects the morning resting heart rate's response to training and correlates well with training results with respect to fitness or fatigue from training. Using the heart rate training manager can also help determine whether you are overtraining.

No athlete should become a slave to his training log, however. In my view, such compulsions influence training in the wrong way. A training journal can lose its effectiveness when an athlete's motivation comes from the entry. Rather than becoming the reason for training, a journal should simply provide a record of results—an opportunity to examine successful as well as other types of training.

Developing Your Own Training Log

A training log is a wonderful history of an athlete's training and competition life. I know of endurance athletes whose training diaries go back nearly 18 years—each offering insight into the life of the athlete beyond what can be gleaned from the numerical data. In addition, the log provides a measure of past training and performance. It can help the athlete design and organize any new strategy and training structures.

For those who want to keep a more comprehensive history, it may be helpful to record the following additional information in your training log:

1. Date
2. Time of workout
3. Environmental conditions (temperature, wind)
4. Course
5. Weight before and after workout
6. Heart rate during separate training intensity zones and/or perceived exertion during separate training intensity zones
7. Injury/overuse status (record what, where, how, and when an injury begins and ongoing status)
8. Goals or significant workout or competition achievements
9. Emotions
10. Equipment and technique modifications (new shoes, wheels, tires, changing seat position, aero setup, etc., or trying a new technique)
11. Change in performance (right or wrong, good and bad)

PART III

SHARPENING YOUR EDGE

8

FUELING THE BODY

Athletes are often misled by promises of athletic excellence with the use of vitamin, mineral, herbal, and any number of ergogenic supplements. As long as athletes have competed, the search for the peak performance nutriment has continued. Does such a quest have any benefit? Perhaps, but only with respect to how nutrient habits and food intake affect performance. The sport food and supplement industry is a multibillion-dollar-a-year business in the United States alone, generating an overflow of misleading and often groundless quasi-medical, scientific, and physiological claims. Despite all that, peak athletic performance is a result of more well-known and sensible approaches to nutrition. The foundations of successful sport performance are found in carbohydrates, fats, proteins, and water, and for some, vitamin and mineral supplements may be necessary.

Although nutrition is a complex area of research, nutritional guidelines exist, and energy and fluid replacement is much less an art than it was 10 years ago. Carbohydrate replacement is important for the endurance athlete, as competitive performance, training, and recovery can be impaired by a low-carbohydrate diet. Fats also take on an important role for the endurance athlete, as they are the largest source of usable fuel in the body. The function of fats as an energy source is well documented; in longer events, they furnish a high percentage of the overall energy requirements during exercise. Protein, which accounts for roughly 20 percent of body weight and is found principally in muscle tissue, is another important, though limited, supplier of energy for the endurance athlete. Each of these areas of energy are reviewed in the upcoming segment of this chapter.

Water helps maintain body temperature through several million sweat glands in the skin. Even small amounts of body water loss cause many adverse changes that lead to reduced endurance capacity and performance. In this chapter, I will discuss the most effective ways to stay hydrated for optimal performance and provide information on liquid carbohydrate and competition fluid replacement strategies.

The chapter concludes with a discussion of vitamin and mineral supplementation for the endurance athlete. In search of the "magic potion," athletes are often influenced by flashy advertisements, elite athlete endorsements, and the promise of performance enhancement without having to do additional training. Although supplementing the diet with vitamins and minerals may be necessary in certain instances, there is no conclusive evidence that nutritional supplements actually enhance performance. In this chapter, I'll provide advice on using supplements for those recovering from illness or injury or those under notable stress.

CARBOHYDRATE: AN IMPORTANT STAMINA FUEL

If carbohydrates were the body's only source of energy, about two hours of moderate exercise would deplete those reserves. Carbohydrates are found in foods containing various types of starches and sugars. These, in turn, are converted to glucose (sugar transported in the blood) and glycogen (carbohydrates in the muscles and liver) to be used by the body for energy. The amount of glycogen stored within muscle is limited, and compared to fats, glycogen is not as abundant an energy fuel. For example, muscles contain up to 400 grams (1,600 calories) of stored glycogen, the liver contains about 70 grams (280 calories), and blood glucose contains 2.5 grams (100 calories). In an average-sized man, fats comprise 90,000 calories, but fats need carbohydrate to metabolize efficiently.

The intensity and length of exercise time, the size of the individual, and the exercise environment all determine how glycogen stores are utilized. In effect, when exercising at intensities higher than 65 percent of $\dot{V}O_2$max, even greater amounts of glycogen are needed to meet energy needs. Additionally, as fitness improves, endurance athletes use less glycogen for energy needs due to improvements in fat oxidation and metabolism. Thus the amount of glycogen required is less due to the athlete's enhanced ability to use fat as an efficient energy source. This is due to the higher fat content in slow-twitch fibers (muscle fibers with high oxidative capacity and low glycogen needs) than in fast-twitch fibers.

Changes in glycogen and fat supplies during endurance training are brought about by repetitive workouts. Glycogen supplies within the muscles are increased with endurance training, thus an athlete can exercise longer. Fat oxidation is also increased within the muscles and further improves fuel utilization. As a consequence, endurance training improves how these fuels are used for energy, and as further adaptations occur, greater improvements in performance are achieved.

Sources and Quantities of Carbohydrates

Endurance training can increase total-body glycogen reserves by 30 percent. Glycogen formations change in response to endurance training, developing more storage volume. That's good news for the endurance athlete. Diet can also significantly affect the amount of glycogen stored within the body, particularly in muscle. For example, consuming an extra 400 to 600 grams of complex carbohydrates in the days before competition increases total-body glycogen reserves, permitting the athlete to extend exercise time.

Quality carbohydrates are found in many types of foods, including breads, bagels, pasta, rice, potatoes, fruits, cereal grains, vegetables, and beans. Carbohydrates contain energy for muscle function and help provide protection against overtraining, staleness, and fatigue. Endurance athletes with training regimens lasting longer than two hours per day are well advised to eat a high-carbohydrate snack (40 to 200 grams) before going to bed. Because sleeping is to some extent fasting, glycogen stores can be increased by using this technique, allowing the body to process this glycogen during sleep. Daily carbohydrate intake should be at least 65 percent of the athlete's total diet, and when training volume and intensity are high, up to 75 percent. Thus an athlete eating 4,000 calories per day needs $4,000 \times 0.65 = 2,600$ calories per day from carbohydrates.

Interestingly, whether by design or default, most endurance athletes eat a similar percentage of carbohydrate, fat, and protein. That's not exactly what is recommended. What's more, many endurance athletes take in far less than the recommended amounts of carbohydrate. W. Mike Sherman, PhD, and David R. Lamb, PhD, (1988) write in *Nutrition and Prolonged Exercise*, "Elite athletes in the United States apparently consume diets in which the percentage of calories derived from carbohydrate is grossly inadequate" (p. 221). Further, they recommend that carbohydrate, fat, and protein intake should be 70, 18, and 12 percent, respectively. I recommend endurance athletes stay within ten percent of these values depending upon the intensity and volume of their exercise.

Of recent interest is what has been called the "40-30-30" diet: 40% protein, 30% carbohydrate; and 30% fat. Numerous chiropractors and applied kinesiologists associate with the "40-30-30" program and, in my opinion, advocate the "fringe" elements in health and nutrition. Barrett and Herbert (1994) write in their article from the eighth edition of *Modern Nutrition in Health and Disease* about misuse, harmful and misleading claims by stating, "Applied kinesiology is based on the notion that every organ dysfunction is accompanied by a specific muscle weakness, which enables diseases to be diagnosed through muscle-testing procedures. Its practitioners, most of whom are chiropractors, also claim that nutritional deficiencies, allergies, and other adverse reactions to food and substances can be detected by placing substances in the mouth so that the patient salivates. 'Good' substances make specific muscles stronger, whereas 'bad' substances cause specific weaknesses. 'Treatment' then consists of expensive vitamin supplements or a special diet. Double-blind studies have found no difference between the results with test substances and placebos. (Kenney, Clemens, and Forsythe 1988)."

Proponents of this diet and makers of products containing this combination of ingredients maintain eating a combination of 40 percent carbohydrate, 30 percent protein, and 30 percent fat will help athletes lose weight permanently, have more energy, and enhance mental and athletic performance. Perhaps of more interest is their position that a high carbohydrate diet produces excess insulin. Insulin is a hormone (chemical substances produced or released in the endocrine glands where hormones are released into the blood stream) that regulates the metabolism (supply and usage) of fuels—control of blood sugar (glucose). This is not the case as endurance exercise and a high complex carbohydrate diet lower insulin levels and increase insulin sensitivity (Fukagawa et al. 1990).

Whether individuals and companies that market and manufacture sport nutritional products have found something that works we'll only know with further research. However, I disagree with diets advocating such low percentages of carbohydrate and high percentages of fat in general. Not much data exist on the *absolute* eating habits of athletes, but it's not uncommon for a typical athlete to eat 14 percent protein, 36 percent fat, and 51 percent carbohydrate (Johnson et al. 1985). This isn't close to the "40-30-30" plan, but is more inline with the 12 percent protein, 18 percent fat, and 70 percent carbohydrate diets referred to earlier. Research in this area is variable, but most agree that carbohydrates are the major fuel in maintaining training for endurance athletes (Costill and Miller 1980; Sherman 1983; Sherman and Lamb 1988).

For the most part, I don't recommend too tight a structure, with athletes counting the dietary grams of every meal. Nevertheless, it's a good idea for the athlete to write down everything consumed at meals for several days to get a clear picture of the percentages. Most eat from a small selection of foods so comparison should be easy. In addition, athletes who are successful tend to eat well even if not by design. Beyond this, watch for symptoms of overtraining such as unexplained poor competitions and workouts, which may indicate something lacking in the diet. If energy levels are strong, recovery from workouts is swift, sleep patterns are normal, eating habits are regular, bowel movements are routine, and weight is stable, there's a very good chance the athlete is eating right.

I recommend eating whole foods (grains, fresh fruits, and vegetables) and reducing or eliminating processed and prepackaged foods, which can be loaded with fats and preservatives the body doesn't need. Stocking the kitchen and lunchbox with healthy choices is my best advice. Athletic performance and overall health will benefit when athletes consume foods from a nutritious variety.

Carbohydrate Loading

Clearly, carbohydrate supercompensation (loading) is effective for endurance exercise. Loading the muscles with glycogen via carbohydrate permits you to exercise longer at your maximum aerobic capacity. One of the best ways to load the muscles with glycogen is to ingest carbohydrates following exercise, when the muscles are most receptive to replenishment. Take in about 0.07 to 3 grams per kilogram of body weight within 30 minutes after completion of training and competitive exercise. Many single servings of sport drinks and high-nutrition bars or a couple of bananas will provide you with this amount.

If you suffer from any of the following symptoms, you should check the amount of carbohydrate you are eating. If you experience ongoing fatigue, have poor workouts, and are easily irritated, you may be suffering from inadequate carbohydrate nutrition or overtraining, which often go hand in hand. Table 8.1 identifies a convenient timetable for carbohydrate ingestion before, during, and after exercise.

FATS: THE ENDURANCE ATHLETE'S ALLY

As a fuel source, fats are virtually an unlimited energy supply for the body, even in the leanest of endurance athletes. A person with 15 percent body fat has approximately 90,000 calories of stored fats. That's enough potential energy to do more than six Ironman triathlons without stopping. By comparison, the body can store only about 1,200 to 1,800 carbohydrate calories for energy and exercise. That amount of carbohydrate will only fuel about 90 minutes of exercise.

TABLE 8.1   Carbohydrate Ingestion Timetable for Exercise

	Precompetition meal	Before exercise	During exercise	After exercise
Timing of intake	3 to 6 hours before competition	30 minutes before	Following first 2 hours	Immediately following exercise
Frequency of intake	NA	NA	Hourly	Each 2 hours after
Amount of intake	1,600 to 2,400 calories	200 to 300 calories	200 to 300 calories	500 to 1,000 calories
Type	Mostly carbohydrate and low fats, proteins	Sport bar or sport drink (combination)	Sport bar or sport drink (combination)	High-carbohydrate replenisher
Carbohydrate grams	400 to 600	±40	40 to 50	0.07 to 2 grams per kilogram of body weight

© Richard Etcherger

Of the dietary fats, saturated fats are mostly of animal origin, and unsaturated fats are found in fish and in vegetable oils. Saturated fats, known as the "bad" fats, are those associated with coronary artery disease and are found in beef, lamb, pork, butterfats (cheese, butter, ice cream), and highly saturated vegetable oils (coconut, cocoa butter, and palm). Some fats have undergone a process called hydrogenation (hard margarine and shortenings), which in effect makes them saturated fats.

The unsaturated group, including monounsaturated and polyunsaturated (omega-3) fatty acids, are known as "healthy" fats and are found in fish as well as olive, soybean, cottonseed, safflower, sunflower, canola, and avocado oils. Although the human body does not need saturated fats in the diet because the body manufactures them, polyunsaturated fats need to be included in the diet and are termed "essential" fatty acids. Fats should account for about 18 percent of the daily food intake for endurance athletes, and for health reasons, I recommend that athletes eat more unsaturated "essential" fats than those of the saturated variety.

Fats (lipids) are associated with unequivocally harmful conditions such as heart disease, arteriosclerosis (fatty deposits on inner artery walls), and obesity. These days, few individuals want to be fat or even have much to do with it. Fat-loss headlines appear on the cover of just about every magazine and tabloid in the grocery checkout line. Yet for the endurance athlete, fats are an abundant source of energy. But remember, to sustain training and competition energy, small and frequently ingested amounts of carbohydrate are needed for fats to be metabolized efficiently.

Trained endurance athletes have higher percentages of slow-twitch fibers and are better able to utilize fats for energy than untrained individuals. The reason is that slow-twitch fibers have more capillaries and greater mitochondrial content to utilize fat for energy. Capillaries are developed through training and surround the muscle fiber. This capillary increase permits a greater exchange of gases, heat, and fuels. Mitochondria are powerful structures located within muscle fibers that use fuel and oxygen to produce large amounts of adenosine triphosphate (ATP). ATP is a high-energy compound the body uses to fuel the working muscles. Interestingly, foods are not used directly for muscle contraction and energy production. With training, however, the muscles use less carbohydrate and more fat for fuel, and the foods we eat are used to produce ATP, which releases energy to the working muscles.

PROTEIN: THE BUILDING, DEVELOPMENT, AND RECOVERY NUTRIENT

Protein is composed of amino acids, the body's "construction material." Protein is an essential food for repair, regeneration, and maintenance of body tissues and protection from disease. The majority of protein is found in muscle tissue and is approximately 20 percent of a person's body mass. In terms of energy, proteins contribute only a small amount to exercise in endurance competition and training.

Vegetable Versus Animal Sources of Protein

Endurance athletes should consider protein an important component of their diet, particularly for repair of muscle tissue damage. With such a high percentage of the diet coming from carbohydrates, endurance athletes frequently overlook the importance of protein intake. Whether your diet is carnivorous or vegetarian, sufficient protein can be found through the foods we eat. Typically, high-protein foods include meats, poultry, eggs, and fish, but vegetarians can easily supply protein needs through nonanimal sources.

Animal proteins do present some concerns if eaten in large quantities, often because sources that are high in protein are also high in saturated fat. Again, saturated fats have been linked to raising blood cholesterol and shown to increase the risk of coronary artery (heart) disease. On the other hand, sources of veg-

etable, plant, and fish protein are high in unsaturated fats. Those fats are healthier for us, but such sources provide less protein than sources containing saturated fats. Thus there has been concern and disagreement over the adequacy of vegetarian diets for the endurance athlete; however, by consuming enough dairy foods (cheese, yogurt), nuts and seeds (pumpkin seeds, almonds, cashews), legumes (dried peas, beans, lentils, soybeans), and grains (rice, oatmeal, whole wheat, pasta), vegetarians can easily meet all of the daily protein requirements without overshooting their optimal fat intake percentage.

Vegetarians (I've been one for more than 20 years) must watch their diets carefully, however, when under particular strain from training, illness, or emotional stress. Stress leads to what Timothy Noakes, MD, describes as increased turnover rate (continual protein replacement); that is, the body's need for proteins is increased with muscle damage associated with endurance training and competitions. If you are a vegetarian, include plant and vegetable foods high in protein when under exceptional stress. For example, spinach is 49 percent protein, broccoli is 45 percent, tofu (soybean curd) is 43 percent, wheat germ is 31 percent, and pumpkin seeds are 21 percent.

Protein as an Energy Source

How much protein is used during endurance exercise? Recent studies indicate protein may make a small contribution to energy used by muscle. The less carbohydrate in the muscle, the more protein is used for energy. Sherman and Lamb (1988) found that 4.4 to 10.4 percent of total energy used by athletes exercising for one hour at moderate intensity comes from protein. Further, their study indicated that as carbohydrate stores are depleted by active muscles, unless the athlete is replacing carbohydrates at frequent intervals and in appropriate amounts, protein can supply up to 15 percent of the energy. However, as an energy source, protein is not as efficient as carbohydrate. The central nervous system needs carbohydrate to function properly.

WATER: THE OPTIMUM FLUID FOR ENDURANCE TRAINING AND COMPETITION

In 1983, I was training for the Hawaiian Ironman. On a typical summer day in northern California—beautiful clear blue skies—I was planning to ride a hundred miles, not too fast, just to get in the "saddle time." Seventy miles into the ride, the temperature had risen to more than 105 degrees—without a breeze. As I began the final 30 miles, my body and mind began behaving with uncertainty. I was very hot, wandering and pedaling bricks, not sweating, and getting light-headed. The water I did have was as hot as the asphalt, tasted like artificial plastic, and had no appeal whatsoever.

I rode sluggishly along, feeling more and more distracted and disoriented. Soon I stopped alongside the road, where just over a hill, a small lagoon awaited my overheated body. I collapsed into the pond of cool water. I felt better, but I was still light-headed and significantly dehydrated. Ten long and impossible miles later I finally got water. I recall it being the best I had ever tasted. Unfortunately, I was still not functioning well. I decided I'd had enough! I laid my bike down and rested alongside the road for a few quiet moments to recuperate and retrieve my strength.

I awoke in near darkness (a few minutes had turned to several hours) when a sheriff's car pulled up and the deputy asked, "Are you okay?" I rolled over, eyes gaunt, and remember saying sarcastically, "Yes." Big mistake! The officer drove off and left me there, in effect, to die! When I finally began riding again, I was not in too bad shape, and the temperature was cooler as the sun had gone down. I was very lucky to come through that day. When I finally returned home, I weighed nine pounds less than my normal weight.

This incident has served me well in the 14 years since. In my personal athletic endeavors and in coaching, I have learned (the hard way) the value of the body's most important nutrient: water. Endurance training, competitions, and high-intensity exercise place great requirements on fluid replacement. When the body gets hot or has not been properly hydrated, its cardiovascular and temperature-regulating systems are under higher levels of stress, work less efficiently, and cause you to slow down.

Temperature, Humidity, and Performance

Exercise produces body heat, which must be decreased for the body to function within optimal temperature zones. Too much body heat dwindles exercise capacity, as oxygen is limited due to increased circulation demands. Body temperature is maintained by moving heat from exercising muscles to the surface of the body via the blood. As the body's core temperature rises, the blood flow to the skin increases, and the body now attempts to cool itself by sweating.

What really happens to body and muscle temperatures when we exercise? The body's temperature rises to as high as 105 degrees, just as when we have a fever. The muscle temperatures also rise, sometimes to more than 108 degrees. These high temperatures make exercise difficult because the body and muscles are now competing for blood: The body's skin surface wants to be cooled and requires blood flow to do so, and the muscles need oxygenated blood to work and perform. This creates a compromising situation for the circulatory system. However, with training and good fluid and energy replacement planning, circulatory system function can be maintained and improved.

In humid environments, such as those found in the Midwest, Texas, Hawaii, and parts of Europe, air humidity affects the body's control of heat dissipation more than high temperatures. When the air is high in moisture, the sweat that normally cools the body's surface no longer evaporates efficiently. Evaporation of sweat is necessary for heat to be removed from the body. In environments where the air humidity is up to 100 percent, sweat cannot evaporate from the skin but merely drips off and does not cool the body effectively.

Some athletes can tolerate high heat demands in extreme environments. Dave Scott is one athlete who can endure high humidity and temperatures in competitions such as the

SHOULD YOU POUR WATER OVER YOUR BODY?

It is common for an athlete to splash or sponge water over the head, face, neck, abdomen, legs, and wrists to cool the body. Ironically, this can lead to further over-heating of the body and subsequently a greater loss of body water (dehydration). Although the feeling is pleasant and psychologically effective for short periods, the temporary coolness of the water and the momentary relief from heat often invite increases in pace. Unfortunately, the increase in pace is short-lived and only results in more slowing down as the body temperature rises further. Additionally, water drips and splashes onto the feet and causes an annoying squishing in the shoes and socks. This also increases the weight of the shoe, requiring more effort per footstrike and causing blisters and a general loss of normal biomechanics.

If you feel the need to splash water over your body, be attentive to momentary increases in effort due to temporary relief and be careful of getting your shoes wet. My recommendation is to first drink the fluids, then, if you must, apply a cold sponge or ice to your wrists, neck, and abdomen rather than splashing your entire body. You could save yourself from painful blisters and other consequences such as soppy running shoes and socks.

Hawaiian Ironman triathlon, where he is a six-time winner. Paula Newby Fraser, the women's eight-time Ironman champion, is another athlete who can adapt to the extreme temperatures along the Kona coast on the island of Hawaii. Whether this ability is due to their unique physiological makeup or to exceptional training and preparation is an interesting question.

For most endurance athletes, exercising in hot and humid conditions presents many problems. In particular, dehydration can significantly affect performance and, in extreme cases, compromise the health of the athlete. If you are going to compete in a hot and/or humid environment, you must train in similar conditions to be fully prepared for competition. If you are unable to do so, arriving five to eight days prior to the race will help you acclimate. However, this is the time when you should be tapering, so exercise volume and intensity should be kept within appropriate ranges based on your individual acclimation needs. If you train in a cooler environment, you must get a certain amount of exposure to heat and/or humidity to perform well.

Dehydration and Thirst

When you sense that you are thirsty, as much as 2 percent of your body water is lost and needs to be replenished. Although this amount is considered within the "normal" range for humans, it is not an optimum condition for the endurance athlete. Armstrong, Costill, and Fink (1985) conducted a study that, rather than inducing dehydration through room temperature control and exercise intensity, induced dehydration by purposefully dehydrating the participants using diuretics. In effect, what the researchers were looking at was "true dehydration" as opposed to dehydration resulting from temperature increases, caloric decreases, or physical stress. The results showed that with only a 1 percent reduction in body weight, exercise times were significantly longer for completing 1,500-, 5,000-, and 10,000-meter runs. For each run in this study, respective increases of 17 seconds; 39 seconds; and 1 minute, 57 seconds resulted. Clearly, even a slight reduction (only 1 percent of body weight) in body water leads to a significant reduction in work capacity.

To maintain functional body temperature during exercise, the heat generated needs to be transferred from the muscles to the body core. With an increase in core temperature, blood flow to the skin increases perspiration, thus cooling the body temperature. However, as this occurs, body water must be replaced to keep an athlete performing optimally. Water has many important contributions beyond body temperature maintenance. It helps dilute electrolytes, glucose, and proteins and delivers oxygen and nutrients to the exercising muscles. Therefore, a watchful endurance athlete will maintain water balance.

There is no organ for notifying us that we are thirsty. This makes rehydrating during training and competition especially important and at the same time hard to manage. Water, the most abundant component of the body, needs to be maintained within a very narrow range for peak athletic performance; that is, fluid deficits should be kept to less than 2 percent of body weight. This is not always easy, practical, or even practiced by many endurance athletes. I've even known athletes who purposefully dehydrate themselves in training as a means of adaptation and acclimation—a foolish practice that should never be done. Prolonged fasting (fluids and foods) before exercise dehydrates the athlete and depletes liver and muscle glycogen stores, causing a serious deficiency in endurance performance. Thus an athlete may perceive that she is exercising at high intensity and her heart rate may indicate this as well, but the specificity and the performance are less than optimal. The best way to stay hydrated is to take in fluids frequently throughout the day before you feel thirsty.

Water is needed for the delivery of oxygen and nutrients to the muscles being used during exercise and for transferring heat from the muscles to the skin for dissipation (in the form of sweat). With increased dehydration, several physical symptoms and potentially serious effects can occur (table 8.2). A simple reminder is that with increased dehydration, there is a corresponding reduction in the amount of oxygen transferred to the muscles. (Obviously, this is not in the best interests of any athlete.) In essence, for the endurance athlete, water is the most important nutrient for optimum performance.

The difficulty lies in knowing when to take in fluids before it's too late. Part of the problem is that humans have a poor sense for knowing when they are thirsty. Often, one does not feel thirsty until 1 percent or more of body water has already been lost. What can you do

TABLE 8.2   Physical Symptoms and Effects of Dehydration

Body water lost	Symptoms
1 percent	Few symptoms or signs of any thirst are present; however, there is a marked reduction in $\dot{V}O_2$max
2 percent	Beginning to feel thirsty; loss of endurance capacity and appetite
3 percent	Dry mouth; performance impaired
4 percent	Increased effort for exercise, impatience, apathy, vague discomfort, loss of appetite
5 percent	Difficulty concentrating, increased pulse and breathing, slowing of pace
6 to 7 percent	Further impairment of temperature regulation, higher pulse and breathing, flushed skin, sleepiness, tingling, stumbling, headache
8 to 9 percent	Dizziness, labored breathing, mental confusion, further weakness
10 percent	Muscle spasms, loss of balance, swelling of tongue
11 percent	Heat exhaustion, delirium, stroke, coma, difficulty swallowing; death can occur

> # DEHYDRATION CAN DECREASE ATHLETIC PERFORMANCE IN SEVERAL WAYS:
>
> - Decreasing endurance duration
> - Increasing heart rate per minute
> - Increasing lactate acid in muscles
> - Increasing body temperature
> - Decreasing strength
> - Causing any of the following medical conditions: heat cramping, heat exhaustion, and heat stroke (possible permanent central nervous system damage, coma, or death)

to ensure that this doesn't happen to you? The best way is to make a habit of drinking something every 15 minutes during exercise. This is especially important when training for prolonged periods (longer than one hour). Swimming can dehydrate you as well, and it is a good idea to have body fluid replacement drinks at poolside. By maintaining fluids, the blood can travel more efficiently (cooling the body, optimizing and regulating body temperature) as the perspiration rate remains at peak levels. Thus your performance is sure to be better for attending to this simple and important aspect of training.

It is important to remember that the sensation of thirst is slowed in humans. In other words, don't rely on feeling thirsty to manage the replenishment of body fluids. By then, it's too late, because you're already starting to become dehydrated. The following are some additional tips for monitoring body water:

- Weigh in before and after exercise. For every pound of body weight lost during exercise, drink 16 ounces of fluid.
- Continually rehydrate during exercise (swimming, cycling, running, and supplemental training).
- Do not intentionally train in a dehydrated condition in hopes of acclimating.
- Consider posttraining rehydration a fundamental component of the training process.
- Drink nondiuretic (caffeine-free) fluids (water, juices, sport drinks) regularly.
- Monitor urination for copious volume and clear color.

Water Versus Liquid Carbohydrates During Exercise

To illustrate the importance of water and carbohydrate replacement during exercise, one study (Pitts, Johnson, and Consolazio 1944) measured the heart rates, rectal temperatures, and sweat rates of men walking on a treadmill up a 2.5 percent grade for one to four hours. Some of the subjects were allowed water any time they wished, others were given no water, others received water at 15-minute intervals, and another group was given a 3.5 percent glucose solution at 15-minute intervals. The subjects maintained an average temperature of 95 degrees and an average humidity of 59 percent. The group that was not allowed any water had heart rates of 22 beats per minute higher than the group that was allowed water at 15-minute intervals. Those taking in the glucose (carbohydrate) had lower heart rates, rectal temperatures, and sweat rates than all the other groups. This is not new information, either; as noted previously, the study was reported in 1944.

Water is likely the most optimal fluid to drink, especially for events lasting less than two hours when a liquid sport drink is not necessary. Simply be well hydrated (clear and copious urine) before the race. However, for events lasting longer than two hours, liquid carbohydrate sport drinks are a better nutrient. These drinks are excellent sources of carbohydrate and electrolytes (sodium, potassium, chloride, phosphorus, calcium, and magnesium). Some argue that, other than sodium, these minerals have no effect on performance and are replaced easily through a well-balanced diet. On the other hand, sodium and glucose concentrations (sport drinks) enhance fluid absorption from the small intestine. Additionally, small amounts of sodium improve the mechanism of thirst, as it is more palatable.

Study after study demonstrates that carbohydrate sport drinks improve endurance performance. Not only do these products help while training and competing, they provide substantial gains in nutrition and postexercise restoration. When ingested after exercise, carbohydrate is readily absorbed, as the body is more responsive to restoring glycogen in the

muscles, liver, and blood at this time. Some guidelines for hydrating are to drink 16 to 20 ounces of water between one hour and 15 minutes prior to competition or training and to consume 16 ounces of your sport drink in the final 15 minutes before the start.

How Much and How Often?

Training or competing with a stomach full of sloshing, gurgling fluids is not comfortable. The stomach has a limited ability to absorb fluids, so I don't advise taking in any more than the prescribed hourly amounts when training or competing. In competition, it is impossible

NUTRITION IN TRAINING AND RACING

Training is the time to test sport nutriments as guided by the product label for mixture, amount, and frequency. Do not wait until race day to learn you cannot stomach the race-day nutrition supplied. For any competition, particularly those longer than four hours, make a point of using the carbohydrate fluid product to be made available during that event. I believe most sensible race directors will be using safe and appropriately mixed quantities of these fluids. Race day, however, is too late to find out that you don't like or can't tolerate the product.

Finally, be suspicious of curious or remarkable statements, affirmations, endorsements by athletes, and ambiguous research references. If it sounds too good to be true, it probably is. On the other hand, there are many well-respected companies supplying the endurance athlete with sound nutritional choices. Use the guidelines described in table 8.3 for selecting a sport nutrition product.

As we approach the 21st century, a wide variety of supplemental training and competition nutrition products is available with contents such as glucose, fructose, sucrose, and glucose polymers (maltodextrin)—types of carbohydrate that are absorbed into the muscles and liver for eventual use as energy. All of these ingredients have proven practical and effective for replacing energy and promoting performance. Glycogen replenishment is an indispensable form of nutritional fitness for training, competition, and postrace recovery—one that endurance athletes must consider to be competitive and healthy.

Sport nutrition products (high-nutrition bars, gels, and liquid carbohydrate drinks) are a mainstay for the endurance athlete. A visit to an endurance athlete's kitchen usually reveals a vast array of these products stockpiled for the next feeding frenzy. It is important to expand carbohydrate reserves and replace losses through convenient and reliable, wholesome foods. Supplemental sport foods can be nutritious, tasty, and a practical method of meeting your energy requirements. Although they don't take the place of eating healthy whole foods, when in a rush, such products can be the insurance you need to get through a busy schedule.

TABLE 8.3   Fluid Replacement Beverage Comparison Chart

Beverage	Carbohydrate ingredient	Carbohydrate concentration per 8 ounces (percent)	Sodium per 8 ounces (mg)	Potassium (mg)	Other minerals and vitamins
Gatorade Thirst Quencher	Powder: Sucrose, glucose, sodium, potassium	6	110	25	Chloride, phosphorus
Powerade	High-fructose corn syrup, maltodextrin	8	73 or less	33	Chloride
AllSport	High-fructose corn syrup	8-9	55	55	Chloride, phosphorus, calcium
10K	Sucrose, glucose, fructose	6.3	54	25	Vitamin C, chloride, phosphorus
QuickKick	Fructose, sucrose	4.7	116	23	Calcium, chloride, phosphorus
Endura	Glucose polymers, fructose	6.2	92	180	Calcium, chloride, magnesium, chromium
1st Ade	High-fructose corn syrup, fructose	6	119	25	Phosphorus
Hydra Fuel	Glucose polymers, glucose, fructose	7	25	50	Chloride, magnesium, chromium, phosphorus, vitamin C
Cytomax	Fructose, corn syrup, sucrose	7-11	10	150	Chromium, magnesium
Gookinaide	Glucose	12	70	70	Vitamins A and C, calcium, iron
Pro Motion	Fructose	7.7	8	99	None
EverlastSports Drink	Sucrose, fructose	6	100	20	Vitamin C
PurePower Energy & Recovery Drink	Fructose, maltodextrin	4.3	50	100	Chromium, vitamin C, calcium, phosphorus, magnesium
Breakthrough	Maltodextrin, fructose	8.5	60	45	Vitamin C, calcium, chloride, magnesium, riboflavin, niacin, iron, thiamin
Coca-Cola	High-fructose corn syrup, sucrose	11	9.2	Trace	Phosphorus
Diet soft drinks	None	0	0	25	Low phosphorus
Orange juice	Fructose, sucrose	11-15	2.7	510	Vitamins A and C, niacin, thiamin, riboflavin
Water	0	0	Low	Low	Low

to breathe and swallow much fluid at the same time. I'll never understand why they put aide stations atop the longest, steepest hills. It just isn't possible for respiratory muscles to work right during high-intensity exercise. Breathing and drinking don't go hand in hand.

Studies of endurance athletes indicate that 150 to 250 milliliters (4 to 8 ounces) or two or three mouthfuls every 10 to 15 minutes is the most effective fluid ingestion rate. Over an hour, this intake rate will deliver approximately 16 to 30 ounces (500 to 800 milliliters). Taking in such small amounts of fluid at this frequency is not likely to cause gasping. In addition, this amount of fluid is emptied most efficiently from the stomach to the intestines, where the rate of absorption to the working muscles is very fast. Drinking regularly and in smaller quantities helps ensure proper absorption and, more important, peak performance.

Endurance athletes often become hyponatremic—a condition also referred to as water intoxication (bloating), the most common type of electrolyte disorder. If an athlete drinks large amounts of water during prolonged exercise, it dilutes, resulting in low blood sodium levels. When combined with increased sweat rates, which cause further sodium losses, hyponatremica (low blood sodium) may follow. During any multihour endurance training or competition, the fear of dehydration along with the plentiful availability of water pose ideal conditions for this problem to occur.

When an athlete's pace slows due to fatigue and dehydration, he is now at greater risk. Lower exercise intensity permits the athlete to take in more fluids because of a lower respiratory rate. The athlete is likely feeling any number of symptoms such as headache, muscle cramps, weakness, thirst, agitation, disorientation, apathy, and lethargy. Drinking too much fluid results in a dysfunction in gastric absorption rate, a decrease of blood flow to working muscles, kidney failure, increased core body temperature, and a decrease in $\dot{V}O_2$max (maximal oxygen consumption). Hyponatremia may be more common than suspected and should be treated under medical supervision. Fortunately, carbohydrate/sodium beverages help reduce this potentially serious condition by maintaining blood sodium levels.

Taking in small quantities of fluids at frequent intervals of 10 to 15 minutes is the golden rule for rehydration during exercise. Remember, just a 1 percent loss in body water can lead to significant decreases in performance. Once you begin competition or training, your most important task is to replenish body fluids. Do so by following the recommended replacement schedule.

The Colder the Better

The temperature of a fluid has a bearing on how quickly it is absorbed in the stomach. Colder fluids increase the smooth-muscle activity of the stomach and therefore will be transferred to the intestines, and thus to working muscles, more rapidly than warmer fluids. A smart endurance athlete will choose colder fluids at every opportunity. When nearing an aide station, let the volunteers know your needs clearly. And although colder fluids are better, those near body temperature also provide protection against overheating.

Sugar in Liquid Carbohydrate Energy Drinks: How Much Is Right?

Liquid carbohydrate sugar quantities greater than 8 percent slow the movement of fluid from the stomach to the intestines and on to the working muscles. Most authorities and product manufacturers recommend mixtures containing 5 to 7 percent carbohydrates for optimal absorption.

Slight differences exist in the effectiveness of most liquid carbohydrate products. In some individuals, fructose causes gastrointestinal problems (nausea, gas, and diarrhea), although it is alleviated somewhat when combined with glucose or glucose polymer. The simple solution for those susceptible to stomach problems is to avoid high-fructose liquid carbohydrate sport drinks (table 8.4). Instead, consume drinks made with a glucose and sodium concentration such as Gatorade.

TRY IT OUT BEFORE COMPETING

Training is the perfect time to test various nutrition products for palatability, digestion, fluid absorption, and energy replacement. Begin using a product to be supplied at a race 8 to 10 weeks prior to the competition. If it doesn't work for you during this trial period, it's very important that you make arrangements with the race director to have a "special needs" container at the competition. Again, *do not* try new food products during competition. I've seen the undesirable consequences of this too many times. You never know what your reaction will be, especially under the physical and emotional stresses of competition. Remember the reasons you are out there, and stay focused on the goals you've set. Don't let another's well-meaning but inappropriate last-minute advice or the circumstances of competition sway you from doing what is right for you. Do what you've done in training, and keep in mind the rule of right practice.

VITAMIN AND MINERAL SUPPLEMENTATION

The nutritional scientific literature, for the most part, continues to cast a long shadow on the role of vitamin supplementation for healthy individuals and endurance athletes. Vitamins and minerals act as catalysts in the presence of carbohydrate, protein, and fats but by themselves are non-energy-producing micronutrients. Although vitamins and minerals are essential to life and needed in small amounts, they are found in abundance in a well-balanced diet.

Distinguished researchers Jack Wilmore and David Costill (1988) write in their third edition of *Training for Sport and Activity:* "There have been a number of studies that found increased endurance with megadoses of vitamins C, E, and B-complex, but there are far more studies demonstrating that vitamins in excess of the RDA will not improve performance in either strength or endurance activities. Experts generally agree that popping vitamins will not make up for a lack of talent or training, or give one an edge over the competition" (p. 230).

Hundreds of thousands of "health food" stores and direct-mail advertisers sell vitamins, minerals, herbs, and other food products for promoting optimum health and athletic performance. The chiropractic physician, too, is often promoting any number of nutritional, supplemental products and herbal medicines. Every week, it seems, news of at least one big food or supplement fad buzzes among endurance athletes. Greater endurance, stamina, unlimited energy, and improved well-being are marketed like multi-level marketing schemes. All too often, the science is manipulated, as few supplements actually have much efficacy when a sound diet is followed. Despite evidence that unhealthy individuals may need vitamin and mineral supplements, especially during periods of illness or considerable stress, those in robust health do not.

People are drawn to the "elixirs of life" by promises of regaining their lost youth and excelling in physical performance. But there are no real secrets, no magic potions or food supplements, that will make you a better athlete. Vitamin supplements do not contain energy and cannot overcome the effects of a steady diet of Coca-Cola and Snickers bars. It's the foods you eat and your exercising, not the pills you take, that help make you strong and capable as an endurance athlete.

Diet affects how we feel, look, and perform in competition and training and how damaged tissue is repaired. Eliminate chemically processed foods, limit saturated fats, eat green, leafy vegetables, fruits, grains, and nonfat dairy products, and include daily protein from any number of plant or animal sources.

TABLE 8.4   Fluid Ingestion Timetable for Events Lasting More Than 2 Hours

	Before exercise	During exercise	After exercise
Timing of intake	60 until 15 minutes before, drink water; 15 minutes before exercise, drink sport drink*	Hourly or as dictated by temperature and intensity	First hour following exercise
Frequency of intake	Until stomach is partially full*	10- to 15-minute cycles	Until partially full
Amount of intake	16 to 20 ounces (500 to 600 milliliters) more than 15 minutes and less than 60 minutes before event*	4 to 8 ounces (150 to 250 milliliters)	16 to 32 ounces (1,000 milliliters)
Temperature	Cold (41 degrees)	Cold (41 degrees)	Cold (41 degrees)
Carbohydrate content	5 to 7 percent	5 to 8 percent	20 to 25 percent
Carbohydrate grams	30 to 40	40 to 50	1.5 to 3 grams per kilogram of body weight

*Based on 8-ounce servings

If you are uncertain about the vitamin and mineral status of your body, your physician can do several blood tests to help pinpoint any deficiency. A complete blood panel (SMAC-24), which measures 24 different chemical characteristics of the blood, can provide useful information. Likewise, blood markers can be assessed and permit training to be analyzed via additional blood tests. Three particular markers found in muscle tissue increase after exercise: creatine phosphokinase (CPK), aspartate transaminase (AST), and lactate dehydrogenase (LDH). These markers are established by analyzing the amounts in the bloodstream. With high-intensity exercise, higher markers leak from the muscle into the bloodstream. A fourth important blood marker is cortisol, which increases following physical activity or psychological stress. Cortisol increases the body's ability to produce energy and, during exercise, is an important benefit for the athlete. However, if cortisol levels remain too high, the body will break down muscle to continue to produce energy, resulting in fatigue and detraining problems. Blood tests can be taken by your physician to indicate the ranges of corti-

sol in your blood compared to "normal" readings.

Finally, when taking supplements or performance foods, the following should be kept in mind:

1. Be cautious, even suspicious, of product claims and endorsements, and fight the urge to start "taking" the goods before you've learned more about them.
2. Don't believe in the "magical qualities" of the product; they simply do not exist.
3. If you have a serious health problem, don't act in desperation to solve it by taking anything and everything.
4. Just because a product is labeled "natural" doesn't mean it's safe.
5. Maintain a healthy degree of skepticism toward both the "scientific" and "health food" communities.
6. Obtain an annual complete blood panel to check if a change in diet or supplementation is needed.
7. Supplements will not overcome the effects of poor dietary habits.
8. Think and eat more whole foods, not "health foods."

PREVENTING IRON DEFICIENCY

Iron deficiency, also called anemia, can be caused by a reduction in food intake, as when an athlete intentionally cuts back on calories, and by vegetarian diets. In training, only a minute amount of iron is lost in sweat, so the likely problem is inappropriate levels of iron in the diet. As iron is crucial to the transport of oxygen throughout the body, it is important to have adequate levels. Additionally, a condition called footstrike hemolysis was discovered more than 100 years ago in German soldiers. This condition—caused by the impact of the feet on the ground when running long distances in uncushioned shoes, on hard roads, or with a stomping gait—lowers the red blood cell concentrations in athletes. However, the condition generally remains mild, and with dietary watchfulness, athletes should not suffer from this problem.

Sports anemia is likely a misnomer, as endurance training expands the plasma volume, which dilutes the red blood cells (oxygen-carrying cells). Therefore, endurance athletes will have lower hematocrit levels (total blood volume percentage of red blood cells).

Careful attention to diet seems to be the best way to prevent iron deficiency. Iron absorption can be increased by eating more red meat, dark chicken meat, decreasing coffee and tea intake when eating cereal and bread, cooking acidic foods such as tomato sauce in iron skillets, and eating poultry or seafood with beans or peas (the animal protein increases absorption in the vegetables). Other sources of iron are egg yolks, legumes, whole grains, dark green vegetables, shrimp, and oysters.

How do you know when you have iron deficiency? The primary symptoms are inadequate red blood cells, low hemoglobin levels, and decreased oxygen-transfer capacity. These symptoms cause you to feel slow, lethargic, and chronically tired.

In the future, I believe vitamin, mineral, and herbal supplementation will likely play a dominant role in the performance of endurance athletes. For now, it remains a "shot in the dark." Keep in mind that there are no secret magic potions or food supplements that will make you a better athlete, and let common sense prevail. As scientists and herbalists expand and refine their respective research, I believe they will find more common ground between them. Perhaps it won't be long before intravenous solutions are somehow ingeniously dispensed during exercise without interrupting performance. After mentioning this to an acquaintance, she replied, "Yeah, instead of aide stations we'll have 'I.V.' stations." An interesting concept, and one that may have future potential.

9

PREPARING THE MIND

Achieving peak athletic performance requires a synergism of three things. First, the athlete must have the physical ability: biomechanics, endurance, strength, and flexibility. Second, the athlete must prepare by training the body properly and thoroughly. This is achieved through right practice, specificity in workouts, implementation of a training plan, and good coaching. Third, and just as important, the athlete must have psychological steadiness—unwavering self-confidence, the will to excel, a positive attitude, and concentration on specific goals. Mark Allen, six-time winner of the Ironman, says it well: "Do I set goals? Yes! You've got to have a clear picture of what you're doing, where you're going . . . a goal is sort of helping align every cell in the body to do this thing on a given day. Goals help bring everything together to a fine point."

Jerry May, PhD, a psychologist at the University of Nevada School of Medicine, told me during an interview for this book, "You cannot separate the mental and physical. Biologically the brain controls both, so when one quits, both stop. However, athletes often place cognitive restrictions [on themselves] that may adversely affect their performance. For example, a golfer might say internally, 'Don't slice this shot.' The result, of course, is a sliced shot. [A preferable] cognitive statement would be, 'Okay, hit the ball straight.' For the endurance athlete, a similar statement might be, 'I am running fast. Stay smooth and composed.'"

World-class athletes accomplish the extraordinary under the most challenging circumstances. When you look into their eyes, you notice something different, something not easily defined. Self-assurance, dominance, and body language make us admire their talents. They, too, are human and have the same feelings and thoughts you and I have, but they differ in how they manage their emotions in the heat of competition. Not only have they learned to master their physical capabilities and to train well, they have also refined their mental skills to a world-class level.

Other athletes are capable of doing the physical workouts and pushing themselves through continuous, exhaustive training, but psychology—not physiology—keeps them from reaching their fullest potential. They regularly underachieve in competition. It is the mental state of the athlete that is most vital in the pursuit of achieving peak performance. In discussing the mental aspects of training and competition, Mark Allen told me, "Yes, everybody does the physical work—that's the easier part. On the starting line, you have the freedom to show completely what you've done . . . allowing all the mental stuff to come together in the right way."

Studies show that athletes can slow down during competition and training as a result of mental fatigue, loss of motivation, and related psychological symptoms. So beyond a doubt, the mental resolve of the athlete plays a vital role in athletic performance. How elite athletes deal with precompetition anxiety and apply mental strategy is an individual process, but similarities do exist. Several of these traits and techniques will be detailed throughout this chapter. I'll also describe some unique relaxation and imagery techniques that, with practice, you can use to improve your mental training and competitive focus.

THE COMPETITIVE BODY AND MIND

It has been said that sport is 90 percent mental. If this is so (and I agree that it is), then why don't we train the mind as much as the body? Well, perhaps we do, but in more subtle ways. I view sport psychology as a means of developing the extra edge needed to achieve one's goals. Positive mental assertions and outlook can't help but affect how an athlete performs.

Elite endurance athletes share certain physiological attributes, training regimens, and tactical methods. Despite slight differences in their physical makeup, they all have similar maximal oxygen capacities. Technically, a race is rarely won because of equipment or mechanical advantages, and tactical strategies differ very little among athletes. Psychological makeup, I believe, is the true differentiator—the essence of the world-class athlete. Even though we do not all possess the necessary physical qualities to excel, with proper physical training we can improve greatly. However, mental training can perhaps make even more of a difference. Anyone is capable of changing how they think about athletic performance. The mind is a powerful tool for visualizing successful outcomes in training and competition.

Motivation: Approaching Success Versus Avoiding Failure

Whenever you face a difficult situation, challenge it head on. To understand and control anxiety, you must first determine where your negative thoughts are coming from and confront them purposefully. Then turn those negative thoughts into positive, earnest affirmations (table 9.1) and repeat them to yourself over and over. Whenever I face a difficult situation, I say to myself again and again, "Things will work out. I know I can be successful." Believe me, I've said this to myself thousands of times. It helps me overcome feelings of uncertainty or the fear of failure.

Few would argue that by modifying our personal thoughts and attitudes, our lives can be substantially changed to a healthier vision of the world, of others, and ourselves (Vealey 1994). For many athletes, the goal in competing is to avoid losing rather than to perform their personal best. I encourage athletes to dare to *succeed*, rather than just to avoid failure. The athlete who succeeds out of fear of failure will ultimately become apprehensive, perform less well, and perhaps even avoid competition. Athletes who are highly motivated to succeed are less anxious about failure, perform at their very best in difficult competitive situations, and compete more successfully than those competing to avoid losing (Gill 1993).

Elite athletes I have coached are definitely more interested in how they performed than in merely winning. Although winning is important to them, it's not the most satisfying aspect of competing. In a questionnaire, I asked Scott Tinley, Dave Scott, and Karen Smyers, "Does losing upset you?" Each said they had dispassionate feelings about losing. I asked if they "hated to lose," and the replies were generally that they didn't strongly agree or strongly disagree with the statement. Finally, I asked, "Is the only time you're satisfied when you win?" Each disagreed with this, and Dave Scott disagreed very strongly.

These individuals are not unlike other world-class athletes in their attitude toward competition. They like to win, of course, and set extraordinarily focused goals to accomplish this. However, the manner in which each balances their satisfaction with winning is similar: Performing to the best of their ability is more important to them. Mark Allen says, " Every race you enter, you must fully accept the fact you may not be the one who comes out on top. That has to be okay even before you start, to have a chance [at doing well]. If it's not okay before you start, then [you won't be prepared] if things start going haywire—which they do in almost every race."

Although winning is important—and a lot more fun than losing—giving their very best each moment is at the very core of why successful athletes do what they do. It's the performance and how it's accomplished that's most satisfying, not money or a championship or getting their picture on the cover of a magazine.

Fortunately, the same mental techniques can help you cope with losses and attain your best results. Goals, imagery training, and positive self-talk can help an athlete through both positive and negative athletic situations. For example, goals direct the training plan in ways that will best result in success. Using imagery training—rehearsing in your mind what your muscles will feel like in a competition or imagining a peak performance—provides positive images and precompetitive rehearsals to prepare you for possible race scenarios. It doesn't take long for the mind to do this, either. In a quiet moment before a race, close your eyes and go through the entire event, imagining everything about the competition. Finally, use positive self-talk to turn negative statements, such as "I can't keep up this pace," into positive ones, such as "This pace is hard, but I know I can do it."

Mental Fatigue Versus Physical Fatigue

Elite athletes tend to perform very well in competition, particularly in close situations. They know how to deal with the pressures of competition and often perform at their best under these conditions. Mark Allen describes it this way: "If you have ten units of energy and give two away [to a competitor or any negative situation or thought], it affects your performance." Don't waste energy on things that are out of your control. Certainly, you must be aware of the competition, but you cannot allow any valuable emotional energy to be absorbed by it.

Triathlete Karen Smyers relates her very real emotional battle in the 1990 World Triathlon Championships when she was passed on the run by Joy Hansen and Carol Montgomery. She vividly remembers "trying to just hang on

mentally, but negative thoughts were flowing: the hot, humid environment, how bad I was feeling, and even feeling sorry for myself." Karen admits, "I was concentrating too much on how bad I was feeling and forgetting the competitors were likely feeling just as bad."

These are very normal feelings, ones we all have. But Karen handled them with one significant difference. She remembers that even though her arms were numb with pain, she somehow found enough strength and began "running for [her] life." She continued to repeat to herself over and over again, "Don't let up, don't let up! Every single second counts!" She won the World Championships! And it was a change of mental statements that brought her around and through the physical pain. This is a kind of pain management in a sense. Positive self-dialogue can take an athlete far beyond physical pain.

Maintaining Balance

A difficult part of endurance sport coaching is seeing athletes tormented by a "compulsive training disorder" or addiction to endurance training. Too often, athletes are more concerned about the quantity of training and not the quality. This can get in the way of living a normal, sensible life. Athletes, especially endurance athletes, have an extremely difficult time letting go of the need to train, even when they must. I've spent a lot of time consulting with athletes and writing programs like the one in this book. During phone consultations, the emphasis is often on psychology; much of the work I do is keeping an athlete focused on realistic goals.

Numerous endurance athletes with extraordinary athletic backgrounds and potential train around the world. Unfortunately, many are training at the expense of everything else in their lives. Sure, it makes sense to give it your all and spend a lot of time training if you want to be the "very best," but reason must prevail. There is nothing wrong with doing everything possible to improve your performance, unless it means jeopardizing your career or losing sight of family and spiritual values. Don't become so focused on training that you cannot make time for other activities in your life.

If you are training full-time and are not really in the hunt for elite status, you're probably better off getting a job, finishing school, and finding things to do athletically that are not related to training. Otherwise, you'll likely only become more narrowly focused on training, caught in an unhealthy cycle of compulsive-addictive behavior.

Endurance athletes who find themselves in a perpetual state of overtraining need to take a hard look at volume, intensity, recovery, and restoration. As outlined in chapter 2, training and competitions need to be organized so as to strike a balance between athletics and personal and professional lives. I've found the most successful athletes are those who can do just that.

GOAL SETTING: THE DESIRE TO SURPASS

Every elite athlete I have coached has set very specific goals and developed plans that focused on fulfilling them. Goals motivate an athlete to excel by establishing training and competitive objectives as measures of accomplishment.

Goals affect performance by guiding a series of actions necessary to move to a higher level. Training goals to improve performance might consist of swimming 20 × 200 meters in 2:30 on a send-off interval of 2:45 or cycling a 10-mile time-trial course in less than 25 minutes or running 8 × 800 meters on the track in 2:45 with a send-off interval of 3:00. Many athletes need to improve technique, so they might set a goal of correcting an aspect of swimming, cycling, or running through technical form training. Although these types of goals are less objective because you cannot measure them, by videotaping your form or getting feedback from your coach, you can see how you are progressing.

Long-term goals are best realized by setting short-term bridge goals. Long-term goals are frequently too far off to affect an athlete's day-to-day motivation (Locke and Latham 1985). The example long-term training goals listed above are more likely to be attained by designing several months of workouts with specific incremental objectives leading up to the target goal. Succeeding at short-term bridge goals keeps the athlete motivated along the way to achieving long-term goals by inspiring self-confidence.

Tom Morris, PhD (1994, p. 286), writes about setting goals in *True Success: A New Philosophy of Excellence*:

- We need a clear conception of what we want, a vivid vision, a goal or set of goals powerfully imagined.
- We need a strong confidence that we can attain our goals.
- We need a focused concentration on what it takes to reach our goal.
- We need a stubborn consistency in pursuing our vision, a determined persistence in thought and action.
- We need an emotional commitment to the importance of what we're doing, and to the people with whom we're doing it.
- We need a good character to guide us and keep us on a proper course.
- We need a capacity to enjoy the process along the way.

Applying these excellent guidelines will help you focus on what undertaking a goal means—a personal commitment to achieving the task, whatever it may require. For the endurance athlete, goals tend to focus on several areas, typically improving endurance, speed, strength, biomechanics, and event times. The psychological mindset is important, too, and an athlete may want to work on this area. Once areas for improvement have been identified and goals defined (which can be as simple as writing them down on paper), the next step is to decide how they will be achieved. That is, the athlete needs to determine the level of commitment necessary to meet each objective.

Goals should be challenging but not unrealistic. Be honest with yourself and set goals that will be gratifying to achieve, but don't set a goal you know in your heart is too lofty. Goals that are too high may cause an athlete to give up, believing that they are only going to fail anyway (Locke and Latham 1985). Conversely, if goals are too easy to attain, the athlete won't take them seriously, and less than optimal performances are likely.

Performing for Yourself

I have listened to hundreds of unhappy athletes (and even coached a few) who dwell on comparing their results to those of others. Measuring one's performance against that of others is a natural ego-driven process, but we can get too caught up with who we've finally trounced at the expense of forgetting to enjoy the process. The real satisfaction comes from performing to the best of our ability.

Mark Allen puts it this way:

> If [I'm] in the race, I definitely have my eye on everyone else. But races where I am so far out of it become purely individual internal focusing experiences. I'm aware of the other guys—keeping an eye on them, gauging them, doing things in relation to them—but I don't give it any energy. If I give it energy . . . it's like [I've] got ten units of energy and two of them are focused on that versus putting all ten into what I am doing. I described it once as [having] to be connected to what is going on but not attached to it. Once you become attached to someone else through ego or fear, energy is lost.

Setting performance-based or task-oriented goals, rather than results-oriented or ego-based goals, provides structure and focus. Examples of these two competitive orientations are shown in table 9.1. Clearly, the ego-based orientation is less desirable as a competitive mental strategy. It takes too much energy to spend time on ego- or results-based thinking.

Setting Specific Training and Racing Goals

"Good performances don't come out of the blue. I have to work hard for each one," says Karen Smyers, women's champion of the 1995 Ironman in Hawaii. Successful athletes like Karen just accept hard work as a known component of training life. But all that hard work will be wasted effort if it isn't channeled into meeting specific training and racing goals.

Setting competitive goals gives an athlete's training form and purpose. Deciding where and when to compete, at what distance, in what disciplines, and so on, will compel you to action. Having targets to shoot for helps in defining the steps needed to reach them. On the other hand, endurance athletes who make no plans for competitions, but just do them whenever they have the urge, have no clear direction for their training. Of course, there's nothing wrong with someone simply wanting to do a few competitions for the fun of it, as long as they are ready physically. However, to achieve one's personal best, goals are needed, and selecting a competition is the way to get started.

TABLE 9.1 Performance-Task Versus Result-Ego Orientation

Performance and task orientation	Result and ego orientation
When I perform my very best, I feel most successful. I try my hardest to win, but my goal is to be the best athlete possible.	I can do better than anyone, including my friends. I can beat any of them. The only time I am satisfied is when I win. I hate to lose.
After I learn a new technique or practice hard at a skill and it feels good, I feel most satisfied.	I can ride faster, probably better, than anyone in the club, race, or nation. My technique is by far better than anyone else's.
I feel most satisfied with my performances when I know I've really worked hard in training.	I am the best. No one can beat me. It would be accidental for anyone to do so. My times are faster than everyone else's in training.
Winning is important to me. I have the most fun when I win, but losing does not upset me much. I simply want to perform to the very best of my ability.	Losing upsets me. I cannot believe I didn't win. It never would have happened had I been able to train as much as they did.

I rarely prescribe the initial training or competition goals for an athlete. It is up to the athlete to be decisive about setting short-, medium-, and long-term goals. Once they have done so, the coach and athlete can manage those goals by creating the optimum conditions for accomplishing them.

For beginner and intermediate endurance athletes, competitive goals should be moderate. I recommend scheduling events over one or more years before taking on competitions requiring more than several hours to complete. Give your musculoskeletal system a chance to adapt to the stress of training and competing. Competitions should be spread at least six to eight weeks apart to permit recovery and proper preparatory training between them.

The competitive and elite athlete will focus similarly, but may also want to set time goals for certain competitions. These provide the training targets to be implemented into the training program and workouts. Again, specific swim, cycle, or running goal times can be incorporated into the workouts by using the IPCs. Also, technical form training and improving biomechanics are fundamental training goals as well. If an athlete wants to run 10 kilometers at a particular pace, the workouts need to be formatted to make it possible to meet those physical demands.

Athletes who set general goals such as, "I'll just do the best I can," do not perform as well as those who set specific goals. If a goal doesn't define exactly what the athlete is supposed to do, the athlete won't know when the goal has been reached (Locke, Mento, and Katcher 1978). Regardless of how you propose to compete, you need a clear understanding of why you are doing what you are doing as well as your strategy for getting there.

Challenging and specific goals are far more likely to produce superior performances than less difficult or more general goals. If you want to improve performance and mental focus, set reasonable but well-defined goals. Write those goals down and read them regularly.

What types of guidelines are used in formulating competitive goals? First and foremost, personal responsibilities need attention. These include family, personal well-being, and work. Athletes must keep these at the forefront main-taining an even balance of competitions, training, and their professional and personal lives. Second, because training and competitions take time away from everything, a time plan must be put in place. It is important to organize a competitive calendar and training schedule, as outlined in chapters 2 and 7, to deal with the demands of training and racing.

Next comes an assessment of what you've done in the past—successful or otherwise. You need to review what got you to where you are: What kinds of training have you done in the past and what were the results? Once your previous training volumes, intensities, rest patterns, and competition outcomes have been analyzed, more clearly defined goals can be set.

At this point, the specifics of your training program and competitive agenda should be more clear. You should know what your training and competitive strengths are and how to capitalize on them. If you have distractions, as many elite and professional endurance athletes do, remember you cannot control all things. So don't worry about things you cannot control and stay focused on those things that are strategic to continued successful performances.

The following is taken from the *Journal of Sport Psychology* (Locke and Latham 1985, p. 209) in an article titled "The Application of Goal Setting to Sports."

1. Distinct, difficult goals surpass and lead to better performances than vague, easy goals;
2. Short-term goals help in accomplishing long-term goals;
3. Goals help performance by affecting the implementation of training to accomplish the goals;
4. Feedback must be related to each goal; and
5. Each goal must be accepted by the athlete to positively influence performance.

Finally, you must be strongly committed to your goals. You must acknowledge and accept the targets you've set and have the will to do what it takes to reach them. Does this mean you have to be serious and grimly focused all the time? Of course not! It only means that to be a better athlete, you need to have firm competitive intentions. However, your goals should not be so rigid that you cannot step aside and perhaps even miss a workout now and then. You need to be flexible, because you never know what may occur that will be beyond your control.

Charting Your Training Goals

You can fine-tune your training goal setting by using Table 9.2 as a guide in identifying and managing specific training goals. For instance, workout goals can be objectively associated with time and/or distance. For swimming, cycling, and running, training goals could be aimed at accomplishing a target pace for a certain distance. However, limit training goals to two per sport—one related to improving technique (skill/action) and the other a time-based training intensity zone goal (such as a time trial on a certain course). As you achieve one goal, set another and work on it until that, too, is attained. Finally, make sure you can measure the results in some way, such as time, distance, speed, or recovery. I recommend entering the goals in a journal. Updated goals can then be added when appropriate.

TABLE 9.2 Training Goal Manager

Sport	Skill/action	Goal	Test 1 result (date)	Test 2 result (date)	Test 3 result (date)	Test 4 result (date)
Swimming	5×200 on 5-minute send-off (VO_2)	Training intensity zone goal: average goal time of 2:18				
	10×100 on 2-minute send-off (LVT)	Technical form drill: average stroke count of 64 p/100				
Cycling	10-mile time trial (LVT) on flat to rolling terrain	Training intensity zone goal: under 29:00				
	2,000 isolated-leg spins in small chain ring	Technical form drill: under 18:00				
Running	$3(4 \times 400)$ on 3-minute send-off form drills: high knee, kick ups, hold up drills	Technical form drill: heart rate under 140 and time under 2 minutes				
	5×1 mile on 6:15 send-off (LVT)	Training intensity zone goal: descend time from 5:45 to 5:15 (count and record footstrikes for 1 minute last one-fourth mile)				

1. Use short-term goals to improve long-term results.

2. Establish difficult goals, but be realistic.

3. Make sure you can measure the results, and do so on a regular basis.

4. Include technical form training drills and training intensity zone goals.

MENTAL COPING IN TRAINING AND COMPETITION

Karen Smyers, told me during a conversation:

> I understand I can control only how I perform, not how others perform. Competition is a positive force, not a negative one, and you cannot control who is showing up for the event either. In an ideal mental state I feel very much at ease prior to the start of the event. This is not something contrived [coming to this mental state]. Rather, I seem to do this naturally. I feel an inner peace, inner calmness. Now, I don't need to be alone or too internally focused. At the starting line, I often tell jokes, smile, and I am friendly.

Coping with the stress of training and competition can be a huge burden for any endurance athlete. This is an area where individual differences are quite striking. Everyone deals with stress in their own unique way; some externalize feelings, others internalize them. No one method works best, but I have found that practicing mental rehearsals in training can be effective for easing competitive anxieties. Athletes should visualize the entire competition beforehand, preparing for as many eventualities as possible. What conditions will you be competing under, how long will it take to complete the event, what environmental conditions, travel considerations, and other factors are involved? Answering these questions by physically and mentally rehearsing a competition beforehand can help performance significantly.

Sharpening the Mind in Practice

An athlete and coach together should examine four questions before each workout:

1. What have you planned to do?
2. What specific techniques or emphasis are you going to concentrate on?
3. How are you planning to do this?
4. What self-talk message are you going to use?

The first question relates to goal setting and the structure of the workout. What is the purpose of the workout? What pace/time/distance are you trying to achieve? The second question focuses on specific physical tasks such as technique and drill practice. The third question invites you to use imagery to visualize how you will apply the technique. The last question asks the athlete to anticipate what specific self-talk statement will be most appropriate during the workout.

Following the workout, the coach and athlete evaluate the session by asking themselves five questions to understand the psychology used during the task and make plans for the next session:

1. What did you feel (what were you saying to yourself) when the workout or interval was over?
2. Did you do what you had intended to do and how did it feel?
3. How hard did you try (1 to 5 ranking)?
4. What needs to be changed?
5. What are you going to do the next time and how are you going to do it?

As you can see, these are all performance-related, task-oriented goals and feedback. They provide a positive setting for implementation and further improvement by

- setting goals,
- applying focus,
- using imagery and visualization,
- using self-talk techniques,
- providing feedback and review, and
- encouraging long-term goal planning.

Imagery Training

A survey of Olympic athletes and coaches found that 90 percent use imagery for training and competition (Murphy 1994). Through imagery, athletes can visualize themselves performing a movement without actually doing it. Imagery techniques include deliberately thinking about tasks related to an athletic movement or the outcome of a competition (table 9.3). For example, a triathlete may "see"

TABLE 9.3   Imagery Training Techniques

1. Dream about successful performances.

2. Internally rehearse (imagine) what the competition will feel like to the muscles.

3. Perform positive preperformance self-talk concerning routine, physical strain, and actions (technique) during competition.

4. Imagine peak performance, an optimal competition where you accomplish a physically and emotionally flawless race, without regard to the competition and end result.

herself swimming and "feel" the water flowing smoothly alongside her body as her strokes become longer and faster. Next, she imagines making the transition from the water to the bike, her every movement swift and controlled. Finally, as the run begins, she imagines feeling energized, powerful, relaxed, and effortlessly fast.

Both internal and external imagery techniques are used to enhance athletic performance. Internal imagery consists of an athlete imagining being inside her own body and feeling the same sensations she feels in an actual competition. Conversely, athletes using external imagery see their performance from the point of view of a spectator, as if watching a film. I find that elite athletes tend to internally visualize their competitive performance and mentally rehearse how the event will feel to the mind, body, and muscles. A study of gymnasts who made the Olympic team bears this out (Mahoney and Avener 1977); athletes who applied internal imagery achieved higher levels of performance compared to those who did not make the team.

Although positive thinking is important in visualization, going over negative outcomes and visualizing yourself dealing with them positively can be useful too. This technique is effective because you can mentally rehearse any number of outcomes before competition. Then, if something does go awry, you will have practiced in your mind how best to handle the situation. For instance, you might imagine what you will feel like after a poor swim start and rehearse how to overcome your disappointment and force yourself to keep going. Or, as so often happens during an open-water swim, you might imagine your distress at having your goggles fill with water. A positive prerehearsal of this situation would have you

calmly replacing the goggles and settling back into your pace. Another image could be that of an exploding flat tire when you're leading the cycling race. You would feel yourself slowing abruptly as you watch your competitors pass. You then imagine your efficient movements as you calmly replace the tire, quickly and without difficulty. Finally, you see yourself composed and in control, regaining momentum and going on to a successful finish. I've witnessed dozens of situations where elite athletes have bounced back from adversity that would doom most of us. These athletes have prepared themselves by knowing they cannot control everything during competition.

Imagery can be practiced and experienced almost any time. I have found this type of mental training to be most successful for my athletes when used in combination with technique training during workouts. Any of the dozens of drills in the respective swimming, cycling, and running chapters can be used for imagery training. Close your eyes and imagine a long, streamlined swimming stroke with a high, relaxed elbow recovery and natural side-to-side body roll. Visualize the pull deflecting water with curvilinear (S-shaped) perfection until pressing gracefully past your thigh. Go through the entire stroke, or focus on imagining one aspect or drill. It only takes a few seconds and can be done between swimming sets, while taking a mental break from work, or in the moments before falling asleep.

Concentrating on areas of technique and performance you need to work on is best. Imagine what it will feel like to be passed on the run by a strong competitor. How do you want yourself to react? Will you increase your pace? Will your form suffer? One thing is certain, everyone has their own way of dealing with

such situations. Do you imagine passing them back, keeping pace, or maintaining your own speed and form? Whatever the outcome, I expect you'll want to imagine dealing with this situation positively. Successful performances are engineered by positive images of performance.

Positive Self-Talk

Throughout my friendship and coaching relationship with Scott Tinley, he has often associated the importance of positive mental imagery with his ongoing success. However, races don't always go the way we'd like, and on rare occasions, even Scott has felt psychologically flat. As we reviewed a disappointing performance while in Switzerland for Powerman Zofingen, he admitted saying to himself before the race, "Oh, no! Not another Ironman!" This represented a rare loss of strength of mind for Scott. It wasn't until the long and difficult final run of this world-renowned duathlon that Scott finally came together mentally. Although he finished in the top 20, he did not have a great day. Yet it was a personal victory, as he overcame his sluggish first run and modest bike split by having one of the fastest second runs of the day. He did this by using a rather simple

positive self-talk message, "Okay! At least I can have the best second run!"

I can't write about coaching and sport psychology without sharing a memorable moment during the 1984 Ironman when circumstances shifted dramatically for Scott. At mile 80 on the bike, Scott was not among the top 50 competitors. As he passed me (I was in a car) riding like he was out for a casual afternoon tour of the Big Island, I was puzzled that he wasn't more aggressive and in contention. I drove away, but couldn't stop looking back at Scott's figure in the rearview mirror. Suddenly, I turned around; I couldn't let Scott give up that easily.

As I pulled alongside Scott again and asked how he felt, a salute with his middle finger was his response. "Scott, focus yourself," I shouted out the car window. "Second place is not that bad. There is still the run! Focus, focus, concentrate!" We had made eye contact, and I knew he understood me. Without hesitation, Scott resolutely lowered himself into an aerodynamic position. I felt the energy change immediately. Once again, he was in his characteristic groove, focusing his energy on pushing to the front. He would go on to make one of the most extraordinary recoveries I have ever seen.

TABLE 9.4   Peak Experience Descriptions of Elite Athletes

1. "In the cocoon," extraordinary awareness
2. In control
3. Mentally relaxed, physically relaxed
4. Confident, optimistic
5. Energized
6. Alert, mentally focused
7. In control, automatic, effortless
8. Mentally calm, physically relaxed, low anxiety
9. Self-confident, optimistic
10. Centered present focus, narrow focus of attention
11. Complete absorption, harmony, and oneness
12. Perfection, noncritical, and effortless
13. Loss of fear
14. Positive preoccupation with sport
15. In control, but not forcing it
16. Self-regulation of arousal
17. Higher self-confidence
18. Determination
19. Commitment
20. Optimal, effortless concentration, selfless observation
21. In total control, no attempt to control
22. Self-control
23. Confidence
24. Mastery: orientation, goal direction
25. Positive attitudes, self-orientation, commitment
26. Merging of action and awareness
27. Centering of attention on a limited stimulus field
28. Loss of ego
29. In control of actions and environment
30. Coherent, noncontradictory demands for action and clear feedback
31. Maintaining composure; not afraid to fail; staying cool, confident
32. Determination
33. Self-motivation, desire, attitude, heart
34. Highly energized
35. Focused on the present

Adapted, by permission, from Y.V. Auweele, B. De Cuyper, V. Van Mele, and R. Rzewnick, 1993, Elite Performance and Personality: Description and Prediction to Diagnosis and Intervention." In *Handbook of Research on Sport Psychology*, edited by R. Singer, M. Murphey, and L.K. Tennant (New York: Macmillan), 280.

At the finish line several hours later, Dave Scott had won his third Ironman World Championship, but the story of the day was Scott Tinley's second-place finish. I remember standing near the medical tent and hearing the loud applause and the energy of the spectators at the announcement of his remarkable achievement. Upon finishing, Scott came directly toward me and offered his hand. Needless to say, it was an emotional moment for us both. For me personally, I only felt lucky enough to have said the right thing. Repeating my simple words to himself throughout the day prompted Scott to refocus on the race and center himself internally. Scott won the Ironman the following year in impressive style.

I have no doubt that thoughts and feelings can be modified to improve performance, as research confirms. Table 9.4 summarizes the findings of studies pinpointing similar mental outlooks among elite athletes during peak performances (Auweele et al. 1993). The athletes were interviewed about how they felt during peak performances and what statements best described those feelings. These statements can be used as effective self-talk messages to enhance your own performance. Select two or three statements that are most appropriate for you. Use them during training, while practicing imagery techniques, or before going to bed.

Dealing With Negative Thoughts

After coaching several hundred elite endurance athletes over the past decade and listening to their preworkout or prerace comments, I could write a book entitled *1001 Reasons Why I Won't Race (or Train) Well Today.* "Coach, I really swam hard yesterday. Can I warm up and let you know how I feel?" Or, "I rode really hard Saturday and my legs haven't recovered, so I'll just climb easy." Or, "Do you know a stretch for sore hamstrings—should I run easy today?" And naturally, "Coach, I really want to do this $\dot{V}O_2$max swim, but I'm not going to be my best, okay?"

I can't help but chuckle at these pronouncements, which are usually nothing more than precompetition anxieties revealing themselves. Once the athlete gets moving, all the aches and pains and emotional upsets take a backseat, although they still exist and require attention.

The important thing is to recognize that these negative or anxious thoughts need to be acknowledged and dealt with honestly.

Everyone has negative thoughts, but in an athletic setting they can have disastrous consequences. Few would disagree that emotions affect our performance. If not managed properly, anger, anxiety, depression, and negative thinking can cause muscles to tense up and heart rate and blood pressure to increase. Negative performances lower self-esteem, in turn leading to more anger, anxiety, and depression.

The way to counter negative self-talk that affects performance is to practice thought control, replacing negative statements with positive mental messages and affirmations. Karen Smyers says, "I understand I can control only how I perform, not [how] others [perform]. Competition is a positive force, not a negative one, and you cannot control who is showing up for the event either."

Affirmations like "I am human, I make mistakes" ring positive in the face of situations that may cause anxiety. Dave Scott, a legendary professional triathlete, fitness consultant, and coach, spoke with me about his 1994 Ironman preparation: "One of the things that really helped me was [that] I had already won the race [six times]. The negatives initially came from the outside media. They were skeptical, doubtful of my chances, and honestly, there were ego and credibility issues for me too. However, formulating a plan consisting of things I could and couldn't control, things that bogged me down, helped me deal with the negative issues."

The way to reverse the tendency for precompetition anxiety is to isolate what thoughts are causing the uncertainty. As the brain can make more than 100 million calculations per second, this can be challenging. The following are a few mental training ideas that I have found helpful in working with athletes suffering from anxiety.

1. No anxiety attack is unexplainable; they are always preceded by some thought or other. If you're having trouble maintaining composure, try to determine what may be causing you to have such thoughts (what you are feeling and thinking about before the anxiety occurs).

2. Thoughts are nothing more than suggestions, and you can choose not to follow them. Every athlete has thoughts, perhaps millions of them, running through his or her mind while training and competing. The trick is to channel your thoughts into positive outcomes.

3. Whenever anxious thoughts begin, immediately challenge them with positive, success-oriented statements like, "I can do it. I am primed to compete!" Take control of your thoughts.

4. Breathe slowly. Try to bring your anxiety level down to mild butterflies. Calmly repeat positive statements to yourself, such as those suggested above.

5. Relax all your muscles.

Of course, those with severe anxiety disorders should seek professional help. Although it's not easy to tell someone they may need help, it can be even more difficult for those with a serious problem to see the signs and symptoms for themselves. One way to handle such situations is to reassure the athlete that addressing their fears and anxieties with the help of a sport psychologist can help improve their performance.

Rebounding From Competition

When an athlete does not perform up to expectations, it is always frustrating for athlete and coach alike. Learning to cope positively with nonfinishes and mediocre performances challenges athletes and coaches to understand their motivation for competing. Perhaps it is to perform beyond individual limits, to find your inner self, or to achieve strength of mind, character, and body. This is why goal setting is important. It helps you understand your reasons for being out there, both when things go well and when they don't.

Sometimes athletes lose sight of why they chose to pursue endurance sports. Conceivably, some may never have examined their motivation in the first place, or even thought it important. Those who aren't in touch with their reasons for competing suffer significant emotional pain when competitions don't go as planned. To achieve emotional balance, endurance athletes need to understand why they go to such incredible lengths to train and race and are so highly committed to improving performance.

In the 1994 Ironman, Ralph Black, a 64-year-old client of mine, did not make the swim cut-off time of 2:15 and was not allowed to finish the rest of the race. It was a huge disappointment to both of us. His training results had indicated a swim time comfortably in the 1:50 range, or an average time per 100 meters of 2:51—not a blistering pace, but fast enough to make the cut. We spoke soon afterward, and although we were both disappointed, the nature of the exchange was positive. Ralph told me that completing the race was important to him, but that he had other reasons for competing in triathlons. "Just because you are older does not mean you cannot be doing these things [Ironman triathlons]. I want in some way to be an example for other senior citizens too. Exercise is a big part of my life. It's fun, challenging, and I think I can be better than I am."

Certainly, this attitude made my coaching less complicated and helped me put things in perspective. I had just wanted Ralph to have a chance at finishing the race. He had done all the necessary training and under different ocean conditions would have done so. I discovered we were both thinking the same thing when he said, "Isn't there an Ironman distance race next weekend in Maui?" When I heard this, I understood why Ralph was able to cope with his great disappointment—his motivations for competing are healthy, balanced, and positive. He is a winner in every sense of the word, finisher or not. I said, "Yeah, Maui would be great. I just want you to have a chance to reach your performance goals!" He finished the Ironman the next year.

DAVE SCOTT: "DO WHAT I CAN DO RIGHT NOW"

Dave Scott has won the Ironman Triathlon World Championship an unprecedented six times. Among his competitors, he is respectfully known as "The Man." Yet, as I spoke with him in a recent interview, I was struck by the "ordinariness" of his feelings—doubt, fear, frustration, anxiety—the same feelings we all share. However, the mental strategies he developed for coping with these feelings are very different from those of the average athlete.

Dave and other elite endurance athletes share similar characteristics: self-confidence, a positive attitude, concentration on task-specific goals, and effective coping strategies for dealing with anxiety and poor performances. Clearly, these athletes have unique psychological capabilities for implementing strategies and dealing with difficult circumstances effectively. As a coach, I believe these characteristics are the most important components in achieving peak performance.

In recounting his peak performance in the 1994 Ironman at 40 years of age, Dave spoke of the important role sport psychology and mental training techniques played in his preparation for the race. There was tremendous pressure on Dave's shoulders as he looked ahead to competing for a possible seventh title, and he felt every bit of it. Would his return to Kona after a five-year absence be a race for himself or for others? Dave's response to the pressure was to adopt a healthy attitude before the race: "I can fail in everyone else's eyes, or I could be the fastest 40-year-old, establishing a long-standing record."

Eighteen months before the 1994 Ironman, Dave began developing a strategy and setting goals for his return to Hawaii. Taking a sheet of paper, he divided it into two columns. One column was headed "Things I couldn't control" and contained items such as "comments from media," "unexpected but important responsibilities," "expectations of others," and most important, "hours in the day." From his extensive experience, Dave knew that time would be a major factor in training for the 1994 Ironman. "I needed a 30-hour day, and I never had enough time in the earlier years. Now, with my family, the time restraints will be even greater." The other column was headed "Things I could control" and contained items such as "training" and "commitments." Jotting down these two lists helped Dave recognize the futility in giving much energy to things he could not control and gave focus to the process of setting goals for the Ironman.

Another of Dave's mental strategies are what he calls "Q's"—his daily self-talk messages. In essence, these are affirmation statements he uses in coping with the demands of being a husband, father, breadwinner, and world-class triathlete. For example, at the start of the 1994 Ironman, the swim was "particularly chaotic," and Dave felt like he was being "trapped by a vise, almost slaughtered" in the turmoil of swimmers, and couldn't see anything. "I had no idea whether I was in with the faster swimmers or not. I was out of control." At that moment, he began repeating over and over, "Do what I can do right now!" He'd said this to himself thousands of times before. He soon regained his composure, and his improved mental state resulted in his swimming fast and at ease.

When he finished the swim, he had no idea of how well he had done. The familiar faces of the 1980s were not there. "[But] my confidence soared as I realized how quickly I was moving up on the bike." As he approached the leaders on the two-lane highway known as the "Queen K," he thought, "Now I am going to set the precedent. You guys are going to follow my actions."

Seven weeks before the race, Dave had begun using relaxation tapes developed by Jeff Simons of Colorado University. The main points centered upon Dave imagining, "How do you like feeling," and how it actually feels to the muscles when in the heat of competition. Both of these techniques played a vital role in preparing Dave's mind. "I knew what it was going to feel like, and this provided a psychological plus for me. When the race produced pain, I was physically prepared because of the psychological work I had done. The physiological stress became a very positive stress."

At mile 19 of the run in Hawaii, there is a section of the course far from town and the finish line where you can get very close to the athletes. Only a few seconds behind the leader at this point, Dave imagined the thoughts of the hundreds of spectators, reporters, and photographers gathered there—both positive and negative—but he clearly remembers the feelings he had: "Gee, I am really in good position. This is the pace I can win with."

"Relax. Do what I can do right now!" was the mantra Dave repeated over and over throughout the run section, where he managed to close the gap to 11 seconds on eventual winner Greg Welch. Dave felt "at peace, relaxed, floating, and that this was a great race," and he still felt he had "a whole other gear" for catching Greg. Suddenly, almost as quickly as the positive affirmations were running through his mind, he lost concentration as he passed an aide station. It reminded him that he needed food, and before long, his energy was vanishing. He felt "weary for the next mile" and recalls thinking, "I need to sit down and eat something, take in more calories." Soon he was slowing down as he "felt [himself] fall off pace," saying "hold yourself together." Yet he could see Greg pull away. Moments later he remembers running near his wife Anna, and in a sincere but self-effacing manner, saying, "I am feeling a bit weary. I need some support!" It was quite apparent he needed all the help he could get. He was facing the pain he had known so many times before—the "moment" in the race when the mind and body no longer respond as willed.

Ultimately, at mile 24, Dave knew he would not win this day. The result: second place. Yet his effort is a classic example of concrete, task-oriented goal setting, sound mental preparation, and positive self-dialogue culminating in peak performance—what Dave calls "my best race ever."

10

COMPETING: PUTTING THE PIECES TOGETHER

Your training is complete and your body and mind are eager to test the limits of your endurance. You are ready to compete! This chapter reviews techniques for fine-tuning your final preparation, including planning your precompetition workouts, meals, and rest, checking your equipment, preparing for traveling and competing at high altitudes, warming up before the event, and thinking through your tactics and transitions. There are countless ways to carry out the process of tapering and getting ready for competition. The competitive edge is often found in the days and weeks preceding an event. What an athlete does during this period can make the difference in having a poor, good, or superior competition.

IN THE DAYS BEFORE COMPETITION

Depending on the importance and distance of the event, an athlete should taper for one to three weeks (see pt phase, chapter 2). During this time, mental visualization of each aspect of the competition—from start to finish—should be included in daily training (see chapter 9). In planning for a competition, it's important to prepare a schedule for the days leading up to the event: What specific workouts will you do leading up to the event? What will you eat before the event? What equipment will you

be using for the event? Has it been inspected to be sure it is in tip-top shape? A list of precompetition guidelines for each of these areas that you may want to individualize to suit your needs is given below. Make sure that you've begun organizing these items two or three weeks before the event. Waiting until the last minute is likely to ruin an otherwise solid preparation.

Massage Therapy

Having a massage immediately before and after competition is a wise choice for the endurance athlete. Fortunately, massage therapists are attracted to endurance athletic events like bees to honey. Some are experienced, but others are just "getting the feel" for working with athletes and perhaps completing certification.

If you decide to have a prerace warm-up massage, don't make the mistake of letting an inexperienced or over enthusiastic therapist penetrate the deeper tissues within the muscle. You'll end up sore or, even worse, injured by an inappropriately administered massage. You may not know it, but you can direct how a massage is to be performed, so tell the therapist you want a 15- to 20-minute massage with no deep pressure.

The reasons for having a massage are to relax mentally, warm the muscles, and activate soothing circulation within them to encourage recovery, all without damage. The same stan-

PRECOMPETITION GUIDELINES

Workout Time Plan

✔ From the time of arrival to the warm-up before competition, plan each of your workouts. The discipline, duration, and training intensity zone should be specified according to the respective sport program managers.

✔ On your workout training manager (WTM), write the exact workouts you'll be doing and the time of day for each session. This will keep you focused on your preparation goals, so you won't get caught doing a workout with a friend where the intensity or distance get out of hand.

Pre-Event Meal Planning

✔ Again, in the three to four days prior to the race, plan each meal, in particular, the type, time, and quantity. This is a good time for visiting with friends and family, so make a schedule that works for everyone but includes the right kinds of nutrition and timing for you. It's a good idea for those you'll be eating with to do the same. Planning these meals haphazardly can be extremely detrimental to your performance by eating foods you are not familiar with (chapter 8).

✔ Eat your last evening meal early (you should be finished eating 2 hours before bedtime and 8 to 12 hours before the event), then relax and drink more fluids (water, carbohydrate sport drink). This final meal and those preceding it should be high in carbohydrates (70 to 75 percent) and low in fat and protein, as discussed in chapter 8.

Restoration Plan

✔ Design a plan for resting (restoration) before competition. Three days before the competition, go to bed an hour or so earlier than normal. Two days before the competition, go to bed early (8:00 to 9:00 P.M.) after an early meal. The day before the race, go to bed at your regular time but take an early-afternoon nap.

✔ During the tapering process, an athlete should plan several full days of complete rest. For race week, depending on the athlete, I usually recommend one to three rest days. My preference is for the athlete to take a full day off two days before the competition, with a light multisport workout the day before the race. The other days off can be scheduled earlier in the week or in preceding weeks.

✔ Many endurance athletes feel better doing some type of exercise, even on rest days, such as a short (10- to 20-minute) swim, bike, or run. Getting the blood circulating helps reduce soreness and warms the muscles for stretching. Although this is probably the right thing to do, I still recommend that athletes experiment with taking full rest days, especially if previous competitions have not gone as expected.

Equipment Selection and Inspection

✔ The condition, length, and environment of a course largely determine what type of equipment an athlete needs. With respect to swimming, cycling, and running combination events, any number of considerations are possible. Here's an essential list:

Swimming:

Goggles (including an extra pair and antifog droplets)
Swimsuit(s)
Swim caps (regular latex and neoprene)
Wet suit
Petroleum jelly (for lightly lubricating neck, crotch, underarms, and chest to prevent chafing)

Cycling:

Bike and wheels
Helmet
Spare tire (clincher or tubular type)
Extra freewheel cassette
Water bottles
Pumps (frame- and floor-mount), plus air cartridges and adapters
Repair tools (Allen wrenches, freewheel remover, lubricants)
Glasses
Clothing (shorts, shirt, socks, and gloves)

Running:

Shoes (training and racing; always have an extra pair)
Socks (plus extra pairs)
Shorts
Singlet (light colored)
Visor or hat (light colored)

Extras:

Watch
Warm-up suit
Marker (for marking name and number on transition bags and self-body numbering)
Nutrition (sport bars, drinks)
Safety pins (for attaching numbers to clothing)
First-aid kit
Lightweight polypropylene or capilene shirt

dards apply to the postrace massage, except you should have it done immediately after finishing the event while you are replenishing fluid or carbohydrates. Both will hasten the recovery process.

Arriving for the Competition

The means of transportation to a competition is an important consideration for the endurance athlete. Often this involves driving considerable distances and being away for several days at a time, or flying and having to contend with layovers and time zone changes. Long hours of travel, jet lag, different foods, an unfamiliar environment, a strange bed—all affect performance. The athlete needs to consider each of these elements when planning for the competition. Training should simulate the environmental conditions (terrain and temperature) of the event as much as possible.

Like all living organisms, we humans are subject to rhythms in our lives. Traveling to different time zones disrupts our patterns of eating, sleeping, and waking. For east-to-west travel, physical and emotional adaptations are easier because the day is longer. Conversely, the day shortens when traveling west to east, and adjusting is more difficult.

There are several things you can do to reduce the effects of jet lag:

CONSIDERATIONS FOR TRAINING AND COMPETING AT ALTITUDE

Research on the effects of long-term training and competition at altitude (elevations above 7,000 to 8,000 feet) is mixed. On the one hand, increases in the number of red blood cell mass are obtained which increase the hemoglobin content of the blood. Hemoglobin and red blood cells aid in oxygen delivery, thus altitude training increases the blood's capacity to carry oxygen to exercising muscles. Athletes training at moderate altitudes can expect about a one percent per week increase in their hemoglobin levels as long as iron stores are ample (Levine and Stray-Gundersen 1992). Conversely, a decrease in aerobic power $\dot{V}O_2$ max (maximal oxygen uptake) begins at about 5,000 feet. This effect changes the way an athlete trains physiologically and biomechanically. The sea level workloads and techniques cannot be achieved.

Does an athlete need to live at altitude to achieve these benefits? No! The benefits of altitude for sea level competition can be achieved through periodic exposure to altitude. I believe, this is the best way to obtain the benefits and still be able to train at high workloads. Some research suggests that two or three 14- to 21-day training periods can produce the same physiological effects.

World-class athletes who train in cities like Boulder, Colorado, may unknowingly expose themselves periodically because of racing and other commitments that frequently take them to lower elevations. So, they may be gaining the advantages of exposure to altitude without even knowing it. Living at sea level and training at altitude for longer periods (two months or more) without going to lower elevations may not be the best way to improve performance through exposure and training at altitude.

If you plan to compete at high altitude but are unable to train in such conditions, it is best to arrive no sooner than 24 hours before the competition. This is not enough time for the compensatory changes resulting from altitude exposure, such as altitude mountain sickness, to fully manifest themselves.

- Arrive at your destination several days prior to the event and let your body adjust naturally. A good rule of thumb is to allow one full day of acclimation for each time zone crossed.

- Before departure, reset your clock to the current time at your destination.

- Eat at meal times for your destination. Eat more protein at morning meals (it helps reset your internal clock). Carbohydrates are more likely to bring on sleep.

- While traveling, sleep or rest at the same time you will when you reach your destination.

- While traveling, wear dark glasses during the day if it's nighttime at your intended destination. This is particularly helpful when traveling by plane, where there is plenty of opportunity to nap. The darkness helps your body begin adjusting to the new time zone.

- Get some light exercise as soon as you arrive (jog, walk, stretch).

- Don't go to bed or confine yourself to your hotel room. Instead, meet with people and begin adjusting to the new time zone right away.

Learning the Course

Don't forget to review the entire course, including land-sighting the swim course (at the time of day the swim will take place) and driving the cycling and running portions of the course. Sometimes the race director will make course changes at the last minute, so you must be prepared to deal with this situation. You are responsible for knowing the course set out by the race organizers. Too often a well-meaning race-day volunteer has sent athletes in the wrong direction. Although this is sometimes unavoidable, it can be prevented with a prerace review of the course.

RACE DAY KNOW-HOW

When to eat, how to get there, when to get there, where to park, and preparing the transition areas are just a few of the race-day consid-

erations an athlete faces. How much time do you need to warm up? How should you set up each transition? How should you race each event individually? These and other race-day questions are answered in the upcoming sections.

Race Day: Getting There on Time

Let's face it, training for a competition, regardless of competitive goals, is a financial, work, and family strain requiring considerable time investment. To be late or even miss the event because of things you can control would be unthinkable. But not everyone will agree on how early to arrive for a competition. Some individuals thrive on chaos and like to arrive at the last minute. Others need to be more structured and organized, preferring to arrive well before the start of the race.

Whether you are a professional or a recreational amateur, it is important to arrive at the competition enough ahead of time to do all that is required. Again, each individual has different warm-up, setup, and related logistical needs. Don't put yourself in the position of rushing through the registration and transition setup unnecessarily.

Precompetition Warm-Up

In 1983, Dave Scott and I were staying at the same condominium complex along the Kona coast for the Ironman triathlon. At 4:00 A.M. on the morning of the race, I heard voices outside my verandah. It was Dave getting ready to take his 30-minute prerace swim, to be followed by a 10-mile bike and a jog. Not everyone needs this much warm-up, but even for longer events, the athlete needs to warm up thoroughly.

According to David Martin and Peter Coe's (1997) *Better Training for Distance Runners*, warming up raises metabolism and muscle temperature, enhances fuel breakdown, and improves muscle elasticity and circulation. A good warm-up also reduces muscle cohesion or stiffness, decreases muscular tension, makes connective tissues more flexible, and prepares the athlete psychologically. It's like warming up the engine, then revving a few times to make sure everything is ready. I am convinced warming up also helps an athlete feel mentally prepared.

How long should you warm up and at what intensity? Your training volume may have an effect on the duration of your warm-up. Athletes with higher training volumes should warm up long enough to break a light sweat (usually 12 to 20 minutes) in each discipline. Some athletes simply need longer warm-up periods than others. In training, each athlete will come to understand their individual warm-up needs. One thing is certain, if you don't warm up, you'll be slower in the initial stages of competition because of starting with cool muscles.

For both long (more than three hours) and short competitions (less than three hours), warm up the body slowly for 6 to 12 minutes in each discipline (stretching between each), then do two to four LAC accelerations of about 10 seconds with 20-second rest intervals. These should be slowly accelerated build-ups, not all-out sprints. I have my athletes use these as a means of feeling the speed and power of the muscles and to ensure that body temperature is fully raised. Some athletes may prefer to lengthen or shorten the warm-up depending on the competition distance and their training history. Again, it's a matter of individual needs, but my athletes do well following the above recommendations.

In extreme conditions (cold, wet, or hot), stretching is the rule, as this may be all that conditions permit. In rain, a cycling warm-up is probably unwise, as the body will chill quickly. In such conditions, jogging and stretching are better choices. For cold-water swim starts, warm up whenever possible. Getting the blood circulating and raising the body temperature will enhance your swim.

Timing is key with prerace warm-ups. Make sure you've allowed enough time so that the last warm-up ends 10 to 15 minutes before the start of the race. The order of the warm-up should be the reverse of the competition. For example, a warm-up for a swim, bike, run competition should start with running, then cycling, then swimming (along with stretching).

Multisport Tactics

Competitive strategy plays a vital role in all sport, but the multisport athlete's strategy is further complicated by the duration, intensity, equipment, nutrition demands, and environmental conditions of the event. The most successful competitions are those in which the precompetition strategies are followed reasonably closely. Competitions present unexpected circumstances, and if the athlete doesn't have competition goals to key on, the race can get out of control.

Time after time at the Ironman, I've watched Mark Allen use the strategy of following Dave Scott through the swim and then pressing to seemingly insurmountable leads on the bike leg. I felt he was the better pure athlete, but he simply couldn't manage his intensity. I also watched Dave repass a struggling Allen and go on to win again and again. Finally, in 1989 Mark broke through this barrier and learned how to race against Dave. He simply stayed with him until the final miles of the marathon, then pulled away. In the following years, Mark would learn to race the course.

Endurance athletes need to trust their precompetition strategies and not be misled or tempted to do what they cannot. Although there are exceptions to this in every race, an athlete is wise to use reason in changing tactics. I suppose the main issue is intensity. There are limits, and once exceeded, an athlete may over time sacrifice immediate results for long-term performance. Judgment of pace, training, and duration of the event guide the athlete's tactics. It's a mistake to try to do more than you've trained for. Certainly, there are exceptions, but for the most part, a consistent energy output is best.

The Art of Transitions

Transitions are races within the race. They are times when the mind and body are making assessments and decisions. In exiting the water, for example, you must guard against sprinting or increasing intensity too much. Instead, stay focused on immediate tasks (wet suit removal, transition bag, location of entry and bike). Before the race, you should have walked the entire transition area—swim finish, swim/bike transition entrance, bike rack position, bike exit, bike finish entrance, run exit transition, and finish line—so that you are familiar with each of these sections. That's a lot to do, but it can make a difference in your overall time. Also, knowing precisely where you need to go settles the mind.

Each of your transitions should be prearranged to optimize speed, control, and effectiveness. Although there are certain style differences, every aspect of the transition should be considered. Where will the wet suit be taken off? Where will it be placed? Will you put your helmet on first or last? Will there be a clothing change? The list goes on and on and is unique to each athlete. You must physically and mentally "walk" through how each transition works and what you will do as you enter and exit each one.

Practicing transitions is a fun group activity as well. You can create an unlimited set of circumstances for you and your friends to rehearse. A triathlon team I once coached would practice and time a series of transition elements—sometimes just swim to bike or bike shoes to running shoes—which was a lot of fun. Each athlete would be timed while the others watched and made every effort to disrupt their teammate with catcalls. After a while, though, everyone became smoother under pressure. Dean Harper, a former professional triathlete and top-10 finisher at the Ironman, would practice transitions in the hallways of hotels. In those days, wet suits were just becoming popular, and we wanted to make sure he could get the thing off quickly enough. Dean would run down the hallway, peel off the wet suit, and put on his cycling shoes while I timed him. It was a strange sight to behold, but it worked. Being familiar with, relaxed, and composed is important in every aspect of the transition.

The transition from one sport to the next also requires physiological change; namely, circulating blood needs to be rerouted to the new set of muscle groups. It takes a few moments for this to occur after each transition. The athlete will temporarily feel sluggish, uncoordinated, and perhaps lack range of motion. However, once the blood has been recirculated to the new muscles, strength and coordination improve.

The Swim Start

The athlete's position for the swim start is important for several reasons. First, the swimmer needs to self-seed with swimmers of comparable speed. Achieving this is a bit tricky, but it can eliminate much of the chaos associated with open-water swim starts. Besides, having to swim over, around, or through people is of no benefit whatsoever. Ask others how they swim, perhaps telling them what swim time you expect for yourself. If you let them know you are trying to seed yourself, you may get some friendly responses. You'll have to deal with a few egos, but you just might get some good information.

Many swimmers only start in front, whether they belong there or not. If you start up front and don't really belong, you take the chance of going out too fast and missing the draft of another swimmer due to fatigue. In addition, a stronger swimmer may have to climb over you, which can cause numerous problems. Don't blow your race by going into oxygen debt simply for a few moments of ego-oriented satisfaction.

The Swim Course

Swimming the wrong course causes poor swim times more often than anything else. One reason is that the paddlers sometimes don't know the exact course and do a poor job of leading. They often move back and forth in a zigzag pattern, adding distance unnecessarily. If the lead swimmers follow the wrong course, the rest of the field is likely to do the same.

It is your responsibility to follow the proper course. Sight landmarks from all angles, and stay in control of your own race. Becoming familiar with the swim course is key to having a good overall day. It sets the tone for the rest of the race and helps you focus on the moment.

Finally, rounding swim course markers (buoys) requires a certain skill, particularly when engaging the marker with a school of other eager swimmers. In this case, it may be best to take the wide path on approaching and avoid the congestion near the buoy. This is equally effective if you are swimming singly or in a smaller group. Approach the marker from a high position and turn into the buoy, rounding the outermost point in the direction of travel.

The Swim Exit

The swim finish and transition is not the time to shift gears and begin swimming too intensely. This time is more appropriately spent preparing your mind and body for the next event.

The last 25 meters of the swim is the time to focus mentally on the swim exit, running the transition area approach, locating your bike, removing the wet suit, and making the clothing change. Physically, it is time to switch from swimming to cycling muscles. When swimming, particularly in wet suits, blood pools in the arms, chest, and shoulders. This concentration of blood now needs to move down into the cycling muscles. To increase the blood flow to your legs, try lengthening your stroke, reducing the intensity of the pulling motion, and increasing the kick during the last few meters. Some athletes use several breaststroke or butterfly kicks just before exiting the water, which also increases the blood flow to the legs.

The Bike

My first advice for the bike portion is to relax. You need to be supple in both mind and body to ride a fast time trial. The goal is to maximize energy output; however, a cyclist's interrelationship with the mechanical features of the bike can affect how this is done (see chapter 4). Aerodynamics, cadence, gearing, and terrain all affect energy and need to be managed by the athlete.

The best plan is to ride as close to the lactate ventilatory threshold as possible. On short climbs and when closing the gap, you'll need to exceed LVT pace; however, yo-yoing intensity is not the way to go. A 40-kilometer and a 180-kilometer ride are performed at slightly different intensities. The perceived exertion for the 40K is at the upper limit of the LVT, or energetically hard. The Ironman distance is also at the LVT but slightly slower.

An athlete can only remain in the VO_2 and LAC training intensity zones for a limited time. By knowing the training intensity zones and

perceived exertions (chapter 1), you'll know the differences between each level of intensity. More important, you'll know how long you can remain at an intensity greater than LVT before too much lactate has accumulated. Cyclists often reach this intensity when climbing short hills as they "power up" to get over quickly. Knowing the training intensity zones and the length of time you can spend in each will tell you how fast to ride and how long you can maintain a given speed. Managing exertion through the training intensity zones is an important tactic every athlete should come to understand.

Finally, the higher the intensity, the more you'll need to replenish carbohydrates and fluids, so when you exceed the LVT for any length of time, you'll need to take in extra nutrition as well (see chapter 8).

The Run

As the run is usually the final event, it is particularly wise to build the pace gradually over the first few minutes. Once again, it will take time for blood to be recirculated to the new muscle group, and going out too fast is sure to take a toll on the eventual outcome of the competition. Relax your shoulders, hands, arms, wrists, facial muscles, and maintain an efficient body posture. This will set the stage for the rest of the run. Try to maintain a steady pace throughout the majority of the race. Certainly, in competitive situations, it will be necessary to surge at times, but I am convinced that maintaining a strong, consistent pace will result in a faster overall time.

As with any other discipline, the athlete needs to measure intensity in terms of terrain and environment. If a hill will take 3 minutes to run in the LVT zone, it will take less time if run in the VO_2 zone. However, to decide which zone is best to run in, you'll need to know the distance to the finish, whether you can recover, and if your nutrition is sufficient. This is another good reason for reviewing the course ahead of time.

AFTER THE RACE

After a competition, replenishing fluids and carbohydrates is a number-one priority (after sharing a moment with loved ones, of course). Chapter 8 describes all the important nutritional concerns for postrace recovery. A warm-down, massage, and stretching will aid in recovery too. After events where the intensity is high, I recommend the athlete take a few moments to swim, bike, or jog as a warm-down. After longer events where the intensity level isn't as high, a several minute walk, stretch, and full massage should be sufficient.

Remember to share the afterglow of competition with family and friends. The entire time you've been competing, your loved ones, friends, and coach have been pulling for you every stroke, pedal, and step of the way. It's time to give back to those who have supported you throughout the long months of training leading up to this day. I've often felt watching a friend doing an Ironman is perhaps more difficult than competing. So, take a few moments and thank each of them for their support.

Another enjoyable aspect of postevent socialization is developing a camaraderie with your competitors as you relive each moment of the day. And as you replay the event over and over in your mind, you'll begin thinking about training and tactics and plans for "next time." Perhaps you'll even begin formulating new goals. This period of reflection is a good time to give some thought to your reasons for training and competing. Understanding your motivation for doing something can make it that much more enjoyable. Ultimately, enjoyment not only fosters success, it also creates a healthy balance in the life of an endurance athlete.

APPENDIX

TABLE A.1   Heart Rate Zone Template

1. Subtract your resting heart rate (RHR) from your maximum heart rate (HRmax).
2. Multiply by the percentage for each intensity zone.
3. Add your RHR.
4. Enter your training HR for the zone.

Percentage MHR	Your training intensity zone HR	Intensity zone
± 100	( )	LAC
95	( )	VO_2
90	( )	LVT
85	( )	LVT
80	( )	O_2
75	( )	O_2
70	( )	O_2

220 - (   ) age = _____ - (   ) RHR = _____ × (%) = _____ + (   ) RHR = _____ training HR

TABLE A.2   Heart Rate Training Manager

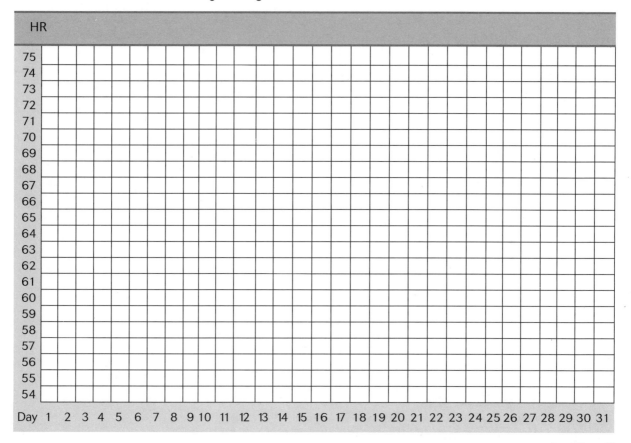

(continued)

TABLE A.2   Heart Rate Training Manager   (*continued*)

HR																														
53																															
52																															
51																															
50																															
49																															
48																															
47																															
46																															
45																															
44																															
43																															
42																															
41																															
40																															
39																															
38																															
37																															
36																															
35																															
34																															
33																															
32																															
31																															
30																															
Day	1	2	3	4	5	6	7	8	9	10	11	12	13	14	15	16	17	18	19	20	21	22	23	24	25	26	27	28	29	30	31

Directions for using Heart Rate Training Manager:

1. Take your resting pulse each morning before rising from bed. Count it for one full minute. While lying down, take your pulse at the carotid artery (base of the neck) by compressing gently. If you press too hard, your pulse count may be lower due to a reflex mechanism.

2. Fill in the square on the appropriate row (HR) and column (day).

3. Record the following psychological and physical symptoms when present in the evening by placing the corresponding letters above the point on the chart. If you experience any of the following symptoms of overtraining, you probably need to reduce the volume and intensity of training for a day or so.

   a. Little enthusiasm; don't feel like training

   b. Lethargic, tired, depressed

   c. Irritable with others (anger)

   d. Poor concentration at work, when reading, and so on

   e. Lower exercise heart rate with higher perceived exertion.

   f. Loss of weight

   g. Loss of appetite

   h. Very thirsty with chapped lips

   i. Poor coordination

   j. Restlessness

   k. Ongoing fatigue, slow workout times

   l. Diarrhea or constipation

   m. Sore muscles

   n. Decline in performance

TABLE A.3   Program Overview Manager

Program Overview Manager					Athlete _____			Season Volume_____				
Wk	Monday	Competition (rank)	Program emphasis/ interval	SP	Swim week target	BP	Bike week target	RP	Run week target	CAL	ISK	IST
1												
2												
3												
4												
5												
6												
7												
8												
9												
10												
11												
12												
13												
14												
15												
16												
17												
18												
19												
20												
21												
22												
23												
24												
25												
26												
27												
28												
29												
30												
31												
32												
33												
34												
35												
36												
37												
38												
39												
40												
41												
42												
43												
44												
45												
46												
47												
48												
49												
50												
51												
52												

TABLE A.4   Annual Volume Worksheet

Month	Swim volume	Swim hours	Cycle volume	Cycle hours	Run volume	Run hours
1						
2						
3						
4						
5						
6						
7						
8						
9						
10						
11						
12						
Total						

TABLE A.5a   Swimming Program Manager

	Swimming Program Manager						Athlete _____					
Wk	Monday	Competition (rank)	Program emphasis	Period	Weekly target	Volume	Pct	O₂	LVT	VO₂	LAC
1											
2											
3											
4											
5											
6											
7											
8											
9											
10											
11											
12											
13											
14											
15											
16											
17											
18											
19											
20											
21											
22											
23											
24											
25											
26											
27											
28											
29											
30											
31											
32											
33											
34											
35											
36											
37											
38											
39											
40											
41											
42											
43											
44											
45											
46											
47											
48											
49											
50											
51											
52											

TABLE A.5b   Cycling Program Manager

Cycling Program Manager					Athlete _____ Season Volume _____						
Wk	Monday	Competition (rank)	Program emphasis	Period	Weekly target	Volume	Pct	O₂	LVT	VO₂	LAC
1											
2											
3											
4											
5											
6											
7											
8											
9											
10											
11											
12											
13											
14											
15											
16											
17											
18											
19											
20											
21											
22											
23											
24											
25											
26											
27											
28											
29											
30											
31											
32											
33											
34											
35											
36											
37											
38											
39											
40											
41											
42											
43											
44											
45											
46											
47											
48											
49											
50											
51											
52											

TABLE A.5c Running Program Manager

	Running Program Manager				Athlete ———— Season Volume ————							
Wk	Monday	Competition (rank)	Program emphasis	Period	Weekly target	Volume	Pct	O$_2$	LVT	VO$_2$	LAC
1											
2											
3											
4											
5											
6											
7											
8											
9											
10											
11											
12											
13											
14											
15											
16											
17											
18											
19											
20											
21											
22											
23											
24											
25											
26											
27											
28											
29											
30											
31											
32											
33											
34											
35											
36											
37											
38											
39											
40											
41											
42											
43											
44											
45											
46											
47											
48											
49											
50											
51											
52											

TABLE A.6 Training Model Week

Week of:　　　　Week number:　　　　Athlete:

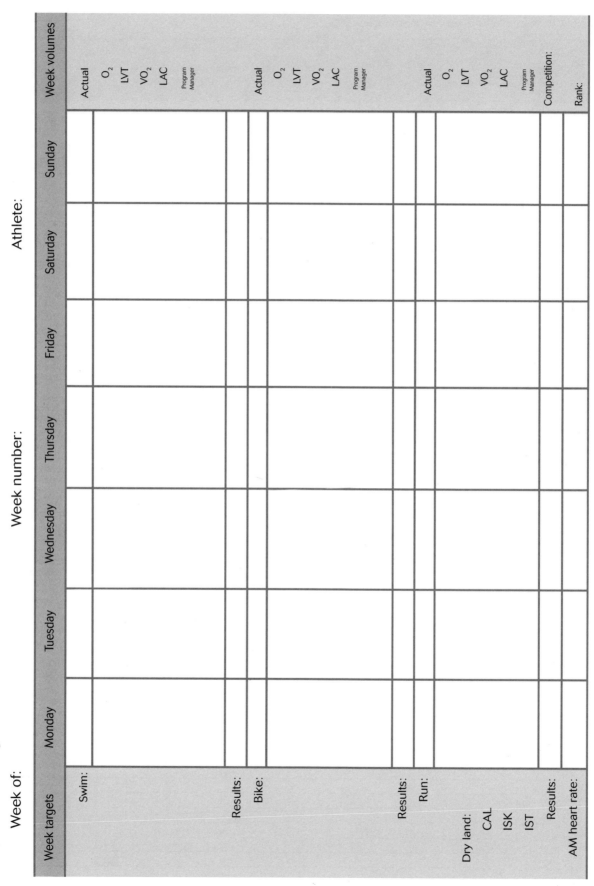

Week targets	Monday	Tuesday	Wednesday	Thursday	Friday	Saturday	Sunday	Week volumes
Swim:								Actual
								O$_2$
								LVT
								VO$_2$
								LAC
								Program Manager
Results:								
Bike:								Actual
								O$_2$
								LVT
								VO$_2$
								LAC
								Program Manager
Results:								
Run:								Actual
								O$_2$
								LVT
								VO$_2$
								LAC
								Program Manager
Dry land: CAL / ISK / IST								Competition:
Results:								
AM heart rate:								Rank:

TABLE A.7   Training Goal Manager

Sport	Skill/action	Goal	Test 1 result (date)	Test 2 result (date)	Test 3 result (date)	Test 4 result (date)
Swimming						
Cycling						
Running						

1. Use short-term goals to improve long-term results.

2. Establish difficult goals, but be realistic.

3. Make sure you can measure the results, and do so on a regular basis.

4. Include technical form training drills and training intensity zone goals.

REFERENCES

Andersen, P. 1975. Capillary density in skeletal muscle of man. *Acta Physiologica Scandinavica* 95 (2): 203-205.

Andersen, P., and J. Henriksson, 1977. Capillary supply of the quadriceps femoris muscle of man: Adaptive response to exercise. *Journal of Physiology* 270: 677-690.

Armstrong, L.E., D.L. Costill, and W.J. Fink. 1985. Influence of diuretic-induced dehydration on competitive running performance. *Medicine and Science in Sports and Exercise* 17: 456-461.

Auweele, Y. V., B. De Cuyper, V. Van Mele, and R. Rzewnick. 1993. Elite performance and personality: Description and prediction to diagnosis and intervention. In *Handbook of research on sport psychology,* edited by Robert Singer, Milledge Murphey, and L. Keith Tennant. New York: Macmillan.

Baldwin, K., G. Klingerfuss, R. Terjung, and J. Holloszy. 1972. Respiratory capacity of white, red and intermediate muscle: Adaptive response to exercise. *American Journal of Physiology* 222: 373-378.

Barr, S.I., D.L. Costill, W.J. Fink, and R.T. Thomas. 1991. Effect of increased training volume on blood lipids and lipoproteins in male collegiate swimmers. *Medicine and Science in Sports and Exercise* 23 (7): 795-800.

Barrett, S., and V. Herbert. 1994. Fads, frauds and quackery. In *Modern nutrition in health and disease, Vol. 2,* edited by M.E. Shils, J.A. Olson, and M. Shike, 1529. Philadelphia: Lea and Febiger.

Bevegard, S., A. Holmgren, and B. Jonsson. 1963. Circulatory studies in well trained athletes at rest and during heavy exercise, with special reference to stroke volume and the influence of body position. *Acta Physiologica Scandinavica* 75: 26-50.

Boileau, R., E. Buskirk, D. Hortsman, J. Mendez, and W. Nichols. 1971. Body composition changes in obese and lean men during physical conditioning. *Medicine and Science in Sports* 3 (4): 183-189.

Booth, F.W., and E.W. Gould. 1975. Effect of training and disuse on connective tissue. In *Exercise and sport sciences reviews,* edited by J.H. Wilmore and J.E. Keough, 83-112. New York: Academic Press.

Borensztajn, J., M. Rone, S. Babirak, J. McGarr, and L. Oscai. 1975. Effects of exercise on lipoprotein lipase activity in rat heart and skeletal muscle. *American Journal of Physiology* 229: 394-397.

Brodal, P., F. Inger, and L. Hermansen. 1977. Capillary supply of skeletal muscle fibers in untrained and endurance-trained men. *American Journal of Physiology* 232 (6): H705-H712.

Burke, E. R. 1995. *Serious cycling.* Champaign, IL: Human Kinetics.

Colwin, C. 1992. *Swimming into the 21st Century.* Champaign, IL: Human Kinetics.

Costill, D.L., E. Coyle, G. Dalsky, W. Evans, W. Fink, and D. Hoppes. 1977. Effects of elevated plasma FFA and insulin on muscle glycogen usage during exercise. *Journal of Applied Physiology* 43 (4): 695-699.

Costill, D.L., J. Daniels, W. Evans, W. Fink, G. Krahenbuhl, and B. Saltin. 1976. Skeletal muscle enzymes and fiber composition in male and female track athletes. *Journal of Applied Physiology* 40 (2): 149-154.

Costill, D.L., and J.M. Miller. 1980. Nutrition for endurance sport: Carbohydrates and fluid balance. *International Journal of Sports Medicine* 1: 2-14.

Ekblom, B., P. Astrand, B. Saltin, J. Stenberg, and B. Wallstrom. 1968. Effect of training on circulatory response to exercise. *Journal of Applied Physiology* 24 (4): 518-528.

Erikson, B., P. Gollnick, and B. Saltin. 1973. Muscle metabolism and enzyme activities after training in boys 11-13 years old. *Acta Physiologica Scandinavica* 87: 485-497.

Fournier, M., J. Ricci, A.W. Taylor, R.J. Ferguson, R.B. Montpetit, and B.R. Chaitman. 1982. Skeletal muscle adaption in adolescent boys: Sprint and endurance training and detraining. *Medicine and Science in Sports and Exercise* 14: 453-456.

Fox, E.L. 1975. Differences in metabolic alterations with sprint versus interval training programs. In *Metabolic adaptations to prolonged exercise*, edited by H. Howald and J. Poortmans, 119-126. Basel, Switzerland: Birkhauser Verlag.

Fox, E.L., R.L. Bartels, J. Klinzing, and K. Ragg. 1977. Metabolic responses to interval training programs of high and low power output. *Medicine in Science and Sports* 9 (3): 191-196.

Frick, M., A. Sjogren, J. Persasalo, and S. Pajunen. 1970. Cardiovascular dimensions and moderate physical training in young men. *Journal of Applied Physiology* 29 (4): 452-455.

Fukagawa, N., J. Anderson, G. Hageman, B. Yound, and K. Minaker. 1990. High-carbohydrate, high fiber diets increase peripheral insulin sensitivity in healthy young and old adults. *American Journal of Clinical Nutrition* 52: 524-528.

Gill, D. L. 1993. Competitiveness and competitive orientation in sport. In *Handbook of research on sport psychology*, edited by Robert Singer, Milledge Murphey, and L. Keith Tennant, 314-315. New York: Macmillan.

Gillespie, L.R., M.L. Pollock, J.L. Durstine, A. Ward, J. Ayres, and A.C. Linnerud. 1976. Physiological responses of men to 1, 3, and 5 days per week training programs. *Research Quarterly for Exercise and Sport* 47 (4): 638-646.

Gollnick, P.D. 1977. Free fatty acid turnover and the availability of substrates as a limiting factor in prolonged exercise. *Annals of the New York Academy of Sciences* 301: 64-71.

Gollnick, P., R. Armstrong, C. Saubert, K. Piehl, and B. Saltin. 1972. Enzyme activity and fiber composition in skeletal muscle of untrained and trained men. *Journal of Applied Physiology* 33 (3): 312-319.

Gollnick, P., R. Armstrong, B. Stalin, C. Saubert, W. Sembrowich, and R. Shepherd. 1973. Effect of training on enzyme activity and fiber composition of human skeletal muscle. *Journal of Applied Physiology* 34 (1): 107-111.

Gollnick, P., and D. King. 1969. Effects of exercise and training on mitochondria of rat skeletal muscle. *American Journal of Physiology* 216: 1502-1509.

Heil, D.P., A.R. Wilcox, and C.M. Quinn. 1995. Cardiorespiratory responses to seat-tube angle variation during steady-state cycling. *Medicine and Science in Sports and Exercise* 27 (5): 730-735.

Hendricksson, J., and J.S. Reitman. 1977. Time course of changes in human skeletal muscle succinate dehydrogenase and cytochrome oxidase activities and maximal oxygen uptake with physical activity and inactivity. *Acta Physiologica Scandinavica* 99: 91-97.

Hermansen, L., and M. Wachtlova. 1971. Capillary density of skeletal muscle in well trained and untrained men. *Journal of Applied Physiology* 30 (6): 860-863.

Hickson, R.C., M.J. Rennie, R.K. Conlee, W.E. Winder, and J.O. Holloszy. 1977. Effects of increased plasma fatty acids on glycogen utilization and endurance. *Journal of Applied Physiology* 43: 829-833.

Holloszy, J. 1967. Effects of exercise on mitochondrial oxygen uptake and respiratory enzyme activity in skeletal muscle. *The Journal of Biological Chemistry* 242: 2278-2282.

Howald, H. 1975. Ultrastructural adaptation of skeletal muscle to prolonged physical exercise. In *Metabolic adaptation to prolonged physical exercise,* edited by H. Howald and J.R. Poortmans, 372-383. Basel, Switzerland: Birkhauser Verlag.

Inger, F. 1979. Capillary supply and mitochondrial content of different skeletal muscle fiber types in untrained and endurance trained men: A histochemical and ultrastructural study. *European Journal of Applied Physiology* 40: 197-209.

Johnson, A., P. Collins, I. Higgins, D. Harrington, J. Connolly, C. Dolphin, M. McCreey, L. Brady, and M. O'Brien. 1985. Psychological, nutritional, and physical status of Olympic road cyclists. *British Journal of Sports Medicine* 19: 11-14.

Karlsson, J., P.V. Komi, and J.H.T. Viitasalo. 1979. Muscle strength and muscle characteristics in monozygous and dizygous twins. *Acta Physiologica Scandinavica* 106: 319-325.

Kenney, J., R. Clemens, and K. Forsythe. 1988. Applied kinesiology unreliable for assessing nutrient status. *Journal of the American Dietetic Association* 88: 698-704.

Kiessling, K., K. Piehl, and C. Lundquist. 1971. Effect of physical training on ultrastructural features in human skeletal muscle. In *Muscle metabolism during exercise,* edited by B. Pernow and B. Saltin, 97-101. New York: Plenum Press.

Kjellberg, S., U. Rudhe, and T. Sjostrand. 1949. Increase of the amount of hemoglobin and blood volume in connection with physical training. *Acta Physiologica Scandinavica* 19: 146-151.

Levine, B.D., and J. Stray-Gundersen. 1992. A practical approach to altitude training: Where to live and train for optimal performance enhancement. *International Journal of Sports Medicine* 13 (suppl. 1): S209-S212.

Locke, E., and G. Latham. 1985. The application of goal setting to sports. *Journal of Sport Psychology* 7: 206-209.

Locke, E., A.J. Mento, and B.L. Katcher. 1978. The interaction of ability and motivation in performance: An exploration of the meaning of moderators. *Personnel Psychology* 31: 269-280.

Mahoney, M.J., and M. Avener. 1977. Psychology of the elite athlete: An exploratory study. *Cognitive Therapy Research* 3: 361-366.

Martin, D., and P. Coe. 1997. *Better training for distance runners,* 2nd ed. Champaign, IL Human Kinetics.

Mole, P., L. Oscai, and J.O. Holloszy. 1971. Adaptation of muscle to exercise: Increase in level of pamityl CoA systhetase, carnitine plamityltransferase, and pamityl CoA dehydrogenase, and in the capacity to oxidize fatty acid. *The Journal of Clinical Investigation.* 50: 2323-2330.

Morganroth, J., B. Maron, W. Henry, and S. Epstein. 1975. Comparative left ventricular dimensions in trained athletes. *Annals of Internal Medicine* 82: 521-524.

Morris, Thomas V. 1994. *True success: A new philosophy of excellence.* New York: Grosset/ Putnam.

Murphy, S.M. 1994. Imagery interventions in sport. *Medicine and Science in Sports and Exercise* 26 (4): 487.

Oscai, L., R. Williams, and B. Hertig. 1968. Effects of exercise on blood volume. *Journal of Applied Physiology* 24 (5): 622-624.

Peripargkul, S., and J. Scheuer. 1970. The effect of physical training upon the mechanical and metabolic performance of the rat heart. *The Journal of Clinical Investigation* 49: 1859-1868.

Pitts, G.C., R.E. Johnson, and F.C. Consolazio. 1944. Work in the heat as affected by intake of water, salt, and glucose. *American Journal of Physiology* 142: 253-259.

Pollock, M. 1973. The quantification of endurance training programs. In *Exercise and sport sciences reviews,* Vol. 1, edited by J. Wilmore, 155-188. New York: Academic Press.

Pollock, M., T. Cureton, and L. Greninger. 1969. Effects of frequency of training on working capacity, cardiovascular function, and body composition of adult men. *Medicine in Science and Sports* 1 (2): 70-74.

Pollock, M., J. Dimmick, H. Miller, Z. Kendrick, and A. Linnerud. 1975. Effects of mode of training on cardiovascular function and body composition of adult men. *Medicine Science Sports* 7 (2): 139-145.

Rtizer, T.F., A.A. Bove, and R.A. Carey. 1980. Left ventricular performance characteristics in training and sedentary dogs. *Journal of Applied Physiology* 48 (1): 130-138.

Rubal, B.J., J. Resentswieg, and B. Hamerly. 1981. Echocardiographic examination of women collegiate softball champions. *Medicine and Science in Sports and Exercise* 13: 176-179.

Sallade, J.R., and S. Koch. 1992. Training errors in long distance running. *Journal of Athletic Training* 27 (1): 50-53

Saltin, B., K. Nazar, D.L. Costill, E. Stein, and E. Jansson. 1976. Nature of the training response: Peripheral and central adaptations of one-legged exercise. *Acta Physiologica Scandinavica* 96 (3): 289-305

Saubert, C., R. Armstrong, R. Shepherd, and P.D. Gollnick. 1973. Anaerobic enzyme adaptations to sprint training in rats. *Pfluger's Archive-European Journal of Physiology.* 341: 305-312.

Sherman, W.M. 1983. Carbohydrates, muscle glycogen, and muscle glycogen supercompensation. In *Ergogenic aids in sport,* edited by M.H. Williams, 3-26. Champaign, IL: Human Kinetics.

Sherman, W.M., and D.R. Lamb. 1988. Nutrition and prolonged exercise. *Perspectives in Exercise Science and Sports Medicine* 1: 222, 225-230.

Smith, D.C., and A. El-Hage. 1978. Effect of exercise training on the chronotropic response of isolated rat atria to atropine. *Experimentia* 34 (8): 1027-1028.

Staudte, H.W., G. Exner, and D. Pette. 1973. Effect of short-term, high-intensity (sprint) training on some contractile and metabolic characteristics of fast and slow muscles of the rat. *Pfluger's Archive-European Journal of Physiology.* 344: 159-168.

Thorstensson, A., B. Sjodin, and J. Karlsson. 1975. Enzyme activities and muscle strength after "sprint training" in man. *Acta Physiologica Scandinavica* 94: 313-318.

Tipton, C.M., R.D. Mathes, J.A. Maynard, and R.A. Carey. 1975. The influence of physical activity on ligaments and tendons. *Medicine and Science in Sports* 7 (3): 165-175.

Vealey, R.S. 1994. Current status and prominent issues in sport psychology interventions. *Medicine and Science in Sports and Exercise* 26 (4): 495.

Wilmore, J.H., and D.L. Costill. 1988. *Training for sport and activity: The physiological basis of the conditioning process.* Dubuque, Iowa: Wm. C. Brown.

Wilmore, J. H., J. Royce, R. Girandola, F. Katch, and V. Katch. 1970. Body composition changes with a 10-week program of jogging. *Medicine in Science and Sports* 2 (3): 113-117.

Zeldis, S.M., J. Morganroth, and S. Rubler. 1978. Cardiac hypertrophy in response to dynamic conditioning in female athletes. *Journal of Applied Physiology* 44 (6): 849-852.

INDEX

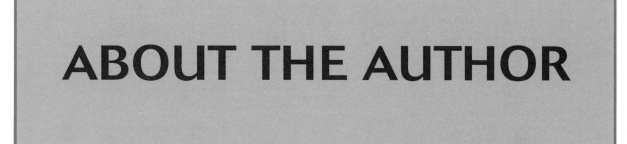

ABOUT THE AUTHOR

Marc Evans is a pioneer in coaching endurance athletes. He got his start in 1981 when he founded Triathletics West and became triathlon's first professional coach. Since then he has coached professional and age group Ironman winners, national champions, and hundreds of other top endurance athletes around the world. In 1989 Evans was named USA National Triathlon Coach for the first World Triathlon Championships in Avignon, France. The following year he was appointed coach of the USA triathlon team at the Elite Performance Testing Series held at the Olympic Training Center in Colorado Springs.

Evans is the president of Endurance Sport Technology Group, Inc. (ESTG), a research, design, and engineering company that specializes in sports training products. Well-known for developing the table of periodization, Evans continues to create new training techniques for both recreational and elite endurance athletes. He was presented the American Medical Athletic Association's Award of Excellence in 1992,

© Jeffrey Dow

and he was named Coach of the Year in 1990 by SECURA Insurance Company.

Evans lives in northern California/Nevada, where he enjoys telemark skiing, swimming, cycling, and hiking with his chocolate Labrador, Edge.

Other Related Books From HK